# Praise for *Free Our Markets*

"Central to economics is the study of how people deal with the scarcity of resources. Unfortunately, among humanity's scarcest resources are crystal-clear, compelling, and correct explanations of how economies work. With this truly outstanding volume, Howard Baetjer makes that vital resource much less scarce."
—Donald J. Boudreaux, professor of economics, George Mason University

"Howard Baetjer takes a new look at economics – neither from the left nor from the right, but from the heart. Baetjer takes a refreshingly holistic approach in exploring how joyously talented and frustratingly limited humans interact to better their lives. You won't find the graphs and equations that unnecessarily alienate so many economics students from this wonderful discipline. Instead, you'll find a story of how people can come together to form a civil society – a story that will resonate with anyone who believes that, for all their shortcomings, humans are fundamentally good."
—Antony Davies, professor of economics, Duquesne University

"In *Free Our Markets* Howard Baetjer demonstrates clearly that increased liberty, not government, is the way to improve our standards of living. Making his case with beautifully explained economic reasoning and a careful and unbiased examination of real-world examples ranging from the housing crisis to education markets, Baetjer has succeeded in producing that wonderful rarity – a book that is both so clear and so important that it really should be read by everyone. If we take the humane lessons of *Free Our Markets* to heart we will undoubtedly make our lives – and the lives of our children – far, far better."
—James Stacey Taylor, professor of philosophy, College of New Jersey

"Howard Baetjer has produced a marvelous introduction to economics that will have great appeal to those who want to understand why economics matters both for making sense of our world and for improving it. In the tradition of the great communicators of sound economics, Baetjer makes complex economic ideas simple, and uses great storytelling and numerous effective examples to illustrate the productivity and humanity of the market. His final section on the housing boom and bust is particularly effective in showing the economic waste and human toll that arise even from the most well-intentioned attempts to intervene in the market. This book is a great place to start in understanding why we need markets that are more free, not less."
—Steven Horwitz, Charles A. Dana Professor of Economics, St. Lawrence University

"*Free Our Markets* enables the educated layman to understand the fundamental reasons why economic liberty is the foundation for prosperity and societal flourishing."
—John Allison, CEO and President, Cato Institute, Washington, DC.

"It's no accident that Howard Baetjer is a highly sought-after speaker far beyond his home institution: few economists – few thinkers in any discipline – are as effective at communicating ideas. His explanations and examples of core economic principles and how they inform our understanding of a free society are clear and vivid; his writing is engaging and uplifting. Baetjer's gifted ability as a lecturer translates nicely to the printed page. Readers of this book will not only come to a better understanding of economics, they will also come away with a better understanding of human freedom."
—Aeon J. Skoble, professor of philosophy, Bridgewater State University

"Howard Baetjer, one of America's great classroom teachers, has now written the definitive introduction to free-market economics for the twenty-first century. Clear, logical, and principled, *Free Our Markets* ranks with Henry Hazlitt's *Economics in One Lesson* as one of the very best books on free-market economics ever written. This book should be read by all Americans who care about prosperity and a free society."
—C. Bradley Thompson, Executive Director of the Clemson Institute for the Study of Capitalism

"We are at this moment in time confronted with the consequences of the perpetuation for decades of economic fallacies that captured the political elite and popular imagination and now have come to threaten the economic future of Europe and the US. We need at this time a massive intellectual correction to defeat popular fallacies and to spread economic literacy. Howard Baetjer is a master teacher of the economic way of thinking, and *Free Our Markets: A Citizens' Guide to Essential Economics* is the perfect antidote to the fallacious reasoning that dominates political speech on the left and the right in DC and Brussels (and everyone in between)."
—Peter Boettke, University Professor of Economics, George Mason University

*Free Our Markets* is that rare treasure—an illuminating book about a complex and important subject that is so clear, so persuasive, and so inspiring that it is an absolute pleasure to read. Professor Baetjer makes the case for economic liberty with a masterful combination of show and tell that leads inexorably to his conclusion: that the way to prosperity, security, and abundance is freedom, not the coercive power of government.
—Clark Neily, Senior Attorney, Institute For Justice

An instant classic... Howard Baetjer's vivid explanation of key economic principles stands out as not only sound and incisive but also humane and generous. *Free Our Markets* makes a clear and compelling case for the restoration of Thomas Jefferson's vision for "a wise and frugal government, which shall restrain men from injuring one another, shall leave them otherwise free to regulate their own pursuits of industry and improvement, and shall not take from the mouth of labor the bread it has earned."
—Robert M. S. McDonald, Associate Professor of History, United States Military Academy

The microeconomic sections of Howard Baetjer's *Free Our Markets*, which are most of the book, are magnificent. He takes you on a voyage of discovery as he reveals the power of free markets to make our lives better. Whether he discusses corn row braiding, how to protect elephants in Africa, why central economic planning doesn't work, or why price controls on water cause people to do without, Baetjer brings fresh energy to his subject. His enthusiasm is infectious. Read, learn, and enjoy.
—David R. Henderson, author of *The Joy of Freedom: An Economist's Odyssey*.

One of the major failings of the economics profession is not making our subject comprehensible to the ordinary person. *Free Our Markets: A Citizens' Guide to Essential Economics* comes to the rescue. Professor Howard Baetjer does a yeoman's job in addressing that problem whilst proving that economics is not only exciting, it's mostly plain common sense. Readable and fun, *Free Our Markets* provides valuable insights and possible solutions to many of the nation's problems.
—Walter E. Williams, John M. Olin Distinguished Professor of Economics, George Mason University

# FREE OUR MARKETS

# FREE OUR MARKETS

A CITIZENS' GUIDE
TO ESSENTIAL ECONOMICS

HOWARD BAETJER JR.

JANE PHILIP PUBLICATIONS, LLC          NEW VIEWS, NEW BEGINNINGS™

Cover and book design by Jordan Zane Brownstein

Grateful acknowledgement is made for permission to excerpt from copyrighted works:

Leonard Read's "I, Pencil." Copyright © 1958, by the Foundation for Economic Education, 260 Peachtree St. NW, Suite 2200, Atlanta, GA 30303.

Russell Roberts's "Gambling With Other People's Money." Copyright © 2010, by Russell Roberts, Mercatus Center, George Mason University.

Publisher's Cataloging-In-Publication Data
(Prepared by The Donohue Group, Inc.)
Baetjer, Howard.
   Free our markets : a citizens' guide to essential economics / Howard Baetjer Jr. -- 1st ed.
   p. : ill. ; cm.

Includes bibliographical references.
ISBN: 978-0-9844254-2-6
   1. Free enterprise.  2. Austrian school of economics.  3. Intervention (Federal government)  4. Economics.  I. Title.

HB95 .B34 2013
330.12/2                                          2013941977

First Edition: July, 2013

Published by Jane Philip Publications, LLC, New Hampshire, USA

*For my mother,*
*...harine Finney Baetjer Hornady,*
*...ion, gratitude, and bottomless affection*

# Contents

## PART III. THE HOUSING BOOM AND FINANCIAL CRISIS

# Acknowledgements

My primary debt of gratitude for this book is to the Institute for Humane Studies (IHS) at George Mason University. IHS helped me pay for my graduate work at George Mason; IHS sponsored the public policy course in which I first gave shape to the ideas presented here; and for the last seventeen years IHS has given me the opportunity to teach at its summer seminars—invariably the high point of my teaching year—where with the help of fellow faculty and many wonderful students I have developed the lectures on which this book is based. In particular I thank my long-time IHS faculty and staff teammates Brad Birzer, Susan Love Brown, Andrew Cohen, Antony Davies, Jerry Ellig, Beth Erber, Christy Rhoton Horpedahl, Mark LeBar, Chris Martin, Rob McDonald, Clark Neily, Aeon Skoble, Frank Stephenson, James Staccy Taylor, Mario Villarreal-Diaz, and Marty Zupan, for their wisdom and friendship.

For explanations of and information on particular policy matters I thank Karol Boudreaux, Urs Kreuter, Jerry Ellig, Sallie James, Bruce Yandle, John Baden, Russ Sobel, and particularly Steven Horwitz, who generously answered questions and also read and commented on early versions of the chapters on money and banking. For helping me better understand mortgage-backed securities and other aspects of the financial crisis of 2008 I thank Alison Granger, Arnold Kling, Joe Pomykala, and Jeffrey Friedman. For information on Children's Scholarship Fund Baltimore I thank Paul Ellis and Beth Harbinson. I thank Alex McCoy for insight into the consequences of the No Child Left Behind Act.

I thank my friends and colleagues who read all or parts of the first complete draft and made many useful suggestions: Jim Dorn, Cheryl Finney, Vin Broderick, Scott Reinhardt, Kerry Brown, Tom Rouse, Jim Vinoski, Art Carden, Greg Muth, and Mike Hanrahan. Tim Stonesifer gave me the benefit both of comments on the manuscript and feedback, over a number of years, on my evolving plans for framing the content. I am particularly grateful and indebted to Ted Winstead for his painstakingly thorough markup of the entire first draft, giving me the benefit of his eye as a professional writer, and his frank criticism as a true friend.

For help with research I thank former students Kathryn Sandstrom, Chad Henson, and Charlie Wieprecht, and also Kai Filipczak. Thanks to Craig Hammond for helping me think through my approach to the education chapter, and to Dr. Alexandre Padilla for identifying the origin of the term "the knowledge problem."

To my colleague and former department chair George Georgiou I am grateful for allowing me to teach money and banking so that I could learn it, even though I had never had a course in it.

For moral support and encouragement in keeping the writing moving I am particularly indebted to Aeon Skoble and Christy Rhoton Horpedahl.

All the graphs in the book were put together by my IHS teammate Antony Davies. He found the data, created the graphs, and altered them in any way I asked, all with astonishing quickness. For that and for his professional and personal friendship I am extremely grateful.

My editor, Deborah Brownstein, has been a joy to work with and a source of constant encouragement and support; I am lucky and grateful we got to team up. Thanks also to Barry Brownstein for his encouragement and insights and the book's title.

I thank all of those who have taught me economics in the Smith-Hayek tradition, a tradition committed to demonstrating that on-going increases in economic well-being for all depend on liberty. These include the great thinkers whose ideas form the foundation of the discipline for me: Adam Smith, Ludwig von Mises, F.A. Hayek, and Israel Kirzner; the great explainers whose lucid prose has clarified for me the essential principles: Frederic Bastiat, Leonard Read, Walter Williams, Henry Hazlitt, Milton Friedman, and Thomas Sowell. They include as well Russ Roberts, via his novels and EconTalk, and (here I hesitate to name names for fear of forgetting some) my teachers at GMU, especially my dear friend and mentor Don Lavoie, Jack High, Dick Wagner, George Selgin, and Don Boudreaux. For a subtle but strong contribution to my intellectual development I thank the trio of inseparable, irrepressible, inspiring grad students in the "class" ahead of me at GMU, who showed me what it was to be immersed in ideas and who continue to teach me through their writings and lectures: Steven Horwitz, Peter Boettke, and David Prychitko. I thank Peter Boettke further for giving me the idea (at an IHS seminar) to write this book.

For intellectual and personal companionship that have helped me develop as a teacher I thank Emily Chamlee-Wright, Mark Steckbeck, Steven Miller, Ben Tisdale, Jonas Merrill, John Ross, Solomon Stein, Jim Vinoski, and other classmates, students, and teachers too numerous to mention. My goal in this book is to pass on to others some of the understanding I have been privileged to gain from all of these.

Not least, I thank my wife, Susan, for putting up with "No, I have to work on the book" and for help with grammar, but mostly for the emotional support of our happy companionship. It sweetened the writing as it sweetens life.

# Introduction

This book had its origin at 30,000 feet in March of 1977. I was a young English teacher and football coach at St. George's School in Rhode Island, assigned to teach an overflow section of a colleague's popular "Utopian Literature" spring elective. During the spring vacation before the term began, on an airline flight with my sister Betsy, I was getting ahead on the course reading. Having finished *The Communist Manifesto*, I opened up the title essay from *For the New Intellectual*, by Ayn Rand. A few pages into it, I turned to Betsy and said, "This is good stuff."

After a few more pages, I turned to her again and said, "This is really good stuff." As I drew toward the end of the essay, my eyes opening for the first time to the right and wrong of government intervention in the economy, I turned to her a third time and said, "This is going to change my life."

Up to that time, my philosophical interests had been limited to a concern about ethics; I had had no interest in economics or political philosophy. But I was intrigued by the idea that business owners have a right to the profits they earn in voluntary exchange with others; that government interference with people's productive activities violates their right to pursue happiness (peacefully) as they wish; and that these peaceful pursuits increase the well-being of *others* as well as the business people themselves.

Excited by this new perspective on human relations, I looked for other writings from the individual-liberty-is-important perspective. I discovered The Foundation for Economic Education (FEE) and went to one of their seminars. Waiting for me in my room when I arrived was Leonard Read's "I, Pencil" (with which we'll begin Chapter 1) and its exhortation to "leave all creative energies uninhibited." Also waiting for me was Frederic Bastiat's *The Law*. I opened it and read,

> See if the law takes from some persons what belongs to them, and gives it to other persons to whom it does not belong. See if the law benefits one citizen at the expense of another by doing what the citizen himself cannot do without committing a crime.

> Then abolish this law without delay... (p. 21)

I was struck by the dignity of principle followed to its logical conclusion. Why had I never thought that before?

I embraced classical liberal (or libertarian) principles easily because they suit my ethics. I had learned at summer camp that one should leave the other guy's tennis balls at his bunk unless one has permission to use them. I believed, and believe still, that a generous concern for others means, first of all, *not* forcing our will on them by preventing them from peacefully pursuing happiness in their own way.

This ethical belief led me logically to a belief in limited government: minimum taxation, no forced transfers of wealth from some people to others, and no regulatory restriction of voluntary exchange. It meant people should be free to do "anything that's peaceful" (the title of one of Leonard Read's books), that no one may justly initiate the use of force on others, and that governmental force should be used only to secure people's rights to life, liberty, and property.

In short, I found myself to be a liberal, in the classical sense. On principle, I believed in unrestricted freedom of enterprise, free markets, capitalism.

But that confronted me with a big problem: I *knew* from high school history that capitalism had caused the exploitation and suffering of workers in the Industrial Revolution. I knew that unfettered capitalism had caused the Great Depression. I knew that abusive monopolies are inevitable in the absence of anti-trust restrictions. I knew, as everyone knows, that strong government regulation of pharmaceuticals via the Food and Drug Administration is necessary to prevent public health disasters. I saw that full freedom of enterprise would mean that anyone could practice medicine without a license, and I knew that would be disastrous. Though I was persuaded that it is wrong to tax people—to seize their property against their wills—even for the laudable purposes of feeding, clothing, healing, or educating the poor; I could not imagine how the poor could be fed, clothed, healed, or educated without such taxation.

My cognitive dissonance was intense. How tragic, I thought, that principles of moral human behavior—respect for others' property and freedom of choice—should have such dreadful practical results. . . . But what I knew turned out not to be so.

I read hungrily: Hazlitt, Friedman, and eventually Hayek. (Henry Hazlitt's *Economics in One Lesson* is the single most valuable book in my economics education; don't miss it.) I thought long and hard for myself. Gradually, on one concern after another, I was reassured. I became persuaded, as Einstein said, that "God does not play dice with the universe." The ethically right system of social rules—the classical liberal prescription of individual liberty, private ownership, and free markets—was also gloriously productive and beneficial to rich and poor alike. Indeed, it is the setting in which the poor become wealthier the fastest.

At the same time, I began to question the efficacy of government for improving human lives. I came to suspect that taxation, restrictions, mandates, subsidies, licenses, tariffs, bailouts, prohibitions and all the rest, even if well-intended, usually protect monopoly, cause recession, burden the poor, enforce racial discrimination (as I learned from Jennifer Roback, the Jim Crow laws were *legislation*), obstruct education, and so on.

My life *had* changed. I found myself driven to participate in the great struggle of ideas I saw being joined. I left my English teaching and threw myself into studying and teaching economics and "the ideas of liberty."

Even before I went back to graduate school to study political philosophy and economics, I took every opportunity I could find to explore and discuss the merits of free markets. For two years I worked for FEE, taking "the freedom philosophy" to schools and colleges. Also I had long, deep talks with a group of wise and thoughtful friends who were willing to engage with me. It was tough going.

It was tough because those I talked with often *knew* the kinds of historical inaccuracies I had known until I started to study. They had been taught, as I had been, that government is necessary to make up for the market's inadequacies and to remedy "market failures" in various areas: poverty, healthcare, wage rates, monopoly, schooling, recessions, sweatshops, trade imbalances, the environment, developing countries, and many more. I tried as best I could to defend economic liberty on each those different issues and concerns.

I went to study at George Mason University and gradually became a better spokesperson for liberty as I learned more economics and economic history, but I grew frustrated at being on the defensive so much of the time, trying to explain why some intervention or other would cause more harm than good. I wanted to make a *positive* case for what Adam Smith called "the obvious and simple system of natural liberty." Often those I talked with about particular policies didn't have the basic understanding I was gaining of why free markets work at all, so I found myself wanting to go back to fundamental principles and start explaining there.

I wanted to help others understand why economic liberty works to make us all better off *in general*, not just on particular issues—but I didn't know how to go about it.

I paid close attention, however, to the different kinds of arguments I heard and read, both for and against free markets. The more I learned, both in courses and in listening to fellow students debate, the more it seemed to me that all the most persuasive explanations of how and why freedom makes us all better off are grounded in three basic principles: One is that the prices generated in free markets communicate the dispersed knowledge people need to coordinate our different activities. The next is that profit and loss in competitive markets guide discovery of what works well to satisfy human wants and needs. The third is that market-based incentives are far healthier than the incentives in government intervention.

When I was invited to teach an undergraduate public policy course, I took the opportunity to organize it around these three categories. My aim was to help my students learn to think about and evaluate public policy as I was learning to—as free market economists do—so that they could understand why free markets tend to generate solutions to social problems, and why government interventions tend to add new problems to old.

The course succeeded. Organizing the case for economic liberty around knowledge, discovery, and incentives worked well enough that Jerry Ellig and I developed a set of summer seminar lectures for the Koch Summer Fellowship program the same way. At one of those seminars Peter Boettke, also there to lecture, suggested that I write up the framework in a book, adding an application or two. That was a good idea!

About ten or fifteen years later (I have lost track), here is the book Pete suggested I write, its ideas fleshed out, refined and polished in many lectures in the intervening years.

*Free Our Markets* aims to show readers that liberty, not the force of government, is the means to achieve the goals we all have for humanity high and rising standards of living, increasing security and abundance for all.

A tragedy of our time is that so many good-hearted people, people generously concerned about the well-being of others, don't believe this. Of course, most people believe in mostly free markets. Since the collapse of the Soviet Union, very few hold that markets should be abolished. Most concede that a large degree of private ownership and freedom of exchange are necessary for society to work at all. But—and the "but" follows immediately—they believe that governments must restrict freedom to make capitalism work properly. They believe that full economic freedom would result in various harms that can be avoided with government intervention.

This belief is tragic and ironic. It leads good people to try to improve on the "simple system of natural liberty" using coercion that they mean to be benign. They try to improve society faster than is possible, by means that can't work, and their efforts set society back.

To an advocate of full economic liberty such as myself, they ask such questions as these: "How can you claim that *X* should be unregulated (meaning unregulated by some *government* body)?" "Doesn't the government have to restrict *Y*?" "How could we possibly leave something as important as *Z* to the free market?"

Like many classical liberals, I am tempted to respond on principle alone. I could stamp my foot and protest, "Darn it! People ought to be free!" meaning free from others' control of their lives and property. But I have learned that many good people—people whose generous concern for humanity I don't doubt—will not endorse that kind of freedom as long as they think it would leave people worse off than they would be with some government intervention.

Hence this book. It explains why, for practical economic reasons, free markets generally produce better results than even the best intended and most carefully crafted government interventions. The ideas presented here are the best of what I have learned from economists whose work I most admire, boiled down to foundational principles and illustrated with stories and examples for the interested layperson. The book offers a mental framework with which to analyze policies, a way of thinking about how and why the underlying institutions of a free market—private ownership and freedom of exchange—allow human beings to flourish, and why it's unwise to compromise those institutions at all. My hope is that if people come to appreciate *why* the free market works to make people better off, they'll encourage their politicians to stop interfering with it, and we'll all become better off.

Thomas Sowell is supposed to have said, when told he had a lot of faith in free markets, "I don't have faith in free markets; I have evidence." I hope readers of this book, in the same situation, will be able to answer, "I don't have faith in free markets; I understand how they work." Put that way, the statement would not be strictly true, because free markets are too complex really to understand. Rather, the statement would mean, "I understand the principles on which free markets work, so I understand why they are indispensable to human flourishing."

Before going further let me clarify what I mean by a "free market": I mean the freedom of all competent adults to exchange their justly-acquired property with one another as they see fit, as long as they respect others' property and equal freedom. *The book is thus pro-market, not pro-business.* In a free market, businesses are subject to the relentless discipline of market feedback: the choices of customers, suppliers, and investors to deal with them *or not.* The crony capitalism we have seen of late in the United States, in which governments subsidize, sponsor, bail out, or otherwise protect certain businesses from the discipline of market profit and loss, is not free markets. It's sort-of free markets, somewhat free enterprise. It's precisely what this book condemns: it's government intervention.

Furthermore, though I focus on *economic* activity and use the term "free markets" to refer to the liberty of peaceful interaction, I am just as dedicated to human freedom to engage peacefully in *non-economic* activity and exchange. Marriages, bowling leagues, religious observance, charities of all kinds, non-profit associations, NFL fan clubs and the like are all valuable human endeavors to which the same basic rules should apply: respect for others' property and freedom of association on peaceful terms. I advocate and work for a free market *in a free society.*

Part I of this book argues that human beings need free markets because of three foundational principles mentioned above. A short-hand summary is as follows:

1. We need the knowledge that free market prices give us;
2. we need the guidance in discovering wealth-creating activities that free market profit and loss give us; and
3. we need the incentives to serve others that private ownership and freedom of exchange give us.

With this information and guidance and with these incentives, people cooperate and create for one another abundantly. Any interference with the free market process, no matter how well-intentioned, is likely to diminish the creativity of the system.

Part II explores regulation. It addresses a challenge to free markets that is so widely accepted as to be treated as a truism: "Yes, free markets are well and good, but they have to be regulated to work properly." Of course markets have to be regulated, but not by *government*, as the challenge implies. Part II applies the principles discussed in Part I to show that bottom-up regulation by market forces outperforms top-down regulation by legislators and bureaucrats, which generally causes more harm than good.

Part III is a case study of the housing boom and bust and the financial turmoil of the first decade of the 2000s. I began writing this book well before these events occurred, so I had no plans for such a section. As the turmoil played out, however, many commentators blamed it on "unregulated free markets." I saw that potential readers would probably not take seriously a book on the virtues of free markets that ignored all that economic distress. Hence, Part III. For the book, the timing worked to great advantage, because the episode helps me make my case. As Part III will show, it is precisely a variety of wrong-headed interventions into the economy—gross failures to follow the principles that make for spontaneous economic order—that caused all that damage to the economy.

Unwilling to end on a negative note, I close with happily imagining all the good that can come from freeing entirely our markets in primary and secondary education. Change in this direction is starting to occur now. It is immensely promising. I hope my readers will help spur it along.

The economic philosophy set out in *Free Our Markets* is not new. My favorite expression of it is Thomas Jefferson's. In his first inaugural address in 1801, he reflected on the many blessings Americans have, such as protection from invasion by the oceans, a bountiful land, an industrious people, and religious tolerance. Then he asked his listeners rhetorically, "What more is necessary to make us a happy and a prosperous people?" He answered his own question this way:

Still one thing more, fellow citizens, a wise and frugal government, which shall restrain men from injuring one another, shall leave them otherwise free to regulate their own pursuits of industry and improvement, and shall not take from the mouth of labor the bread it has earned. This is the sum of good government, and this is necessary to close the circle of our felicities.

Note how radically limited a scope for government Jefferson defines. Its job is to "restrain men from injuring one another." That's all. It should "leave them otherwise free." As to regulation, government should let people "regulate their own pursuits of industry and improvement." As to taxation, government "shall not take from the mouth of labor the bread it has earned." Are there other government functions? No: "This is the sum"—the totality—"of good government." It should "leave [us] otherwise free.... "

Jefferson implicitly rules out any role for government in educating children; in providing for the poor, the sick, and the old; in regulating wages, what people ingest, health care, or the financial industry; in subsidizing exports, agriculture, the arts, or foreign governments; in bailing out banks, insurance companies or car companies. All of this is unwise and unfrugal.

Educating children; providing for the poor, sick, and old—these are "pursuits of industry and improvement" that people should undertake as they see fit in mutual association with like-minded others. It is not for government to "take from the mouth of labor the bread It has earned" in order to care for the poor, sick, and old. That care lies in the personal responsibility of the citizens.

Regulating industry likewise should be left to people in free association with one another. Government must always "restrain men from injuring one another," but where there is no injury, where people freely consent to their own regulation of their affairs, government has no role. "This is the sum of good government, and this is necessary to close the circle of our felicities."

That was wise in 1801; it's just as wise today. What follows explores why.

# Part I

# Principles of Spontaneous
# Economic Order

Does any one person know how to make a pencil? How much profit is too much? Should price gouging after hurricanes be banned? Is there any social value to profit? Does the U.S. Forest Service sell out the National Forests? How did an oil company get permission to drill for oil and gas in a bird sanctuary owned by an environmental group?

In these first three chapters, with questions like these and stories from real life, we investigate three broad principles that, taken together, explain why free markets are so effective at helping people flourish, and not just rich people, rich and poor alike. By free markets I mean liberty in the economic realm: liberty for all of us as individuals to do as we please with our talents and property, in peaceful interaction with others.

Free markets are wonderfully productive, peaceful, and orderly. And, marvelously, their order is spontaneous, not planned. Let us try to understand in principle (not in detail; the detail would overwhelm us) how this order emerges.

# Chapter One

# Prices Communicate Knowledge

Prices are precious.

The economy is a fantastically complex, world-wide system of human cooperation. We all pursue our own purposes; no one is in charge of the whole system; and yet we cooperate. We all cooperate daily with countless people we don't know, but whose specialized knowledge of ever-changing circumstances we must somehow take into account in order to coordinate our actions with theirs. Prices make this knowledge available and this cooperation possible.

We need free markets because we need the information that free market prices give us about what others know. We have no other way to communicate this information to all who might use it. This is the first of three principles of spontaneous economic order that account for why human beings need free markets:

> *Market prices coordinate the actions of billions of people pursuing their myriad goals, by communicating the changing, particular knowledge of everyone about the availability and potential uses of everything.*

This chapter explores this principle. It looks at how prices coordinate all our different plans and how helpless we would be without market prices to guide us. It examines how the nature of human knowledge makes prices necessary and explains why prices should always be allowed to go to their free-market levels, even after natural disasters.

## Three Lessons from "I, Pencil"

We begin our discussion of knowledge with a classic—Leonard Read's wonderful 1958 article, "I, Pencil." As you read the excerpt below, please note:

- how many different skills are required to make a pencil,

- how many different materials are used, and

- in how many different places around the world these skills and materials are found.

I, PENCIL

MY FAMILY TREE AS TOLD TO

Leonard E. Read

I am a lead pencil—the ordinary wooden pencil familiar to all boys and girls and adults who can read and write.

Writing is both my vocation and my avocation; that's all I do.

You may wonder why I should write a genealogy. Well, to begin with, my story is interesting. And, next, I am a mystery—more so than a tree or a sunset or even a flash of lightning. But, sadly, I am taken for granted by those who use me, as if I were a mere incident and without background. This supercilious attitude relegates me to the level of the commonplace. This is a species of the grievous error in which mankind cannot too long persist without peril. For, as the wise G.K. Chesterton observed, "We are perishing for want of wonder, not for want of wonders."

I, Pencil, simple though I appear to be, merit your wonder and awe, a claim I shall attempt to prove. In fact, if you can understand me—no, that's too much to ask of anyone—if you can become aware of the miraculousness which I symbolize, you can help save the freedom mankind is so unhappily losing. I have a profound lesson to teach. And I can teach this lesson better than can an automobile or an airplane or a mechanical dishwasher because—well, because I am seemingly so simple.

Simple? Yet, not a single person on the face of this earth knows how to make me. This sounds fantastic, doesn't it? Especially when it is realized that there are about one and one-half billion of my kind produced in the U.S.A. each year.

Pick me up and look me over. What do you see? Not much meets the eye—there's some wood, lacquer, the printed labeling, graphite lead, a bit of metal, and an eraser.

Just as you cannot trace your family tree back very far, so is it impossible for me to name and explain all my antecedents. But I would like to suggest enough of them to impress upon you the richness and complexity of my background.

My family tree begins with what in fact is a tree, a cedar of straight grain that grows in Northern California and Oregon. Now contemplate all the saws and trucks and rope and the countless other gear used in harvesting and carting the cedar logs to the railroad siding. Think of all the persons and the numberless skills that went into their fabrication: the mining of ore, the making of steel and its refinement into saws, axes, motors; the growing of hemp and bringing it through all the states to heavy and strong rope; the logging camps with their beds and mess halls, the cookery and the raising of all the foods. Why, untold thousands of persons had a hand in every cup of coffee the loggers drink!

The logs are shipped to a mill in San Leandro, California. Can you imagine the individuals who make flat cars and rails and railroad engines and who construct and install the communication systems incidental thereto? These legions are among my antecedents.

Consider the millwork in San Leandro. The cedar logs are cut into small, pencil-length slats less than one-fourth of an inch in thickness. These are kiln dried and then tinted for the same reason women put rouge on their faces. People prefer that I look pretty, not a pallid white.

The slats are waxed and kiln dried again. How many skills went into the making of the tint and the kilns, into supplying the heat, the light and power, the belts, motors, and all the other things a mill requires? Sweepers in the mill among my ancestors? Yes, and included are the men who poured the concrete for the dam of a Pacific Gas & Electric Company hydro plant which supplies the mill's power!

Don't overlook the ancestors present and distant who have a hand in transporting sixty carloads of slats across the nation from California to Wilkes-Barre!

Once in the pencil factory—$4,000,000 in machinery and building, all capital accumulated by thrifty and saving parents of mine—each slat is given eight grooves by a complex machine, after which another machine lays leads in every other slat, applies glue, and places another slat atop—a lead sandwich, so to speak. Seven brothers and I are mechanically carved from this "wood-clinched" sandwich.

My "lead" itself—it contains no lead at all—is complex. The graphite is mined in Ceylon [now Sri Lanka]. Consider these miners and those who make their many tools and the makers of the paper sacks in which the graphite is shipped and those who make the string that ties the sacks and those who put them aboard ships and those who make the ships. Even the lighthouse keepers along the way assisted in my birth—and the harbor pilots.

The graphite is mixed with clay from Mississippi in which ammonium hydroxide is used in the refining process. Then wetting agents are added such as sulfonated tallow—animal fats chemically reacted with sulfuric acid. After passing through numerous machines, the mixture finally appears as endless extrusions—as from a sausage grinder—cut to size, dried, and baked for several hours at 1,850 degrees Fahrenheit. To increase their strength and smoothness the leads are then treated with a hot mixture which includes candelilla wax from Mexico, paraffin wax, and hydrogenated natural fats.

My cedar receives six coats of lacquer. Do you know all of the ingredients of lacquer? Who would think that the growers of castor beans and the refiners of castor oil are a part of it? They are. Why, even the processes by which the lacquer is made a beautiful yellow involves the skills of more persons than one can enumerate.

Observe the labeling. That's a film formed by applying heat to carbon black mixed with resins. How do you make resins and what, pray, is carbon black?

My bit of metal—the ferrule—is brass. Think of all the persons who mine zinc and copper and those who have the skills to make shiny sheet brass from these products of nature. Those black rings on my ferrule are black nickel. What is black nickel and how is it applied? The complete story of why the center of my ferrule has no black nickel on it would take pages to explain.

Then there's my crowning glory, inelegantly referred to in the trade as "the plug," the part man uses to erase the errors he makes with me. An ingredient called "factice" is what does the erasing. It is a rubber-like product made by reacting rape seed oil from the Dutch East Indies [now Indonesia] with sulfur chloride. Rubber, contrary to the common notion, is only for binding purposes. Then, too, there are numerous vulcanizing and accelerating agents. The pumice comes from Italy; and the pigment which gives "the plug" its color is cadmium sulfide.

At this point, please pause and recall some of the skills, materials, and places involved in the making of a simple pencil. (I list a few in the figure on the next page.)

* * * * *

At this point, Leonard Read, author of "I, Pencil," asks his readers a question:

> Does anyone wish to challenge my earlier assertion that no single person on the face of this earth knows how to make me?

How about it? Would you challenge his assertion? Please pause to consider it before you read on. Is it true that no one person knows how to make a pencil?

**Figure 1.1 The Making of a Pencil**

| Skills | Materials* | Places |
|--------|-----------|--------|
| logging | cedar | California |
| carting | tint | Oregon |
| mining | wax | San Leandro, CA |
| growing (hemp) | glue | Wilkes-Barre, PA |
| cooking | graphite | Brazil |
| raising foods | clay | Sri Lanka |
| shipping | ammonium hydroxide | Mississippi |
| flat car making | sulfonated tallow | Mexico |
| rail making | candelilla wax | Indonesia |
| railroad engine making | paraffin wax | Italy |
| milling | hydrogenated natural fats | |
| kiln operating | lacquer | |
| tint making | castor oil | |
| kiln making | carbon black | |
| pouring concrete | resins | |
| string making | zinc | |
| chemistry | copper | |
| lacquering | factice | |
| castor oil refining | vulcanizing agents | |
| resin making | accelerating agent | |
| carbon black making | pumice | |
| metallurgy | cadmium sulfide | |

* This list includes only those materials that become part of the pencil, not the many others mentioned that are used to process these inputs.

"I, Pencil" continues:

Actually, millions of human beings have had a hand in my creation, no one of whom even knows more than a very few of the others. Now, you may say that I go too far in relating the picker of a coffee berry in far off Brazil and food growers elsewhere to my creation; that this is an extreme position. I shall stand by my claim. There isn't a single person in all these millions, including the president of the pencil company, who contributes more than a tiny, infinitesimal bit of know-how. From the standpoint of know-how the only difference between the miner of graphite in Ceylon and the logger in Oregon is in the type of know-how. Neither the miner nor the logger can be dispensed with, any more than can the chemist at the factory or the worker in the oil field—paraffin being a byproduct of petroleum.

Here is the first of three fundamental lessons about economic life that "I, Pencil" teaches: The human knowledge that is essential for producing the things we want and need is fantastically dispersed around the world. It is in the heads and hands of thousands—or millions—of people. There is so much knowledge in these processes that no one person or group could possibly know more than a tiny fraction of it. Now for the second lesson:

Here is an astounding fact: Neither the worker in the oil field nor the chemist nor the digger of graphite or clay nor any who mans or makes the ships or trains or trucks nor the one who runs the machine that does the knurling on my bit of metal nor the president of the company performs his singular task because he wants me. Each one wants me less, perhaps, than does a child in the first grade. Indeed, there are some among this vast multitude who never saw a pencil nor would they know how to use one. Their motivation is other than me. Perhaps it is something like this: Each of these millions sees that he can thus exchange his tiny know-how for the goods and services he needs or wants. I may or may not be among these items.

Everyone aims at his or her own purposes. This is not to say that people are selfish and inconsiderate of others, but rather that we all care more about our own purposes and families and, indeed, our favorite charities, than we care about those of others. Almost no one involved in the process cares much about getting pencils made; all have their own purposes in mind. We are self-interested. That's the second fundamental lesson about economic life that "I, Pencil" teaches; the third follows:

> There is a fact still more astounding: The absence of a master mind,
> of anyone dictating or forcibly directing these countless actions which
> bring me into being. No trace of such a person can be found. Instead,
> we find the Invisible Hand at work. This is the mystery to which I
> earlier referred.

No one is in charge. There is no mastermind, no boss. In a very real sense, the process is out of control! People work together to produce pencils and printers and sewing machines and smart phones, but nobody manages their production from start to finish. Nobody *could* manage these processes *as a whole*, because they are too complex for any person or group even to begin to grasp, much less direct. Indeed, where people have tried to direct production processes, as in the old Soviet Union, they have failed utterly. Production must happen spontaneously—without central direction—if it is to go forward smoothly.

A market economy is a *spontaneous order*; its orderliness and coherence happen, without any design or plan, in response to the behavior of its constituent parts. Language is like this—it was not invented or designed; rather language evolves out of the interactions of people seeking to communicate. Snowflakes are spontaneous orders. They are beautiful, even perfect in their way, but not designed. They happen as a consequence of the interaction of water molecules under certain conditions of temperature, humidity, and air pressure. The Internet is a spontaneous, undesigned order that is constantly evolving in response to human desires and innovation.

Together these three lessons about the economy raise the key question for this chapter, whose answer is the first of the three principles that explain why people flourish better the freer is the economy they live in.

If

1. the knowledge necessary for production is spread all over the globe, and
2. everybody whose knowledge and skills we need is self-interested, and
3. nobody is in charge,

then

how can it all work so smoothly and dependably? It would seem to be a recipe for chaos! *What provides the coordination that keeps a decentralized market economy running so smoothly and productively?*

We take the coordination for granted: Is there anyone of us who doubts that if we wanted a pencil today, we could go to the university book store or local drugstore and find one? Of course not—we would be surprised if there were not a supply of pencils there. But how does it come to be that there are pencils for sale, in about the right quantities, in lots of stores all around (the commercialized part of) the world—with no one in charge of getting them there?

Consider the wood of the cedar trees that goes into the pencils: Why do the lumber companies cut about the right amount of cedar, rather than too much oak or maple instead? How do they know how much of each to cut? Once the cedar is harvested, there are many different uses for it. My wife has been equipping our closets with cedar hangers, our backyard fence is cedar, some picnic tables are cedar. Why doesn't too much cedar go to fencing and picnic tables, and too little go to hangers and pencils?

What provides the coordination? There is perhaps no more important insight in all of economics than the answer to this question. Answer for yourself before reading on.

\* \* \* \* \*

*What provides the coordination* among the millions of people who contribute directly or indirectly to the making of pencils and every other good or service?

Prices do.

*Market prices coordinate the actions of billions of people pursuing their myriad goals, by communicating the changing, particular knowledge of everyone about the availability and potential uses of everything.*

Market prices are necessary to allow societies to function. Without market prices—not just any prices set arbitrarily, but prices determined in free exchange—human society would regress to savagery, because we would not know what to do to use our scarce resources sensibly. Prices provide us with essential information about the current and anticipated state of things in society, as understood by everyone involved. They communicate concisely, to everyone interested, the specialized knowledge that is spread all over society. They need never be exactly "right" to do their job well; in fact, most prices are "wrong" to some degree most of the time because they reflect people's mistakes, misjudgments, and misinformation as well as their good judgments and sound information. Nevertheless, market prices do a marvelous job for us, and there is nothing else that can take their place.

Perhaps the best way to understand this point is to consider what a fix we would be in if we had no prices to communicate to us, in usable fashion, the knowledge of myriad others. Let's consider such a situation next, with a thought experiment.

## A Railroad Thought Experiment

Imagine yourself the Commissar of Railroads in the old Soviet Union. It is the early days after the Revolution of 1917; you and your comrades are trying to eliminate markets and money relations, to do away with the anarchy of markets, and to plan directly for the good of the people. Suppose you are truly dedicated to your task, as many of the old Bolsheviks were—they worked long days for little pay, burning with desire to make communism work. You are not out to line your own pockets, you are genuinely striving to do what is best for the Soviet Union.

Now suppose you want to build a railroad line connecting City A to City B. Standing between the two cities is a mountain range that presents you with a choice: you may build the railroad either through the mountains or around them. There are advantages and disadvantages to both choices. If you go through the mountains, you will save greatly on the amount of steel you use, because that route would be much shorter than going around. At the same time, however, going through the mountains will require a great deal of engineering to design the bridges and tunnels and elaborate grading necessary to get the railroad through the mountains. By contrast, if you go around the mountains, you will need to use very little engineering because the line can be laid out simply on level ground. But you will have to lay much more steel rail because the route is far longer.

Which route would you choose? Would you go through the mountains, saving on steel but consuming more engineering? Or would you go around the mountains, saving on engineering, while consuming more steel? You are the Commissar of Railroads, and the choice is entirely up to you. Remember, we assume that you care only about what is best for the nation as a whole. Which would you choose?

To keep the thought experiment simple, let us ignore all considerations other than the consumption of engineering and steel. Of course, much more is involved in building a railroad than just steel and engineering; there are the ties and gravel, explosives and excavating equipment, labor of many sorts, fuel, machinery, and so on. Let us ignore these or assume that the same amounts would be needed on both routes. Once the railroad is built, there are different advantages to each route. For example, the route through the mountains would be shorter and hence provide a quicker trip between the cities. On the other hand, going around the mountains would allow the road to serve more towns and farms and factories along the way. Again, let us ignore all these considerations, or assume that they come out even, so that we have a manageable problem to think about.

Would you go through or around? How would you make the decision?

Consider the kind of information you would need to take into account. You know that there are very pressing needs for steel all around the country. Steel is needed to make girders for new hospitals, pots and pans, vehicles of all descriptions, surgical instruments, and thousands of other valuable goods. If you use more steel on your railroad line, less steel will be available for all these other important uses.

At the same time, engineering services are urgently needed all around the country. Engineers' time and expertise is needed to design and build irrigation systems, mines, harbor installations, and thousands of other systems that will improve the country's productivity. If you use a great deal of engineering building your railroad, the country will wait precious months for those other systems and their services.

So there is your problem: If, when you build your railroad line, the alternative uses of steel—the girders, pots and pans, vehicles, surgical instruments, etc.—are more important and pressing to the nation than the systems and services that need engineering, then you should put the engineers to work building the railroad through the mountains. That way you would save on the relatively scarce and precious steel, and use more of the relatively abundant engineering. By contrast, if the other uses of engineering—the irrigation systems, mines, harbor installations, etc.—are more important and pressing than the other uses of steel, then you should run the line around the mountains, to save on the relatively scarce and important engineering services and use more of the relatively abundant steel.

What would you decide?

\* \* \* \* \*

When I ask this in lectures, most of my audience has no answer. And that's the right answer.

Think what you would need to know in order make the judgment: In order to know the value of steel in other uses, you would need detailed information on the value of the uses to which it would be put. Consider a new hospital that might be built with new steel girders. What is its value? In order to answer that question, you would need to know what the various doctors and nurses and hospital administrators know about currently available space, the state of repair of existing hospitals, the benefits of the new location, and so on. In order to know the value of steel in making pots and pans, you would need to know what various householders and restaurateurs know about the condition of their existing pans, their expectations of need for more pans or pans of different sizes, their preferences for steel pots and pans as opposed to copper, and so on. You would need similar kinds of knowledge to assess the value of steel for manufacturing different kinds of cars and trucks.

Think how dispersed and interconnected is the information you would need with respect to even one vehicle. In order to know the value of, say, a new truck, you would need to know what the trucker knows about the value of the shipments he could make with the truck. In order to know the value of particular shipments, however, say, of produce to grocery stores in the region, you would need to know what the grocer knows about the value of fresh groceries on his shelves. In order to know that, you would need to know what the customers know about the value of the dinners they mean to make with those groceries.

The same kinds of considerations hold on the engineering side. What would you need to know in order to assess the value of engineering used to construct, say, an irrigation system? You would need to know what the farmers know about how much the yield of their fields would increase with irrigation. Of course, to know the value of that increased yield, the farmers need somehow to know what consumers know about the importance to them of the additional food produced.

In short, in order to make a sound assessment of whether steel or engineering is more important in other uses, and accordingly whether to build your railroad line from City A to City B through or around the mountains, you would need an overwhelming amount of detailed knowledge held by thousands, nay, millions of people throughout your society. How would you get that information? Would you send out surveys? As Commissar, you hold absolute power; you may execute anyone who does not tell you promptly what you ask.

But do people even know what they prefer until they are faced with an actual choice? Often they don't, so they might not even be able to answer survey questions accurately. And how would you aggregate all this information, if you could get it all? How much time would it take to get answers back? And by the time you got it all and aggregated it, wouldn't conditions have changed? Your information would constantly be going out of date. Isn't it clear that you simply *could not get the information you need* in a manner timely enough to make it useful?

Furthermore, even if you could get complete and timely information about what everyone knows that's relevant to the use of steel and engineering, you would still need to deduce from it where to build your railroad. How could you possibly know what all that information means for your decision? How would you begin to make sense of all that data?

If you could not say which route you would choose for the railroad from City A to City B, you gave the right answer. It is simply not possible to decide on any rational basis. In the words of Ludwig von Mises, who first pointed out this problem to the socialists, you would be "groping in the dark." You would have to guess. Even though you have absolute power as Commissar of Railroads, and even though you have the best will in the world and a burning desire to make communism outperform capitalism, you would be simply unable to determine the best route, because you could not possibly know which route would be less costly to society overall. The knowledge you would need is too vast, too dispersed, too specialized, and too changeable; and too much of it is inarticulate anyway. (We discuss inarticulate knowledge below.)

This is *the knowledge problem of central planning*. It explains why comprehensive socialism must necessarily always fail: the central planners cannot get the knowledge they need in order to plan effectively.

Now, let's change the thought experiment slightly. Instead of Commissar of Railroads in the old Soviet Union, you are now the chief operations officer of a for-profit railroad company somewhere in the capitalist West. You face the same problem. You want to run a railroad line from City C to City D, and there is a mountain range between them, so you must go either through or around. How would you decide on your route? Again, assume that all the other costs and benefits come out the same on both routes, so that the only variables to consider are the different amounts of steel and engineering you would use. Answer for yourself before you go on.

* * * * *

Unless you are quite unusual, you would decide according to what's cheapest. You would calculate the total cost of each route, in each case multiplying the amount of steel required by the price of steel, and adding that to the amount of engineering required times the price of engineering. Whichever route gives the lower total is the one you'd choose.

Typical, greedy capitalist! All you care about is the company's profits, the bottom line. Like capitalists the world over, you would give no consideration to the overall good of the nation. You would ignore the question of whether steel or engineering is more valuable in other uses, even though that question is crucial to the overall productivity and living standards of your society. You would just do whatever is cheapest, focusing on your company's profits and ignoring the well-being of other people.

But— and here's the marvel—in doing whatever is cheapest in a free economy, you unwittingly do take into consideration every single piece of information and every bit of human knowledge about the values of thousands of alternative uses of steel and engineering. You learn from examining a few numbers all that the central planner would be powerless to find out In months of investigation. And choosing the cheaper route saves what's more valuable in other uses for those uses. How? Because all the relevant knowledge available is embodied in the *prices* of steel and engineering. The lower total cost of one route, as compared to the other, tells us that the combined total of steel and engineering needed for the cheaper route is less valuable *in other uses* than the combination needed for the more expensive route.

Suppose many existing hospitals are small and out of date (in a free market for hospital care). The stronger the desire for new space, the more health care companies and philanthropists will be willing to pay contractors for the erection of new hospitals; and therefore, the more the contractors will be willing and able to pay, if necessary, for the steel girders with which to build them. The price of steel, likewise, reflects the number of house-holders desiring to buy new steel pots and pans and the urgency of their desires. It reflects the amount any trucker will pay for a new delivery truck, which reflects the value of the produce deliveries he makes, which reflects the value of the groceries on the shelves, which reflects the value of the final consumer's dinner. The number and urgency of all these direct and indirect desires for steel is reflected in the price offered for steel, as the various would-be buyers compete for the limited quantity of steel.

The price of engineering at any time is determined in the same manner. If new irrigation systems would improve farm output only a little, then farmers would not be willing to pay much for the engineers' time, and the price of engineering would be correspondingly lower.

This railroad example illustrates the essential point that market prices give us a reliable gauge of the value of productive resources. To see why this is so, consider how market prices are determined: A particular price at a particular time results from competition among buyers and among sellers. Competing bids from would-be buyers push the price upward; competing offers from would-be sellers push the price downward. Each would-be buyer makes his bids based on his particular knowledge of the value of the resource to him. In a kind of implicit auction, he bids as little as he can to still remain in the running, and he never bids more than the good's value to him. At the same time, each would-be seller makes her offers to sell based on her own particular knowledge of her costs—what she must give up to provide the good for sale. She asks as high a price as she can and still remain in the running, and she never asks a price lower than what it costs her to offer the good for sale. Out of that ongoing competitive process of bids and offers emerges the ever-fluctuating market price of the resource. In economic terminology, this is the process of price determination by the interaction of supply and demand. Notice that no individual really *sets* the market price; it emerges out of the interaction of many individuals. As economist Antony Davies says, "Prices are metrics that reflect value, not levers that set value."

The market price reflects the value to the last buyer just barely willing to pay that price, and the cost to the last seller just barely willing to accept that price. Thus the market price (at that moment—remember prices constantly fluctuate) is the actual value in society of one more unit of that resource—what (someone in) society gives up in providing one more, and the benefit (someone in) society realizes from gaining one more.

Stated differently, the market price tells us what one more unit of a good is worth to others. Only with this knowledge can we calculate the least costly ways of producing the things we want, and thereby satisfy as many different human wants as possible.

With market prices to guide us, we can make use of the knowledge of everyone in society about the supplies of and uses for every different resource. In George Selgin's useful term, prices serve as knowledge surrogates. They distill the knowledge of millions of people into a number. With market prices to guide us, each of those millions of people can stay well coordinated with all the others, never using for a less-important purpose what someone else needs for a more important purpose. Without market prices, however, we would be helpless, unable to coordinate our innumerable activities.

## The Nature of Knowledge

The necessity of market prices arises out of the nature of human knowledge. The great Austrian economist F. A. Hayek laid out the connection in his famous article, "The Use of Knowledge in Society." Hayek distinguishes two broad categories of knowledge: *scientific knowledge* and *local knowledge*. Scientific knowledge is much more systematic. It can be written down. It is relatively enduring, though scientific ideas sometimes are overturned by a new paradigm, as in the shift from earth-centered to sun-centered astronomy. Scientific knowledge can be effectively shared, passed wholesale from one person to another.

While scientific knowledge is of course very important, it is not the only kind of knowledge. The other sort, the local knowledge on which we focus here, is equally or more important to social well-being. This is what Hayek calls "knowledge of the particular circumstances of time and place." Real estate agents, for example, specialize in knowing what various houses are for sale in their areas at what prices. Shipping agents know what space for freight is available on different trucks or trains headed for different destinations on different days. Farmers must know the moisture content in their recently-cut hay in order to bale it at the proper time. Each person in the job market knows his or her own aptitudes and qualifications better than anyone else.

In each of these cases, some particular individual (or perhaps just a few individuals) has specialized knowledge about some particular productive resources, and how they might be used to greatest advantage. The knowledge is valuable, but it's local. It can't be looked up. It is available only to that individual or a few individuals.

Local knowledge has several characteristics that lead to the knowledge problem for central planning, and make prices necessary for communicating knowledge.

First, knowledge is dispersed. Think, for example, of the knowledge needed to make a pencil. It is dispersed from Northern California to Sri Lanka to Wilkes-Barre to Indonesia. More important, it is dispersed among thousands of individuals who specialize in everything from logging to mining to chemistry to metallurgy to operating a kiln. Hayek emphasizes that each of us has special knowledge, known only to the individual you or me; good use might be made of that special knowledge if only we can somehow get it into the system.

Second, knowledge is incomplete. We are always learning, filling in the gaps of our understanding, discovering something we did not know the day before. (We pursue this point at length in the next chapter.)

Third, much valuable human knowledge is inarticulate, or tacit. That is, we know it, but we can't say precisely what we know. For a trivial example, we all know how to tie our shoes. But suppose we were asked to write down precisely what we do, so that someone who did not know how to tie her shoes could read and follow our instructions. Could we do it? Probably few of us could make better than a bad job of it. Of course, we know how to tie our shoes, but we don't know it in such a way that we can put it into words. Our knowledge is tacit, inarticulate—it is in our fingers, not in our heads.

This point deserves emphasis because so much important knowledge is tacit. Consider the tacit knowledge of a skilled personnel officer, the sort of person who, year after year, manages to size people up in their interviews, assess how well they'll fit into the enterprise, and consistently hire the right people for the various jobs. Picture that person coming up to retirement. The boss says to her, "Stephanie, we are sure going to miss you. We don't want to lose your skills, however, so in your last few weeks here, would you please write down what you do to size people up so well, so that we can fully instruct your replacement?" What an absurd request! No one can write down how she sizes someone up. The knowledge is a matter of hunches, judgment, interpreting hundreds of non-verbal clues. It is almost entirely inarticulate.

Here is a final example, taken from Hayek, of how tacit knowledge is: What do we mean by the knowledge of the skilled engineer? It is the knowledge of how to solve problems. It is not the knowledge of how to solve some particular problem, because once a particular problem has been solved, the solution can be written down and passed on. No, the knowledge we value in a skilled engineer is knowledge of how to figure out how to solve new problems. Picture the focused face under the hard hat, looking at a new construction or reinforcement problem, or the software systems engineer faced with integrating incompatible programs and operating systems. What sort of knowledge does such a person draw on to solve such problems? Surely it is not the kind of knowledge that can be written down. It's experience. It's what Hayek calls a technique of thought. It cannot be articulated.

A fourth characteristic of local knowledge that leads to the knowledge problem for central planning is that much human knowledge is latent at any particular time. That is, we know, but we are not aware that we know.

In such cases, we do not become consciously aware of our knowledge until it is somehow brought to our attention. I remember my high school physics teacher telling our class that we all "knew" the Doppler Effect—that the sound made by a moving object seems higher pitched to us when the object is approaching than when it is moving away. We all drew a blank. He smiled and made the sound every child makes when imitating a fast car or airplane going past. Sure enough, the pitch goes from higher to lower. Of course I knew that, but I had not been aware that I knew it.

Because local knowledge is dispersed, incomplete, tacit, and latent, it is not possible for the people who have that knowledge to communicate it clearly to some central planner. If that knowledge is to be used effectively, the people who have it must make the decisions that depend on it.

In order for overall coordination to be maintained, each local decision-maker must somehow take into account the relevant local knowledge of everyone else. In our example of building the new railroad line, the chief operating officer of the railroad company must somehow take into account the local knowledge of all the users of steel and engineering, and that of the users of all the goods and services produced with steel and engineering. Prices give us that vast amount of local knowledge. Or, rather, they do not give us the knowledge itself—that is so vast that it would overwhelm us—but instead, prices serve as surrogates for that knowledge. They embody in that simple number, the price, all we need to know of the vast amount of local knowledge held by others.

Hayek uses the example of a change in the supply of, or demand for, tin to illustrate how prices communicate to all, in a manner usable by all, the special knowledge of all. The long passage deserves quoting in its entirety:

> Fundamentally, in a system in which the knowledge of the relevant facts is dispersed among many people, prices can act to coordinate the separate actions of different people.... It is worth contemplating for a moment a very simple and commonplace instance of the action of the price system to see what precisely it accomplishes. Assume that somewhere in the world a new opportunity for the use of some raw

material, say, tin, has arisen, or that one of the sources of supply of tin has been eliminated. It does not matter for our purpose—and it is very significant that it does not matter—which of these two causes has made tin more scarce. All that the users of tin need to know is that some of the tin they used to consume is now more profitably employed elsewhere and that, in consequence, they must economize tin. There is no need for the great majority of them even to know where the more urgent need has arisen, or in favor of what other needs they ought to husband the supply. If only some of them know directly of the new demand, and switch resources over to it, and if the people who are aware of the new gap thus created in turn fill it from still other sources, the effect will rapidly spread throughout the whole economic system and influence not only all the uses of tin but also those of its substitutes and the substitutes of these substitutes, the supply of all the things made of tin, and their substitutes, and so on; and all this without the great majority of those instrumental in bringing about these substitutions knowing anything at all about the original cause of these changes. The whole acts as one market, not because any of its members survey the whole field, but because their limited individual fields of vision sufficiently overlap so that through many intermediaries the relevant information is communicated to all.

Hayek continues, "We must look at the price system as such a mechanism for communicating information if we want to understand its real function." Prices are "a mechanism for communicating information." Few insights in all of economics are more important than this one. Prices—ever-adjusting market prices—are our indispensable means of communicating to one another knowledge that is radically dispersed among us all, incomplete, changing, tacit, and latent.

Hayek stresses how wonderfully efficient the price system is—it shields us from information overload:

The most significant fact about this system is the economy of knowledge with which it operates, or how little the individual participants need to know in order to be able to take the right action. In abbreviated form, by a kind of symbol [that is, the price], only the most essential information is passed on and passed on only to those concerned. It is more than a metaphor to describe the price system as a kind of machinery for registering change, or a system of telecommunications which enables individual producers to watch merely the movement of a few pointers, as an engineer might watch the hands of a few dials, in order to adjust their activities to changes of which they may never know more than is reflected in the price movement.

I illustrate Hayek's point to my students at Towson University, where we have excellent lacrosse teams, by considering how and why our lacrosse players might react to the disturbance in the tin market. Do our lacrosse players monitor the tin market? Of course not. But will they adjust their behavior appropriately? Yes, they will, if the price system is allowed to do its work.

We trace an illustrative scenario from tin to lacrosse sticks this way: The price of tin rises, either because "a new opportunity for the use of ... tin has arisen, or [because] one of the sources of supply of tin has been eliminated." Again, "it does not matter for our purpose—and it is very significant that it does not matter—which of these two causes has made tin more scarce." As the price of tin rises, the makers of tin cans need to charge a slightly higher price to cover the higher cost of tin. Some users of cans, perhaps juice producers, respond to the slightly higher price of tin cans by putting some of their juices into aluminum cans instead. They compete for the limited supply of aluminum cans by offering slightly higher prices for them, and as the price of their product rises, the makers of aluminum cans respond in turn by increasing their output. In order to do that, they need more aluminum; and their increased demand for aluminum (and, of course, the increased demands of other manufacturers switching to some degree from tin to aluminum) tends to bid up the price of aluminum. Because the price of aluminum is a bit higher, the makers of lacrosse sticks, whose handles are aluminum, must charge a slightly higher price for their sticks, to cover their slightly higher costs. And finally, the slightly higher price of lacrosse sticks leads one or two of our Towson lacrosse players not to buy that extra stick he or she has been considering. Lacrosse players in Towson do not monitor the production and use of various metals; they don't need to. They need only the information they receive through prices to persuade them to adjust their behavior as appropriate to the new relative scarcity of tin, and therefore of its substitute, aluminum.

What is really wonderful about all this—Hayek calls it a "marvel"—is that the lacrosse players—and can makers and juice producers and lacrosse stick makers and aluminum producers—all react as they would if they knew directly of the new scarcity of tin and wanted to be socially responsible. But they don't know, they don't need to know, and they need no sense of social responsibility. Prices guide them to appropriate adjustments of their actions. Hayek continues:

> Of course, these adjustments are probably never "perfect" in the sense in which the economist conceives of them in his equilibrium analysis. But ... the marvel is that in a case like that of a scarcity of one raw material, without an order being issued, without more than perhaps a handful of people knowing the cause, tens of thousands of people whose identity could not be ascertained by months of investigation, are made to use the material or its products more sparingly; *i.e.,* they move in the right direction. This is enough of a marvel even if, in a constantly changing world, not all will hit it off ... perfectly.

With market prices to guide us, we are all led to use resources in nearly the best available ways. We don't put engineers to work designing trestles and tunnels when they are more urgently needed designing irrigation systems; we don't use aluminum in spare lacrosse sticks when it's more urgently needed in cans to replace tin cans made more expensive by some disturbance in the tin market.

Prices are precious. If we are to use scarce resources to satisfy people's wants in the most economical way—to achieve the greatest possible human satisfaction for what we give up in the process—prices are the knowledge surrogates we rely on and cannot do without.

## Should Prices Ever be Controlled?

How far can we push this insistence on the value of market prices? Is it *never* in the public interest for governments to control prices?

Let's seek answers to these questions by considering an extreme case— price gouging after a hurricane. Many people condemn *those* market prices as unjust, and support price controls. For example, after Hurricane Hugo hit Charleston, South Carolina, in September of 1989, prices of many needed goods shot up. Because the storm surge had polluted the city water system, bottled water was in great demand, rising drastically in price. Because power lines were down all over the city, gasoline-powered generators that had sold for a few hundred dollars before the storm were going for several thousand dollars afterwards. Ice that had sold for $1 a bag was selling for $10 a bag.

Should grocers be prevented from raising bottled water prices from, say, $1 a gallon to $10 a gallon? Should hardware store owners be prevented from raising gasoline-powered generator prices from, say, $300 to $3,000? Or is it best for the people of Charleston, generally considered, to let those prices rise, to let the market prices prevail?

In Charleston after Hurricane Hugo, anti-gouging sentiments carried the day politically. The mayor and city council passed legislation making it a crime to sell goods for more than they had sold before the hurricane. The punishment for this crime was up to thirty days in jail and a $200 fine.

Let us leave aside the important philosophical question of whether it is right or wrong to charge such high prices, and focus instead on the economic consequences of letting prices rise sky-high, versus holding them down to pre-storm levels.

Suppose the Charleston politicians had left the markets free and allowed grocers to sell their bottled water at, say, $10 a gallon, up from $1 a gallon. What would that $10 a gallon price have communicated? What would it have "said" to those who first arrived at the stores?

It would have communicated—in the summary form of that shocking $10 per gallon price—the combined knowledge and judgments of many people in and around Charleston as to the extent of damage to the city water system, the amount of bottled water available on store shelves, how long it would probably take to get the system fixed, and how hard it would be to bring new bottled water into the city. To those arriving at the store, the $10 per gallon price would have boiled all this information down to this message: "Clean water is very scarce right now; lots of people want some; don't take much."

One excellent characteristic of market prices is that at the same time they communicate dispersed knowledge, they provide an incentive to act on that knowledge. In the wonderful phrase from Professors Tyler Cowen and Alex Tabarrok, "a price is a signal wrapped up in an incentive." What incentive would the $10 price give buyers arriving at grocery stores, eager to stock up on clean water? Of course it would give them an incentive to buy less, which is exactly the response needed by other people who have not yet had a chance to get to a grocery store. It would give the early-arrivers a strong incentive to leave some water for the late-arrivers. Here again, the market price brings about coordination: while bottled water is precious and scarce, its high price motivates people to share the short supply with others.

By contrast, consider what actually did happen in Charleston in 1989 after the price controls were enacted. People who arrived first at the grocery stores bought all the water they could carry, quickly stripping the shelves. When those from harder-hit areas finally arrived, there was no water for them. Market prices were forbidden, so coordination broke down.

Notice how this phenomenon puts the issue of fairness in another light. Observers of the high price might ask themselves *who* would buy water at that price? "The rich," they think, and that seems unfair to people with less money. But if instead we ask *how much* water people would buy at that price, the answer is that probably all buyers, rich and poor, would buy less than they otherwise would, and thereby leave more for others. The pre-storm price of $1 a gallon was certainly unfair to those who couldn't get to stores early, because a price of $1 a gallon meant they got no water at all—it was all sold out. Had a high market price been allowed to do its essential job, it would have deterred both rich and poor from buying more than they considered essential, and spread out the available supply among more of the residents of Charleston. In an important way, it would have been fairer for everyone to have a chance to buy some water at $10 a gallon than for a lucky few to buy up the whole supply at $1 a gallon.

What happened when price controls were put into place is really worse than what we have described so far, because some people bought what water they could at the low, controlled price inside Charleston, and then took it *outside* the price-controlled area to sell it at higher prices. Perversely, the price controls gave people an incentive to move water away from where it was needed most!

Prices provide information and incentives to both consumers and suppliers. What would a price of $10 a gallon have communicated to suppliers, including potential suppliers who would not ordinarily be in the bottled water business? To alert and enterprising people in surrounding states who had the ability to truck water to Charleston, the price would have said, "Bottled water is much more valuable in Charleston than here; take a truckload to Charleston!"

The high price of $10 a gallon would have provided a powerful incentive for people outside the storm-damaged area to bring bottled water to Charleston, and thereby relieve the scarcity and bring prices down. We can imagine college students in Virginia and Georgia hearing of $10 per gallon water in Charleston, renting a truck, buying all the water they could from their local Walmarts, loading their rental truck, and driving all night with precious supplies of clean water. As soon as they open up their truck and start selling, they begin to relieve the scarcity, and prices start heading back down. Indeed, they might find that as the day goes on, and others with the same idea appear, they must offer their water for $9 a gallon, then $6, then $4, and so on. The high price of $10 a gallon creates the incentive for actions that bid it down.

By contrast, what did the enforced pre-hurricane price communicate? It said that there had been no change in the relative desire for and availability of bottled water in Charleston. That message, we might say, was a lie. And it carried no incentive for people to go out of their way to take bottled water to Charleston.

Consider the case of gasoline-powered generators, whose prices went up from hundreds to thousands of dollars before the price controls were imposed. Again, the free-market price—let's call it $5,000—would communicate that people's desire for power generation was urgent while the availability of generators was low. The high price would signal potential suppliers of generators to bring them to Charleston, but we can't really say that the market price would do what it does with bottled water—cause people to buy fewer generators than otherwise. At a price of $5,000, it seems most people would simply have to do without a generator and the electricity it would supply. In this case, it's appropriate to ask who *would* buy at that price?

Think about it before reading on to the next paragraph: Who would be willing to spend $5,000 on a portable generator? Try to "think outside the box." The seemingly automatic response I usually receive from my students is that "the rich" would spend $5,000 for a generator, because they are rich, while "the poor" would have to do without. "The rich" would have the benefits of electricity, then, and "the poor" would not. Try to go beyond this first answer, because it's not a good one. Read on when you have an answer you like: Who would buy a generator for $5,000?

* * * * *

One way to approach the question is to consider what kinds of people in Charleston have the most to gain from a supply of electricity and therefore would bid the most for a portable generator. Is that homeowners? Probably not. What would a grocery store owner pay for a generator if she had two thousand dollars' worth of frozen food in her freezers and three thousand dollars' worth of perishables in her refrigerated cases, all beginning to warm up? What would a filling station owner pay for a generator if he had five thousand dollars' worth of much-needed gasoline in his underground tanks, inaccessible because he had no electricity to power his pumps?

Suppose the grocer and the filling-station owners had been able to buy the generators, because a $5,000 price tag deterred any homeowner from buying a generator that was much more useful to the community at the grocery store or filling station. Who would have had the benefit of the electricity generated? Certainly the grocer and the filling station owner would have benefitted, but all their customers would have benefitted, too. Because electricity was much more valuable keeping perishables cold and gasoline flowing, a high price for generators was just what the people of Charleston needed to maintain coordination among them all, by giving everyone an incentive to get electricity to where it could do the most good.

What happened, in fact, when the price controls were imposed and generators could legally be sold for no more than the $300 they sold for before the storm? If you had been a hardware store owner with a couple of generators, what would you have done with them? Again, think it through before reading on.

* * * * *

What was the effect of preventing "price gouging" on portable generators? I have one illustrative story from my friend Professor Russ Sobel, who was there at the time:

> My neighbor was high school best friends, years ago, with the now owner of a local hardware store. The store had two generators. He didn't get the store open before the price controls took effect. So he was faced with them. He kept one for his family and sold the other at the controlled price to my neighbor (like 1/10th of the free market price). My neighbor's daughter (who was my age...the "girl next door" cutie) was blow-drying her hair on it, and my dad was going over to use his

electric shaver. In the meantime, the gas station, the grocery store, the bank (with an ATM), and K-Mart were all without power.

What a dreadful waste of precious resources!

## Summary

Freely-determined market prices are society's essential means of communicating the vastly dispersed and ever-changing "knowledge of the particular circumstances of time and place." We should free all our markets because we need market prices to give us this essential information in order to coordinate our various activities. Prices tell us what to do, or how to do it, by telling us indirectly what others know and what they are doing. Prices communicate to all, in a manner usable by all, the dispersed knowledge of all. Without market prices we would face chaos and poverty. With market prices, we cooperate, coordinate our infinitely varied purposes, and prosper.

Supporters of government intervention in markets may object, saying that the knowledge problem of central planning is irrelevant to public policy in countries such as the United States, where *comprehensive* central planning is not tried, where our economy is largely free. While of course we are free of *comprehensive* central planning, we nevertheless have lots of individual policies that constitute *degrees* of central planning. While our governments do not try to do without market prices, as in the old Soviet Union, they impose many policies that distort or even forbid market prices. Such policies inevitably hinder prices from communicating dispersed knowledge accurately. To that extent, such policies are a problem.

Hayek writes that "we must look at the price system as such a mechanism for communicating information if we want to understand its real function—a function which, of course, it fulfills less perfectly as prices grow more rigid." When public policy makes prices more rigid or distorts prices away from market-determined levels, that policy impedes the communication function of prices, reduces the coordination among different people that market prices make possible, and thereby reduces overall well-being.

Interventions such as minimum wage laws (wage rates being the prices of labor services), rent controls, subsidies to reduce mortgage interest rates (interest rates being the "price of time"), price ceilings on gasoline, price supports on milk and cheese, subsidies for alternative energy sources such as wind and ethanol—all these distortions of prices block communication and hinder coordination. In each case, the intervention brings about the kind of waste (though perhaps harder to detect) that occurred when Russ Sobel's neighbor dried her hair, and his father used his electric shaver, with electricity that could have kept thousands of dollars' worth of food from spoiling.

Every price has an important story to tell. Every single one should be left free. Good government will protect all people's freedom to negotiate whatever prices they see fit for the purchase or sale of their property, in peaceful negotiation with others.

Though market prices are essential to human flourishing, they don't guide us all by themselves. If we are to cooperate as well as possible in a society based on division of labor and exchange, we must use prices to discover how best to create value for others. That is, we must use prices to pursue profit and avoid loss, because profits—in a free market—come from creating value for other people. While that is not a generally held opinion, it is as true as arithmetic. To profit and loss, and to their all-important role in making the world a better place, we turn in the next chapter.

Chapter Two

# Profit and Loss Guide Innovation

I n a world of endless possibilities but limited resources with which to try out those possibilities; in a world where many people have business ideas but it's not clear which of those ideas are sound and which unsound; in a world where no single person even knows how to make a pencil, much less predict what new products, processes, and technologies will best serve people's needs a year or five years from now—in such a world, we need some means of sorting out the good ideas from the bad, for discovering which products and processes actually do serve us better than others.

We need free markets because free markets give us profit and loss, and profit and loss guide innovation. They are imperfect guides, to be sure, but they are the best available to us. Hence the second of three principles of spontaneous economic order that account for why we should free our markets:

> In free markets, profit and loss help entrepreneurs discover the most
> value-creating uses of scarce resources by providing them feedback
> about how well they are serving others: profit rewards value creation;
> loss punishes value destruction.

This chapter explains what profit and loss are and what they signify. It lays out the indispensable role they play in innovation. It distinguishes

admirable from blameworthy profit. It explains that profits are more important as guides to future action than as rewards for past action, and draws
conclusions for public policy.

## Opposing Views of Value, Exchange, and Profit

Let us take a moment at the outset to appreciate the astonishing creativity
of market economies. Contemplate all the delightful goods and services we
enjoy—if we live in the economically freer regions of the world. How did
it all come to be?

Some who enjoy rock- and ice-climbing may value life in nature and
scorn workaday, commercial enterprise. Yet their joyful recreation in the
mountains is vastly enriched by their crampons and ropes, their high-fric-
tion-soled rock climbing shoes, their high-tech alloy ice axes, their pitons
and carabiners, all of which are created through an immense network of
enterprises in mining, manufacturing, metallurgy, chemistry, materials science, transportation, insurance, and the like. The luxurious wealth that is
rock-climbing gear is provided for them by entrepreneurial industrial and
commercial enterprise.

Closer to our daily lives, we have contact lenses, air conditioning,
Tylenol, and hot showers. We have music, at minimal expense, that in both
quality and variety far surpasses what kings and queens of old could enjoy.
And we can listen as we go for a run, or fly through the air at 35,000 feet.
When the snow flies in the winter and nothing is growing for hundreds of
miles around, we have fresh grapes and kiwi fruit.

An academic, I revel in the immediate availability of information of
all sorts via the Internet, and I shall be eternally grateful to the Microsoft
programmers who gave me automatic formatting of footnotes in Word.

This abundance is astonishing, enriching, glorious.

What makes developed economies so creative? What guides that creativity in socially useful directions? We begin to answer these questions with
the help of some basic economic principles.

How would you answer each of the following questions? Please think them through before going on; I'll give my answers in the discussion that follows:

- What determines something's value? (economic value, not spiritual or moral value)
- When a sale is made, who benefits and who loses, the buyer or the seller?
- Can wealth be created simply through trade?
- How much profit is too much?

* * * * *

What determines the value of a product? For a long time economists had the answer wrong. They believed that the value of a good was determined by the labor that went into producing it, directly or indirectly. The great Adam Smith got this wrong in chapter five of *The Wealth of Nations*, where he said, "Labour, therefore, as it appears evidently, is the only universal, as well as the only accurate measure of value."

Karl Marx picked up on Smith's error and developed it into his labor theory of value, which underlies all of Marxian economics.

A crucial implication of the labor theory of value is that value is inherent in the good itself and, hence, is *objective*. It implies that a good's value can be measured or calculated; it does not vary; it is fixed as a consequence of the labor that went into producing the good. The value is in the good itself.

The labor theory of value has been discredited in economics since the 1870s. Even most Marxists now reject it. A little thought will make clear that the labor theory of value must be wrong. A house that falls down is not a good house, regardless of how much work went into building it. As a professor, I run into the labor theory of value frequently when students who have failed tests plead for a passing grade on the grounds that "I studied so hard!" If the labor theory of value were true, then mud pies should be worth as much as apple pies, as long as the same amount of labor went into each.

Value is not determined by labor input, but by the judgment of the valuer. We say, accordingly, that value is *subjective*, determined by the person (the subject) doing the valuing, not the object being valued. A mud pie is not worth as much as an apple pie because people like eating apples and dislike eating mud.

An important implication of the subjective theory of value is that different people value things differently. Accordingly, when considering the value of something, it is wise to ask, "value to whom?" A pick-up truck is generally of more value to a Wyoming rancher than to a New York City accountant. Some people prefer pepperoni pizza to plain cheese; for others, it's the reverse. For vegetarians, a hamburger has no value at all.

Of course, the same person will value the same thing differently in different situations. An obvious example is food. When we have just eaten, we put a much lower value on a nice meal than when we have not eaten all day. Value is subjective.

Here is a quick quiz to check the reader's understanding of this principle: Suppose, one evening, you and your friend go into a Pizza Hut hungry and buy a large pepperoni pizza for $11.00. What is value of that pizza? Not the price, the value; the price is easy; it's $11.00. But what is the *value* of the pizza? Please answer before reading on.

\* \* \* \* \*

If you answered that the value of the pizza is $11.00, then you fell into the trap. We can be certain that neither you nor the Pizza Hut values the pizza at exactly $11.00. If the pizza were worth exactly $11.00 to you and your friend, then you would not have bothered to give up your $11.00 for it. Why take the time to make a perfectly even trade? Similarly, if Pizza Hut valued the pizza at exactly $11.00, they would not take the trouble to produce and sell it for the identical $11.00 value in return.

We can be certain that the pizza is not worth $11.00 either to you and your friend or to Pizza Hut. We can be certain that the pizza is worth more than $11.00 to you and your friend, because otherwise you would not have given up $11.00 for it. Similarly, we can be certain that the pizza is worth less than $11.00 to Pizza Hut, or else they would not have accepted $11.00 for it.

The point is important: Voluntary exchange occurs only when both parties to the exchange expect to be made better off by it. It's not a zero-sum game with a winner and a loser; it's a positive-sum game in which both trading partners win. In an important sense, wealth is *created* through exchange, in that both parties to the exchange become better off in their own opinion—wealthier—as a result of the trade. You and your friend are better off (especially if you are ravenously hungry and would have paid $15 or $20 for the pizza if you had had to) *and* Pizza Hut is better off, because the overall cost to them of producing and selling one more pepperoni pizza is less than $11. Both buyer and seller gain. Wealth is created though trade, as long as the trade occurs in free and open exchange.

These different theories of value have decisive implications for how we understand the nature of exchange and of profit and loss. Marxists and others who hold the labor theory of value necessarily conclude that market exchange is a pernicious business in which some people exploit others. For those who hold the subjective theory of value, by contrast, market exchange means benefit for both parties involved.

If the value of a good were determined by the amount of labor needed to make it, as in the Marxian view, then that value would be objective and fixed, and the buyer and seller could not both gain. Their exchange would be zero-sum—the sum of their gains and losses must be zero. "One man's loss is another man's gain."

On this view, profit is an ugly thing because it can result only from exploitation. To simplify slightly the Marxist viewpoint, profit is the difference between the objective, labor-determined value of the capitalist's product and the wages he pays his laborers. Because the laborers who produced it are the sole source of the product's value, the argument goes, laborers should be paid the whole value they create; but they aren't.

Consider a simple example. Suppose you are the capitalist owner of a tractor factory. In a year, you buy $4 million worth of inputs—steel, tires, glass, copper wire, etc.—that your workers assemble into tractors that sell for $5 million. According to Marxist theory, your workers have created $1 million worth of new value. You pay them, however, only $900,000. Your

$100,000 profit was created by the workers, but you did not pay them for it. Your profit means you exploited your workers. You live as a parasite, at others' expense. Shame on you ... if the labor theory were correct.

But it is not correct.

Next, consider the implications of the subjective theory of value. Because the value of a good is subjective—because different people value things differently—exchange is (except when we make mistakes) value-creating for both parties. As long as each person gives up what she values less for what she values more, exchange creates value for both trade partners. Each person gets more (according to her values) only when the other person also gets more (according to his different values). You and your friend benefit when you buy the $11.00 pizza; so does Pizza Hut.

In the tractor factory example, the wage rates the company must pay emerge from competition among workers for jobs and competition among various companies for workers' services. The workers value their wages more than the time and effort they give the tractor company, and the tractor company values the workers' time and effort more than the wages it pays. Both sides benefit from the exchange, whether the factory makes profits or losses. Notice that the wages to be paid are determined by contract long before the entrepreneur finds out whether he has made profit or loss on his enterprise for any period of time. His profit or loss is irrelevant to his wage bill (except that if losses go on too long, the wages must cease altogether).

Voluntary exchange is positive-sum. Wealth is created through trade, as long as we judge people's wealth by their own subjective valuations. One man's gain, in free and voluntary exchange, means another man's gain. Hence profit is *good*. It results not from exploitation, but from creating new value for other people.

## The Source and Meaning of Profit and Loss

Exactly what are profit and loss, and where do they come from?

To begin with, we should always keep profit and loss together in our thinking, like the two sides of a coin. Think of the market process not as a profit system, but as a *profit-and-loss* system. Think of business people not as profit makers, but as people who risk loss in the hope of profit; frequently they just make losses. The future is always uncertain; no one is guaranteed a profit.

Here's the definition: Profit or loss equals *yield* minus *cost*:

*Yield*

*– Cost*

*Profit or Loss*

This is the broadest definition of profit or loss. In everyday terms, it is the difference between what we get out of an effort (its yield) and what we put into it (its cost). If that difference is positive, it's profit; if it is negative, it's loss. Note the general applicability of this definition: it can apply to everything we undertake. When we go to a movie with friends, the yield is the enjoyment of the film and the companionship; the cost is the next best use we could have made of that time and the money we paid for the ticket. If the movie and companionship are delightful, we profit from going to the movie. If the movie is poor and our companions are dull, we lose by going to the movie.

Yield comprises not just monetary yield. People care about innumerable things other than money; so in figuring yield, we must pay attention to non-monetary benefits. As a college professor I am paid less than I could earn in other professions; and if the money were all I got from teaching, I would not teach. A great part of my yield from teaching comes from its many non-monetary benefits: I get to think about interesting ideas, I get long vacations, I get to spread understanding of ideas I care about, and I get a captive audience six or eight times a week!

Profit and loss are concepts generally applicable to human experience, as is made clear by the many non-business activities to which we apply the terms. One classic use of the terms comes from the Bible, in which Jesus asks, "For what is a man profited, if he shall gain the whole world, and lose his own soul?" Jesus clearly considered such an exchange a losing proposition. Moving from the profound to the commonplace, when I ask my students if they have ever been in an unprofitable romantic relationship, many nod ruefully and others laugh. They all know what I mean. The yield of some relationships is just not as large as all we have to give up to maintain them.

Even for business owners, monetary return is rarely the whole of the yield they seek. Many business owners could make more money working at a salary for some other enterprise than they can make working for themselves. Nevertheless, they prefer working for themselves because the non-monetary satisfactions of being their own bosses and of following their own creative visions provide enough additional reward to make up for the money income sacrificed. Money is rarely the only object of human endeavor.

But money is important. Let us restrict our thinking about yield, for present purposes, to *monetary yield*. The money part of yield is *total revenue*, the money customers pay the enterprise for its product. Cost is *total cost*, everything they spend or otherwise give up (such as alternative uses of the owners' time) to produce that product. Monetary yield represented by *total revenue* minus *total cost* equals profit or loss:

$$\begin{array}{l} \textit{Total Revenue} \\ \underline{-\ \textit{Total Cost}} \\ \textit{Profit or Loss} \end{array}$$

Let's consider the elements of this difference one at a time. First, what determines an enterprise's total revenue, its monetary yield, in a true free-market setting? In very general terms, what's the source of an enterprise's revenue?

The size of the (monetary) yield is determined by the customers who buy; their valuations of the good or service determine the monetary yield to the entrepreneur. In other words, customers will pay for something only what it is worth to them (or less). What they'll pay for the entrepreneur's output is an approximation of the value of that product to them. In short, the entrepreneur's total revenue reflects the amount of *value* she has provided her customers.

Significantly, the value of a product to the customers is almost always *more than* what they have to pay. At the going price, some people get what they consider a decent bargain; some get what they consider a good bargain; and others get what they consider a great bargain. (The difference between the most customers are willing to pay and the price they actually do pay is called *consumer surplus*.) This means the value the entrepreneur provides her buyers is usually substantially more than the revenue she receives. Hence, total revenue is a conservative indicator of the value the business provides to customers.

Now, what determines a business's cost? To economists, all costs are properly understood as opportunity costs, the values of the best opportunities foregone when an action is taken. The cost of production, then, is the next best use of all the resources used in production; it is the value of what does not get produced instead.

Profit or loss expressed in terms of value, then, is the difference between the value an entrepreneur produces for customers and the value of the resources she uses in doing so:

*Value of the output to customers*
*−Value of resources in their next best use*
*Profit or Loss*

The arithmetic is simple, isn't it? But look what a profoundly important insight about enterprise it reveals: Entrepreneurs make profits by increasing the value available from resources, that is, by creating value. On the other side of the coin, entrepreneurs make losses by destroying value.

Again, let's illustrate with an example. Suppose Alice comes up with an idea for a new line of women's sportswear. She goes into business producing it. She incurs a variety of costs. Among other things, she must rent space, purchase cloth and thread, rent or purchase sewing and cutting machines, buy electricity, and hire people to help her. All of these productive resources could be used to produce other things whose value is reflected in the price she must pay for these resources. For each resource she uses, she must out-bid other entrepreneurs who would like to use them for other purposes. Her space could be used to house some other business; the cloth and thread could be used to produce some other kinds of clothing; the sewing and cutting machines could be used to produce sheets, upholstery, or whatever; the electricity could be used for myriad other purposes; and the skills and energy of the people she hires could also be used in all sorts of ways. Don't forget alternative uses of Alice's own talent and energy; the most valuable service she could provide some other employer is the cost of Alice's being in business for herself.

The cost of Alice's sportswear, then, is the value to consumers of the best other things that might have been produced with the resources Alice uses on sportswear instead.

Now suppose Alice's total cost in a year is $100,000, but her customers pay her $120,000 for her sportswear. She makes a $20,000 profit. How? By taking resources worth $100,000 in their next best uses and transforming them into sportswear worth … $120,000! Alice has *created* $20,000 worth of new value for other people. She has put those resources to a higher-valued use than their best (known) alternatives. Her actions are profoundly creative. Her $20,000 profit is a consequence of her creating at least $20,000 worth of new value for her customers.

So now, how much profit is too much?

No amount. There can't be too much profit *if it's made in a free market*.

Suppose Alice were to make far more profit than $20,000. Suppose she had taken $100,000 worth of resources and transformed them into sports-wear worth, say, $500,000. (I don't know how she would do that; using some miraculous new technology, perhaps.) Would her now $400,000 profit be "too much" in some meaningful sense? How could it be? Too much for whom? Her profit means she has produced for consumers *far greater value* out of existing scarce resources than others expect to be able to produce. That creativity is a great thing, not a bad thing. It serves others.

Or suppose that Alice manages to partner with Harry Potter, who waves his wand and conjures the sportswear out of thin air, so that her cost is zero. Suppose he conjures up sportswear for which people will pay Alice $120,000, but Alice uses no scarce resources of buildings, machines, electricity, labor, etc. in doing so. Her profit would be the entire $120,000 she gets paid. Would that be bad for others? Of course not. In that case, we would have sportswear we willingly pay $120,000 for without having to give up any other goods that we would have had to give up if Alice required scarce resources in order to produce.

The more profit, the better for society, as long as that profit is made in a free market.

Next, consider loss. Suppose Alice takes resources worth $100,000 in other uses and transforms them into sportswear for which people will pay only, say, $70,000. She thereby makes a loss of $30,000. What does this loss mean? It means she has destroyed $30,000 worth of value to others. In place of a variety of other goods and services worth $100,000 to us consumers, we now have sportswear worth only $70,000. Our society is $30,000 worse off than we would have been if Alice had never tried her enterprise.

The huge losses that some companies make represent huge losses to society overall. Consider the dramatic true story of Iridium, a satellite phone company that went bankrupt in 1999. Their concept was wonderful: A person with an Iridium phone could call from anywhere in the world to anywhere in the world. The phone would beam a signal up to one of a ring of satellites in low-earth orbit. Computers in the satellites would beam the signal around the ring to a satellite over the person being called and down to his Iridium phone, or to a receiving tower located near him, with the call completed over land lines.

The money cost of the Iridium system was estimated at between $5 billion and $7 billion. The company actually developed communications satellites, put up sixty-six of them, designed and debugged the software to run the system, built ground towers, negotiated with governments around the world for permission to build those towers and run land lines, and so on. It was a tremendous undertaking. All the resources they used—the time and energy of the satellite designers and manufacturers, the rocketry for launching, the time and expertise of the software designers, the computers,

the construction of the ground towers, the time and expertise of the nego-
tiators—all these resources could have been used producing other things
that you and I would have valued. Instead they were used to produce the
Iridium system.

In the end, the system could attract only a few thousand customers,
instead of the millions it needed to turn a profit. The phones were very
expensive; they were large and heavy ("like bricks"); and they performed
poorly indoors. More important, the people at Iridium grossly underesti-
mated the rates of growth and improvement of their main competitor—cell
phones. Iridium could not compete. Around the time of bankruptcy in
2000 they were even preparing to de-orbit the satellites, letting them fall
into the atmosphere and burn up, rather than clutter the space around
Earth with useless junk.

Iridium was a stunning technical success, but a staggering economic
failure. Their losses were in the multiple billions. Why? Because they
destroyed value. They took resources valued at between $5 billion and $7
billion in other uses and transformed them into satellite phone services
valued at only a few million. It was a minor tragedy.

Profit, then, is a consequence of the entrepreneur's creating new value;
loss is the consequence of the entrepreneur's destroying value. More profit
means more new value created. In the same way that prices reflect information about how badly people need things and how easy (or hard) it is to
produce those things, profit and loss reflect information about how much
value people have created or destroyed. Accordingly, there is simply no such
thing as too much profit, *as long as that profit is made in voluntary, free-
market exchange.* The more profit, the better.

## Most Profits are Fleeting

The benefits of profit and loss in a market economy are heavily weighted
toward consumers, not businesses, because of competition. Competition
is the consumer's friend. In a free market, when one company finds a way
to make large profits, competitors quickly arise who seek to earn some of

those profits for themselves by imitating or improving on the strategy of the innovator.

Consider Alice from our example above (without the help of Harry Potter). When she introduces her new line of attractive sportswear she earns profits because customers are willing to pay a price substantially above her cost of production. But then what happens? To the extent that Alice has success, she will attract competitors who make similar sportswear and offer it for sale at around the same price. That competition will cut into Alice's sales; she will have to respond by lowering her price a little. But if her competitor is making some profit he can lower his price a little also. The competition tends to go on until Alice and her competitor just can't afford to lower their prices any further, because they are charging just what it costs, or a razor-thin margin above.

Meanwhile the consumers benefit from more choices and lower prices. So it is for most products and processes: the companies that produce or use them make profit for a while, and then prices are pushed down by competition, benefiting the consumers and eliminating profits *on that product or process.*

But entrepreneurs are endlessly ingenious and innovative, so they come up with still new products and processes and the cycle begins again.

The pattern is clear in the computer and telecommunications industries over the last decades: Consumers have benefitted from ever better, faster, cheaper, lighter, smaller computers, smart phones, laptops and tablets; and ever faster, higher band-width, more mobile and widespread telecommunications. The companies that have produced these have made profits, but those profits are very short-lived. As I write these words Research in Motion (RIM), the maker of the Blackberry, once the leading smartphone, is in trouble. So is Nokia, once the leading manufacturer of cell phones. At present, the Apple iPhone is the leading smartphone, but Google is doing its best to take away Apple's market share with its Android technology. Apple's iPad is the leading tablet, but Amazon offers the Kindle Fire, and Microsoft has just brought to market the Surface. The profits, or losses, to be made on all these products as time passes are uncertain and certainly temporary, but their benefits to consumers are certain and lasting.

And competition squeezes profits and lowers prices for consumers not just in high-tech products. Both Michael Rothschild's *Bionomics* and Russell Roberts's novel, *The Price of Everything*, describe in some detail the extraordinary innovations that producers in search of profits have made over the years in the production of an ancient product, the hen's egg. The innovations have driven down and down the inflation-adjusted price of eggs to consumers; but again, the profits producers earned have been temporary, because all big egg producers imitate the best practices of others as well as they can, and compete on price.

It is true that there are some products that are assured profits, at least for a while, because there are no substitutes, or substitutes that are few and imperfect. Actors and actresses have monopolies on their personal good looks; great athletes have monopolies on their extraordinary skill, grace, and strength. Hence they can charge astonishingly high prices for their performances with very limited competition to bring down the prices their customers pay. But these are exceptions that prove the rule. The main beneficiaries of profit and loss are consumers, not producers.

## The Social Role of Profit and Loss

Clear now on what profit and loss mean, we turn to the indispensable role they play in helping people innovate—discover new and better ways of satisfying human wants—in a world where resources are scarce and the future is uncertain.

Because productive resources such as human talent, machinery, energy, and raw materials are scarce, whenever we use resources to produce one thing, we thereby give up all the other things we could have used those resources to produce instead. (The value of the most valuable bundle of those other things foregone is called the *opportunity cost*, as we have seen.) In order to live as prosperously as possible, therefore, we need to put resources to their most valuable uses.

But just what the most valuable uses are at any time and place is uncertain, both because of the limitations on what any one individual can possibly know (remember that no one even knows how to make a pencil) and because the future is inherently uncertain.

There would be no need for profit and loss *if* the world were not uncertain—*if* everyone could know for sure the most value-creating use of every resource at every time and place, and know that her action was perfectly fitted with the actions of everyone else with every other resource. We could all simply take the action that we directly perceive to be the most value-creating. But we can't have such omniscience, so we need profit and loss to help us discover what to do to get the greatest possible value out of our scarce resources. There are three categories of discovery, the first is ordinary, the second and third are dramatic.

## Discovery of the Best (Known) Uses of (Known) Resources

For illustration of the first kind of discovery, which we have already touched on in another context, let's do another thought experiment: Suppose you are a farmer with a field that's good for crops that grow down in the soil, such as carrots and potatoes. It is nearly planting season, so you need to decide what to plant in that field—how best to use that resource. To keep it simple, suppose you can grow equal quantities of carrots or potatoes in that field, say, one thousand bushels of one or the other. Suppose, as shown in Table 2.1, you expect that the market price for carrots at season end will be, say, $80 per bushel. You can't know that for certain, of course; prices fluctuate constantly. You must use your experience and judgment to interpret past and current prices for clues about what prices to expect at harvest time. Suppose you also expect the cost of producing carrots—for wear and tear on your machinery, for paying your farmhands, and for fertilizer and pesticides—to be about $70 per bushel. Hence you expect a profit of around $10 per bushel or $10,000 in all if you plant carrots.

You make the same kind of calculation for potatoes. Suppose that you expect the price of potatoes at season end to be lower, at around $60 per bushel, but you expect costs to be lower still, at around $45 per bushel. Your expected profit for potatoes, then, is $15 per bushel or $15,000 in all.

Note that all this calculating is in terms of market prices (including wages, the price of labor services) which communicate, as we saw in the last chapter, the vastly dispersed and specialized knowledge, experience, and judgment of all the participants in the markets for carrots and potatoes, and for farm machinery, fertilizer, pesticides, farm labor and the rest. The price you must meet for each resource is the most some *other* farmer (or other enterpriser) will pay for the machinery, fertilizer, and so on, based on his judgment of the value he can create for his customers with it. That is, their market prices give a pretty good indication of the opportunity cost of your use of all these resources.

#### Expected Profit or Loss on Different Crops

|                        | Carrots   | Potatoes  |
| ---------------------- | --------- | --------- |
| Expected Revenue       | $80,000   | $60,000   |
| Expected Cost          | $70,000   | $45,000   |
| Expected Profit or Loss | $10,000  | $15,000   |

Given these expected costs and prices and your expected output of a thousand bushels of either crop, what would you plant?

You would plant potatoes, of course, because you expect potatoes to give you a profit of $15,000 instead of the $10,000 you expect from carrots, as shown above. That greater profit, if it comes to pass in reality, would be a consequence of your creating more new value for your customers growing potatoes than growing carrots. Accordingly, growing potatoes would be best for your customers just as it would be best for you. Indeed, as we have seen, it would be best for you *because* it would be best for your customers: it would give them the greatest difference between the value (to them) of the food you grow for them, as reflected in its price (at least $60,000 worth) and the value (to them) of the next best other things they could have had from those resources instead, as reflected in their various prices ($45,000).

Note that even though you expect you can provide $20,000 more value to your customers growing carrots in your field instead of potatoes ($80,000 worth as opposed to only $60,000 worth), you expect you can do that only by giving up an even greater value—$25,000 worth—of other things that could be produced with those resources instead ($70,000 worth as opposed to only $45,000 worth). In a world of scarce resources, the trick is not to produce whatever is most valuable regardless of cost, but to produce whatever will give customers the greatest increase of value. That increase (or decrease if it's a loss) is reflected in profit and loss calculations.

Calculations of expected profit or loss, based on expected market prices, are indispensable for helping entrepreneurs try to discover how best to use scarce resources to satisfy the wants of others.

Of course entrepreneurs' *forward-looking* estimates of profit and loss are not their only means of discovering the most value-creating uses of scarce resources in an uncertain world. That discovery also occurs through *backward-looking* calculations of the actual profits or losses they make on their different projects. Businesses tally up their actual revenues based on the prices at which they were actually able to sell, tally up their actual costs based on the prices they actually had to pay for productive resources, and subtract. In reading the profit or loss on that bottom line they discover whether they have used scarce resources well or badly, whether they have created or destroyed value. Then (if they have enough cash flow to continue in business at all) it's back to their entrepreneurial judgments: What does the profit or loss mean? Why was it different than expected? How might losses be cut, or profits increased? Should we try to improve the product to increase the value to customers or try to cut costs by improving our production methods? Or some of both?

Realized profit or loss never tells an entrepreneur what to do next, of course; it only makes clear the past project's success or failure in creating value for others. But that feedback from the market, that discovery of whether past efforts have created value or not is essential in guiding entrepreneurs as they try to judge what to do next.

## Innovation: Discovery of the New and Better

So far in this section we have talked about discovery of how best to use our scarce resources to get as much as possible of the things we want, when we know both what we have and what we want. It is discovery of how best to use known means to achieve known ends.

The second, more dramatic kind of discovery that profit and loss direct is discovery of previously unknown ways of satisfying human wants: new products, new resources, new productive techniques, tools, and processes. This is innovation, discovery of real novelty that helps us make more out of life. For innovation also, profit and loss are indispensable.

The great economist Joseph Schumpeter coined a famous term for this kind of discovery: "creative destruction." He meant the destruction of goods, processes, and enterprises that once served people well, by means of the creation of new goods, new processes, and new enterprises that serve people better. Schumpeter wrote:

> The fundamental impulse that sets and keeps the capitalist engine
> in motion comes from the new consumers, goods, the new methods
> of production or transportation, the new markets, the new forms of
> industrial organization that capitalist enterprise creates....
>
> [T]he ... process of industrial mutation—if I may use that biological
> term— ... incessantly revolutionizes the economic structure from
> within, incessantly destroying the old one, incessantly creating a new
> one. This process of Creative Destruction is the essential fact about
> capitalism.

For example, consider how we light our buildings. Only one hundred fifty years ago the primary source of light was whale oil lamps. The discovery that petroleum could be refined into kerosene destroyed the role of whale oil in lighting and, with it, large portions of the whaling industry. (By some accounts the advent of kerosene sank the whaling centers of New England into recession for two generations.) This destruction was creative—it resulted from the creation of a lamp fuel that was cheaper and burned brighter and cleaner than whale oil.

Of course kerosene's role in lighting was creatively destroyed, too, by the development of electric lighting, in its own turn cheaper, brighter, and cleaner still. What will creatively destroy electric light bulbs and fluorescent tubes? We can't say, of course, but we should expect it before too long. As of this writing, light-emitting diodes (LEDs) look like the leading contender.

Consider telecommunications. Fifty years ago, when someone in the United States called someone in Australia, the signal of her voice was carried by copper wire—tons and tons of copper torn from the mountains of Peru and Utah and Montana—stretching in a cable across the Pacific. The call could be made, but quality was poor; there were delays and clicks as repeaters amplified the steadily degrading signal.

Now, when we make a phone call to Australia, the signal of our voice is carried either by an optical fiber cable or by microwave. Optical fiber cables are also stretched across the Pacific, but they carry thousands of times as many calls as copper for their weight, and they are made of cheap and abundant sand. Microwave communication requires even less physical stuff: we just bounce the signal off a satellite floating in geosynchronous orbit. Whether the signal is carried by optical fiber or microwave, the call is much cheaper, there are no notable delays, and the quality is almost perfect. Telecommunication via optical fibers and microwaves are creatively destroying communication via copper cable.

Innovation, then, beyond the discovery of how best to use known resources for known ends, is discovery of new and better resources, or new ways to use them, or formerly *unknown* ends. Profit and loss feedback continuously motivates and guides entrepreneurs who seek to innovate.

Profit and loss feedback are not just helpful to human advancement; they are indispensable. Or, rather, perhaps society could advance without profit and loss, but it could only do so much more slowly. The reason has to do with scarcity and uncertainty.

Resources for experimentation are scarce. Lots of people have ideas for new products and processes, but most of those ideas probably won't work, and we don't have unlimited free capital to invest in any and every idea. There is not enough capital to go around. Machinery, energy, and human talent invested in one idea are unavailable to invest in another idea; only some ideas can get tried out.

At the same time, just what are the best new ideas—best in how they satisfy others' wants—cannot be known ahead of time.

As some wag has said, "The future is hard to predict because it hasn't happened yet." The future is uncertain; it is unpredictable, though not unimaginable. In consequence, profits are never assured, because businesspeople can never be certain that their ideas will work. They must try to figure out, to imagine, to project what will work; what will work well enough and at low enough cost so that the price it earns will cover that cost.

Human beings simply don't know for sure what products and processes will fit well into the ever-unfolding future. The following quotations should help to make this clear:

> "This 'telephone' has too many shortcomings to be seriously considered as a means of communication. The device is inherently of no value to us." – William Orton, president of Western Union, 1876

> "The wireless music box has no imaginable commercial value. Who would pay for a message sent to nobody in particular?" – one of David Sarnoff's associates in response to his urgings for investment in radio in the 1920s

> "Who the hell wants to hear actors talk? The music—that's the big plus about this." – H.M. Warner of Warner Brothers on the prospect of sound tracks in movies, 1927

Note the date on the next one; the comment must have been made by summer, because things changed in the fall:

> "Stocks have reached what looks like a permanently high plateau." – Irving Fisher, Professor of Economics, Yale University, 1929

"Computers in the future may weigh no more than 1.5 tons." – *Popular Mechanics*, forecasting the relentless march of science, 1949

"We don't like their sound, and guitar music is on the way out." – Decca Records, rejecting The Beatles, 1962

"So we went to Atari and said, 'Hey, we've got this amazing thing, even built with some of your parts, and what do you think about funding us? Or we'll give it to you. We just want to do it. Pay our salary, we'll come work for you.' And they said, 'No.' So then we went to Hewlett-Packard, and they said, 'Hey, we don't need you. You haven't got through college yet.'" – Apple Computer Inc. founder Steve Jobs on attempts in 1974 to get Atari and HP interested in his and Steve Wozniak's personal computer.

"What would I do? I'd shut it down and give the money back to the shareholders." – Michael Dell, CEO of Dell Computer, before a crowd of several thousand IT executives, when asked what could be done to fix Apple Computer, 1997

All these remarkable quotations show that even people in the best position to judge what sorts of products and processes to try often get it wrong. Who was better able to assess the prospects of a satellite phone system than Motorola? Yet they misjudged. More than one major publishing house rejected J.K. Rowling's idea for the Harry Potter series. Think what a dreadful misjudgment *that* was. In general, it's just very difficult to determine what enterprises will really create value for others: over half of all new businesses fail within the first five years. Human beings are woefully ignorant about what to do today to improve our standard of living tomorrow. Because we just don't know, we have to experiment.

Profit and loss guide the experimentation. An entrepreneur with an exciting new idea peers into an uncertain future and applies her judgment about likely developments in consumer tastes, production technologies, labor costs, shipping costs, and all the other considerations she expects to affect the success or failure of the project she is considering. Based on past and present prices she estimates future prices of everything relevant and thereby estimates the project's profit or loss. That calculation, backed up by varying measures of wishful thinking or lack of faith, by greed for gain or fear of loss, and by plain old hunches, determines whether the entrepreneur goes ahead with the effort, tying up scarce and precious productive resources of human talent, machinery, energy, materials, office space, and the like in the inescapably uncertain venture.

We want entrepreneurs to take risks because, when the risks pay off, we all benefit from the new products and lower costs: think of the iPhone, iPod, iPad, eBay, miracle rice, automatic formatting of footnotes, EZ Pass, Lasik surgery, digital photography, and containerized shipping. But we don't want entrepreneurs to waste society's resources on foolish risks. The lure of profit encourages entrepreneurs to take risks, while the fear of loss discourages them from taking imprudent risks.

Most of the time in a market economy, where entrepreneurs must continually pass the market's test of performance to hold onto their position as entrepreneurs, projects expected to make losses are left unattempted. Projects expected to make profits cannot all be attempted (in a world of scarce resources), so entrepreneurs compare the best prospects with one another, weighing expected profit with relative risk.

In this way, forward-looking profit-and-loss calculations guide entrepreneurs to discover which among an infinity of possible endeavors promises best to create new value for customers.

The consuming public needs some means of sorting out the good ideas from the bad. We need a feedback system that tells entrepreneurs when they are creating value and when they are destroying it, and motivates them to do more of the former and less of the latter. By piling up losses, a new product or process—like Iridium—shows that it's unlikely to serve society well; and its backers are thereby "told" to stop wasting resources on it. On the other hand, when a new product or process serves the public well at low cost, profit rewards its backers and encourages them to develop it further.

These reactions from the market are society's indispensable guidance system for economic activity.

Economic development is an evolutionary process. All evolution consists of variation and selection. In the natural world, variation occurs though
genetic mutation and sexual recombination, producing all the wondrous
variety of creatures we observe, both across and within species. The means
of selection, of course, is reproductive success, or "survival of the fittest."

The economic world works the same way. Entrepreneurial innovation
provides the variation—the myriad new products, materials, production
techniques, and approaches to management, marketing and business organization. These changes can be great or small, ranging from introduction of
an entirely new product such as the personal computer to little refinements
such as a more comfortably shaped mouse.

The all-important means of selection is profit and loss. Through profit
and loss, society sorts out the good ideas from the bad, those goods and
services that satisfy us at acceptable cost from those that don't. Profit and
loss are society's crucial means of guiding human creative energies in directions that actually satisfy people's wants and needs.

The profit and loss system of a free market is ultimately directed by
consumers. In a free market, only those goods and services for which consumers willingly pay, directly or indirectly, get rewarded. Through profit
and loss we say yes to cell phones and no to Iridium.

In a society based on private ownership and freedom of association,
profit and loss in their broad senses determine the fortunes of non-profits
and even informal associations as well as those of for-profit enterprises.
Consider churches. Like corporations, they must generate enough value
for their "customers"—parishioners—to induce them to support the enterprise. If they don't, they fail. A weak and uninspiring church, or one in
an area losing population, may not be able to attract enough productive
resources from its congregation. If people don't come to church and put
money in the plate to pay for an inspiring pastor, if they won't contribute
their time and effort to the church's activities, the church will fail. Straight
economic reasoning applies: If a church does not create enough value for
its members—in fellowship, inspiration, service to the greater community
and the like—to exceed the value of the next best use of parishioners' time,
effort, and money, the church will make losses and fail. By contrast, success-

ful churches provide their congregations with spiritual and social benefits and opportunities to serve the greater community in satisfying ways. For these benefits their parishioners will gladly donate time, effort, and money. The church creates more value than it consumes; it profits and thrives.

The same reasoning applies to private-sector non-profits such as schools, soup kitchens, recreational sports leagues, symphony orchestras, fan clubs, medical clinics, environmental protection organizations, drug and alcohol treatment centers, summer camps, the Boy Scouts, book clubs, and the myriad other kinds of voluntary associations and enterprises that people create for themselves in pursuit of some shared vision of the good life. In a free society, these succeed and flourish when, in the broad sense, they are profitable for those concerned—when they create benefits for the targeted population greater than the opportunity cost of the resources used. When they make losses—when supporters believe the benefits created fall short of the value that could be created using the time and money another way—they weaken and eventually disappear.

## Discovery of Capable Entrepreneurs

Evolutionary selection operates not just at the level of goods and processes, but also at the level of the entrepreneurs generating those goods and processes. This is the third kind of discovery guided by profit and loss. In the words of Ludwig von Mises,

> Profit and loss are the instruments by means of which the consumers
> pass the direction of production activities into the hands of those who
> are best fit to serve them.

Those entrepreneurs who make good decisions, or even those who are just lucky, will be rewarded with profit. They may then invest that profit in still other new production activities. Accordingly, those who generally serve the public well get the chance to try again.

In our time, Bill Gates and the late Steve Jobs are notable examples of such successful entrepreneurs. Bill Gates started with Microsoft DOS (disk operating system) for early personal computers. It was a good product that earned him profit. He reinvested that profit in improved versions of DOS, then the new Windows operating system and other programs such as Word and Excel. The success of each new product and version has meant more profits that he has invested in still more improvements and other new products.

The story of Steve Jobs is similar. Each good investment he made in his extraordinary career at Apple meant profits that Jobs used to develop new products and improve existing ones. He admitted that sometimes he made mistakes, causing losses that reduced his investable funds; the Lisa computer comes to mind. But by and large he made good decisions, investing scarce capital resources in products that surprised and delighted consumers. Each time he did so, the consumers rewarded him with profits that he used to work further wonders.

By contrast, those who serve us poorly and thus make losses see their funds available for reinvestment shrink. If they make losses big enough for long enough, they are left with nothing to invest at all. They join the rest of us earning wages or salaries.

Mises describes this process as a kind of ongoing election:

> The consumers by their buying and abstention from buying elect the entrepreneurs in a daily repeated plebiscite as it were. They determine who should own and who not, and how much each owner should own.... The ballot of the market elevates those who in the immediate past have best served the consumers. However, the choice is not unalterable and can daily be corrected. The elected who disappoints the electorate is speedily reduced to the ranks.

Note that while the consumers' judgment—their "election"—of entrepreneurs is decisive in a free market, it is not instantaneous. Entrepreneurs must therefore look into the uncertain future and try to foresee consumers' eventual judgments. Their personal stake in the outcome motivates them to peer into the future as discerningly as possible. Whether a given enterprise will become profitable or not can remain uncertain a long time. But always the prospect of profit or loss motivates entrepreneurs to try to make correct judgments for the long term. Those who believe that their enterprises will eventually increase value for consumers have an incentive to invest more and more money and time into it until it does, even though they first make losses for a long time. Through its first many years of existence, Amazon made losses while the enterprise gobbled up the huge quantities of investment necessary to build it. Nevertheless, the entrepreneurs investing in it believed enough in Amazon's prospects of eventual success that they continued to support it. Those who held on, at least until this writing (2013), have been rewarded.

In contrary cases, when entrepreneurs with their own money at stake become convinced that their enterprise will never provide benefits to customers in excess of its costs, they have an incentive to cut their losses by closing it down, even if they have already sunk a frightful amount of money into it. Remember Iridium.

## Market-based Profit v. "Legal Plunder"

This chapter has sung the praises of the profit-and-loss system: Trade creates wealth. Profit results from creating new value. The more profit the better for society. In each case we have added a crucial proviso: *as long as that profit is made in a free market*. The underlying discipline of the free market's basic institutions—private property and freedom of exchange—will direct profit-seeking activities in socially useful, mutually-beneficial directions. (Part II develops this idea.)

When government intervenes, however, or property is not privately owned, or property rights are not protected, profit may come from seizing wealth rather than creating it. In those circumstances, where governments transfer property from those who own it to those who don't, or restrict freedom to engage in mutually agreeable exchange, or fail to enforce contracts; or where government ownership allows one party to pollute, despoil, or deplete what "everybody owns," then profit can be made at others' expense. Such profit-making merits not praise but condemnation.

The crucial factor for distinguishing the good kind of profit from the bad is consent of the parties involved. In a (classical) liberal society, in which governments, in Jefferson's words, "prevent men from injuring one another, … leave them otherwise free to regulate their own pursuits of industry and improvement, and … [do] not take from the mouth of labor the bread it has earned," people interact with one another only when they find it mutually beneficial. Hence any exchange occurs only when both parties (expect to) benefit. The interactions are by what Franz Oppenheimer calls "the economic means"—free and voluntary exchange.

In contrast to the economic means are what Oppenheimer calls "the political means" of transferring goods without the consent of those concerned: taxing, restricting, granting monopolies, licensing, subsidizing, and the like. When political means are used, it is not necessary to get the consent of those one deals with; those possessing governmental power simply compel others. In such circumstances, those we interact with may not find the interaction beneficial to them; they may find it harmful.

In his superb essay, "The Law," Frederic Bastiat called this kind of interaction "legal plunder." It is legal in that legislation permits or requires it, but it is plunder nonetheless because it involves taking without consent.

Ayn Rand, the great Russian-born American novelist, celebrated in this regard the American idea of "making money." When one makes profit in a free and open market, in a very real sense one does *make* money—one creates new wealth for himself and others. But when one profits by the political means, one creates no new wealth, but simply gets wealth that rightly belongs to someone else. In free markets, where property is private and protected, exchange is free, and contracts are enforced, relationships among people are symbiotic: each person benefits the others she deals with. By contrast, where governments require interactions or forbid them, relationships among people can become parasitic, with some benefitting at the expense of others. In such cases it is not clear that profit indicates new wealth created for others.

**Figure 2.1 Profit on a Free Market versus Profit by Political Means**

| Market-based Profit | "Legal Plunder" |
|---|---|
| Economic Means | Political Means |
| "Make Money" | Get Money |
| Create Value | Transfer Value |
| Symbiotic | Parasitic |

Here are some examples we will take up at more length in later chapters:

*Subsidies to logging companies in the National Forests*: The logging companies do not have to pay for the roads they use for access to the timber in the Tongass National Forest and other national forests; you and I and other taxpayers pay for those roads. Because we cover a substantial portion of the cost of their operations, the profits of logging companies are correspondingly higher. These extra profits (or profits where otherwise there would be losses) do not represent new value created; they are a consequence of our being forced to pay for logging roads. That profit is legal plunder.

*Hairdresser licensing*: Licensing law prevents you and me from paying someone to cut our hair if that person does not have a license. The arbitrary and costly requirements of licensing (many of which are unrelated to professional competence or customer safety) make it difficult for people to get licenses. Licensing law further prevents us from hiring even a licensed hairdresser to do our hair in any place but a licensed salon or barbershop. The consequence of these restrictions is less competition and, accordingly, higher profits for established hairdressers and salons. But again, these higher profits do not result from new value created for consumers; they result from political restrictions on choice. That profit is legal plunder, plunder taken from both consumers and the capable would-be hairdressers excluded from the business.

*Milk marketing orders*: Because these state laws hold the price of milk higher than it would otherwise be, some dairy farmers make more profit than they otherwise would. Indeed, that is the goal of the policy. But is this additional profit an indication of additional value created for consumers? No. Here political means are used; dairies are forbidden to compete with one another on price, as they would have to in free competition. The resulting addition to the profits of dairy companies comes not from benefitting consumers, but from the laws requiring dairies to charge more than competition would allow them to charge.

We could fill many books with such examples, but these three illustrate the point: We should endorse and celebrate profits that are earned in free markets, because they come from creating value for other people. We should condemn profits made through the political means, because they come from transferring rather than creating value, and they provide misleading signals about where human effort and other resources should be applied to help humanity flourish. *Crony capitalism* is a helpful term that has come into use since the many government bailouts of the financial crisis of 2008. We should applaud free-market capitalism but condemn crony capitalism. This book is not pro-business; it's pro-market.

## Guidance for the Future, Not Reward for the Past

Before we close this discussion of profit and loss, I want to acknowledge many good people who are put off by free enterprise because of a concern about the morality of profit making. The concern is that sometimes profits (or losses) earned in a truly free market just aren't fair; and therefore, actions that lead to profits (or losses) should be restricted.

To return to the previous chapter's discussion of price gouging, for example, consider the high profits made by merchants who sell bottled water and generators after a hurricane for five or ten times the normal price. Those profits don't seem fair. The store owners have done nothing brilliant to merit those high profits; they just got lucky. And they got lucky because others got unlucky. Why should the economic system reward them?

Some ask the same thing about the large profits made in recent years by oil companies. If prices go up just because of increasing demand from India and China, and through no foresight or hard work of the oil companies themselves, why should the economic system reward them?

On the loss side, as I write these words following the financial turmoil and Great Recession of 2008, many claim that it is unfair for various firms or industries to be driven to bankruptcy by economic forces beyond their control. Why should the economic system punish them? These firms or industries are said to deserve a bailout at taxpayer expense.

I leave to other writers and other books the (to me compelling) philosophical and ethical reasons for not interfering with free-market profit and loss, and focus on the practical, economic reason. That is, *what society requires from profit and loss is not reward for past action, but guidance for future action.* Forward-looking profit and loss projections together with backward-looking profit and loss accounting give entrepreneurs indispensable (though not infallible) guidance for what to do today to make the world a better place tomorrow, and we can't have that guidance for the future without rewarding past results—even results of dumb luck.

Profit and loss do reward or punish past actions, true, but that is not their essential effect in society or the crucial job they do for us. Their essential effect is to guide *future* action by entrepreneurs. As we have seen, the high prices of bottled water and generators right after a hurricane—and the high profits they promise—tell anyone watching to bring bottled water and generators to the stricken area. The high prices of gasoline as I write these words—and the high profits they bring—tell oil companies to expand exploration and production *and* tell other entrepreneurs to develop substitute energy sources. The losses suffered by thousands of investors in mortgage-backed securities who credulously relied on the securities' AAA credit ratings tell everyone watching to weigh risk more carefully before investing, lest they lose their capital. (Of course that lesson is weakened to the extent that investors are bailed out with taxpayers' money. See Part III.)

The main job of free-market profits and losses is not to do moral justice for past action but to give practical guidance for future action. Their crucial role is future-oriented. Reward or punishment for past actions is the incidental means, not the essential end. Looking backward at profits or losses realized from past projects, entrepreneurs see how well they created value for others. Based on that information, their own judgment, and current and expected prices, they make profit-or-loss estimates for various other projects they might undertake in the future. When they choose the ones they expect to be most profitable, *in the expectation that they will enjoy the profit or suffer the loss*, society benefits.

## Summary and Implications for Policy

We need free markets because advances in human well-being depend on innovation, the discovery of new and better ways of satisfying human wants and needs, and innovation requires free-market profit and loss to guide it. Profit rewards the creation of value and loss punishes the destruction of value insofar as prices are market prices that "tell the truth."

The implications of this insight for public policy are straightforward: We should free our markets, all of them. Policies that leave entrepreneurs free to innovate and get accurate profit-and-loss feedback from the consuming public will foster rapid discovery of new and better ways to satisfy the public's wants. Policies that restrict entrepreneurs' freedom, limit the profits of those who serve the public well, or shield from losses those who serve the public poorly, will slow down rates of increase in overall well-being.

Society has no better gauge of the contribution an enterprise makes to the world than its profit or loss in an unhampered market. The profitability of an enterprise is a kind of summary judgment that comprises the individual judgments of literally everyone concerned. Potential customers contribute by their decisions to buy or not to buy at various prices, thereby registering the current value of that product to actual people. Potential investors in the enterprise contribute by their decisions to invest or not, at different stock prices or lending rates of interest, thereby registering their judgments of the enterprise's ability to create wealth in the near and distant future. Potential suppliers to the enterprise contribute by their decisions to sell or not to sell the various inputs the enterprise needs at various prices, thereby registering the judgments of other users of those inputs as to the value of those inputs in other uses.

Accordingly, the ever-changing profitability of an enterprise is the continually-updating outcome of a vast social calculation of its usefulness, based on the knowledge, insights, and judgments of thousands or millions of people to whom the product and enterprise matter. The knowledge content, so to speak, of this process is immense.

Government interventions in the economy substitute the judgments of political bodies, based on the limited view of a relatively few people, for the judgments of the whole market. Rarely, if ever, will such a substitution be justified.

As for subsidies or bailouts: no! Policy should not shield an enterprise from the salutary feedback that is loss. Those in charge of the enterprise need that signal to motivate improvement in their products, production processes, or both. If they can't return to profitability, that *means* the resources they are using would be better used elsewhere, in the judgment of actual consumers. The enterprise ought to close down and release those resources to uses that serve others better.

At the same time, public policy should not penalize (tax) profits made in free and open competition. With those profits consumers signal producers to do more of what they are doing and provide producers the means with which to do it.

In judging which enterprises should be tried out, which should expand and which should close down, we can't do better than leave it to entrepreneurial innovation and profit-and-loss selection in a free market.

Though this chapter has emphasized the informational role of profit and loss in telling businesspeople what to do and how, profit and loss play a motivational role also. In a free market, where interactions are voluntary on both sides, people can profit only when they create benefits for others. Hence in free markets everyone has a strong incentive to perform well in the service of others. In government interventions in the economy, by contrast, where legal force is used to compel or forbid some interaction even against another's will, incentives to serve others are weak or absent. And incentives matter. This brings us to the third main reason why we should free our markets, the subject of our next chapter.

Chapter Three

# Free Market Incentives Foster Service to Others

Human beings are a remarkable blend of knowledge and ignorance, foresight and blindness, good and bad. We have seen that market prices help us overcome our individual ignorance by serving as surrogates for the knowledge of countless others, and that profit and loss feedback in a free market help us discover the value-creating uses of our time, ingenuity, and other scarce resources.

Free markets also help us overcome the inclination to be selfishly inconsiderate of the desires of others. Free markets push us to cultivate a respectful attention to those desires. The incentives inherent in the key institutions on which free markets are based—private ownership and freedom of exchange—restrain and even penalize our baser instincts and require people to consider the well-being of others. Because property rights must be respected in free markets, stealing and cheating are out, whether perpetrated by an individual or a mob ... or a legislature. Accordingly, if Tom desires some part of Jane's property, the only way he can acquire it is with Jane's consent. Such consent usually must be acquired by offering Jane something she desires. And that means Tom must try to satisfy Jane's wants. In the words of my teacher at George Mason University, Walter Williams, "In a free market, you get more for yourself by serving your fellow man. You don't have to care about him! Just serve him."

Freedom of exchange means freedom to exchange with *anyone* (any adult) a person might choose, independent of permission from any government body or other meddler, and also freedom *not* to exchange if one does not like the terms or can get better terms elsewhere. That means that, in a free market, businesspeople must constantly strive to serve others better than their competitors (or potential competitors!) can do; no legislature, licensing board, union, or professional association protects them from the rigor of market competition.

We should free our markets because we need the incentives that private ownership and freedom of exchange give us to serve one another. The alternative is to give some people the legal authority to compel others, and people with such power lose the incentive to consider the desires of others. Human beings don't handle well the power to coerce, not even when the power is meant to be used to benefit society. Thus, the third of three principles of spontaneous economic order that account for why human beings need free markets:

> *Private ownership and freedom of exchange, the foundational institutions of a free market, lead people to serve others in order to benefit themselves, whereas government interventions tempt people to benefit themselves at others' expense.*

In this chapter we illustrate this principle with two natural resource management examples, then contrast directly the incentives people face in free markets and those they face in government intervention.

## Subsidized Waste in a Government-Owned Forest

The Tongass National Forest blankets the Pacific coast of southeast Alaska. The nation's largest national forest, larger than West Virginia, it is also the largest temperate-zone rain forest in the world; while there are larger tropical rain forests, the Tongass is the largest cool-weather rain forest. It is a magnificent land of densely wooded islands, bays and inlets. It is home to grizzly bears, wolverines, Sitka black-tailed deer, bald eagles, and eight hundred year-old Sitka spruce rising 250 feet to the sky. Some 30 percent of all Pacific salmon spawn in its streams.

There has been a major industrial logging operation in the Tongass for about the last four decades. The US Forest Service builds logging roads into the forest and leases to private companies the right to take timber. The logging companies then sell the timber on the open market.

The logging causes environmental damage. Much of the old-growth timber in the virgin rain forest has been cut down. Thousands of miles of heavy logging roads—heavy because the thin, moist soil cannot support the heavy logging equipment—crisscross the forest. For years the loggers clear cut right down to stream beds, allowing erosion to silt up the streams. According to the *Anchorage Daily News*, one stream, "locally called Fubar Creek, was so filled with sediment that water hadn't flowed in it for 13 years." The siltation makes it harder for salmon to spawn. This is a serious economic problem for the region because its main industry is fishing. Sometimes the logging crews would drive excavators right down the stream beds and drag logs through the channel. This practice also damaged habitat where salmon rest as they make their upstream swim because it eliminated the pools of slow-moving water that naturally occur where fallen trees impede the flow.

As painful as this damage to the Tongass is to most of us, it could conceivably be justified if the value of the timber taken out of the Tongass were sufficiently high. After all, as I point out to my students when we discuss this topic, you are taking notes on paper made from trees, writing on desktops made of particle-board, sitting in a building framed up with wooden two-by-fours. We value wood products.

In the case of the Tongass, however, the economic value of the timber taken out is less than the value of the resources used up in getting it out. In the words of economist John Baden,

> [T]he economic costs of securing the timber far exceeded any
> commercial value the timber had.... Roads funded at taxpayer expense

allowed access to timber that was too sparse, too marginal, or too slow-growing to justify the high price of the roads and other development costs. In essence, taxpayers are subsidizing environmentally destructive behavior that no private timber company or private landowner would ever consider.

Lest the reader misunderstand these facts, let me repeat for emphasis: Much of the logging in the Tongass causes environmental damage at a net loss. The market value of the timber that comes out of the forest is less than the cost of building the logging roads into the forest and otherwise managing the logging. Timber companies' lease payments to the Forest Service are far smaller than the Forest Service's expenditures on the logging roads. Consequently, the U.S. Treasury loses most of every dollar it spends on the program. No profit-seeking company would carry on such an operation because it would mean ruinous losses.

The quotation from John Baden above is from 1986, but the logging has continued for decades. As of 2004, the latest year for which the US Forest Service's website provides information, the logging companies paid an average of $42.54 per thousand board feet of timber they extract. But the Forest Service spends on average "between $300 and $400" per thousand board feet. By those estimates, the program loses between 85 and 89 cents out of every dollar. The website attributes the dramatic difference to the "low value of western hemlock lumber," the cost—"as high as $500,000/mile pending stream crossing needs and a host of other high cost items"—of logging roads "that will support a loaded truck over muskeg or floating bog soils," and generally "difficult access since the land consists of forested islands."

Fortunately, the logging operation in the Tongass has been scaled way back in very recent years and loggers are cutting secondary-growth rather than old-growth timber. The Forest Service and private conservation groups are restoring some of the damage. But the question remains: Why would the Forest Service sponsor this environmentally damaging, economically senseless logging in the Tongass decade after decade? Why?

To help you think this question through, here is a useful technique for policy analysis that distills much of the wisdom of public choice economics, the branch of economics that studies the choices made by people in the public sector:

Of any policy, ask two questions:

1. What groups are primarily affected?
2. What are their incentives?

Those incentives will determine (or strongly influence) the outcomes.

The answers to that pair of questions often give one a very good start at understanding the consequences of any public policy, and even its reason for existing in the first place; we'll applied this technique for analysis in this and future chapters. How would you answer these questions for the Tongass? Think it over before continuing.

\* \* \* \* \*

The groups with the most obvious financial interest in the logging program are, of course, the logging interests—the logging companies, loggers, and local sawmills. The logging companies lease the right to take timber from the Tongass, and because they don't pay for the logging roads as they would if they owned the land, a large part of their costs is born by taxpayers. Their profits and those of the local sawmills are far larger than they would be if the logging companies had to build their own roads; more to the point, they are profits instead of losses. Both the loggers and mill workers themselves benefit from high-paying jobs, and the owners of the logging companies benefit through higher (or positive) profits.

Follow the money. Who funds the thousands of miles of roads the logging companies use? The funding comes from another group with a major interest in the Tongass logging program—the United States Forest Service, which administers the program. What is the Forest Service's interest? Well, the program is huge, and a source of substantial revenue to the US Forest Service (even as it is a large drain on the US Treasury). In fact, as early as 1985, "about 342,000 miles of roads [had] been constructed [in all national forests combined] under the auspices of the Forest Service ..., more than eight times the total mileage of the U.S. interstate highway system." The program means a huge budget, many jobs, many offices, many studies to do, and many subordinates for Forest Service officials.

We can suppose and hope that many Forest Service personnel feel guilty about this program. We can imagine, for example, a young college graduate newly hired to the agency and full of idealism about protecting America's forests, when he first learns the reality of this logging program. We can imagine him going to his superior in dismay and saying, "This is terrible; this program should be eliminated, or at least cut back to areas where it makes economic sense!" His superior smiles patronizingly and says, "Really, Joe? And where will you look for your next job if that happens?" We can imagine the young man recoiling, realizing the implications for himself personally, trying to reconcile the conflict between his environmental values and his career plans, and perhaps mumbling something about making the program more efficient. Troubling though it may be to accept, the Tongass logging program is in the economic self-interest of many Forest Service employees; they accordingly have a strong financial incentive to support and build the program.

Follow the money back another step to find another group with an interest in the program: Who provides the Forest Service's funding? Congress does. What benefit does Congress realize from logging the Tongass at a loss? Who might support Congress for supporting this program? The logging companies and those in related industries do. Alaska's senators and representative receive substantial campaign contributions and other political support from the logging interests, to encourage them to keep the logging subsidies coming to Alaska. The representatives have a strong incentive to vote for the logging program to please their constituents and keep those campaign contributions coming.

Of course there are only a few members of Congress in Alaska, but they and the politicians from other timber states gain majority support for the logging program by promising to vote for the pet programs of their colleagues in non-timber states in return.

These are the incentives that have sustained the cycle of money and favors, year after year. The loggers support their congressmen, the congressmen support the Forest Service, and the Forest Service supports the loggers. Each group has strong financial and career incentives to keep this program going.

There is, of course, one other important group hidden in this picture—the taxpayer-citizens. Our role is to surrender to the IRS the money that finances the whole works. Because the loss-making logging in the Tongass is so much *against* our interests, both financial and environmental, we may ask, "Why don't we stop it?" Public choice economics gives a persuasive answer to this question that we will examine in Chapter 7 on the special interest effect. For now, however, let us simply ask a key question crucial to understanding the perverse incentives driving the spoliation:

### Who owns the Tongass?

I generally receive three different, but equivalent, answers to this question. The first answer is "We do," or "Everybody owns it," or "All the citizens." Of course that is true in a sense: The National Forests are held in trust by the government for all the citizens of the nation. We all have some right to the National Forests and the privilege to use them according to guidelines set out by the Forest Service.

The second answer, at first, sounds very different: "Nobody." This, too, is true in a sense: there is no identifiable person or group with exclusive right to use, control, and dispose of the National Forests as they see fit.

The third answer is "the government." Ultimately, these three ostensibly different answers turn out to be different versions of the same one. What everyone owns, no one owns. That everyone owns something means that no one person or group has the privileges of ownership—the right to use, control, and disposal. You are an "owner" of the Tongass, but can you sell your share? Do you have any say in the decisions about how it is used? No. The Tongass is best understood as government-owned, because the government determines its use, control, and disposal.

That, I will suggest, is the problem. But first, let's consider a counter-example.

## Multiple Uses of a Privately-Owned Wildlife Sanctuary

The Paul J. Rainey Wildlife Sanctuary is a 26,800 acre marshland on the Gulf coast of Louisiana, owned by the Audubon Society. According to John Baden, in his book *Destroying the Environment: Government Mismanagement of our Natural Resources*, the sanctuary "is a home for deer, armadillo, muskrat, otter, [and] mink" and 100,000 migrating snow geese use it to rest and feed. Baden tells an interesting story about Rainey, however, that helps us understand the incentives of private ownership. He writes that "since the early 1950s, thirty-seven wells have pumped natural gas (and a small amount of oil) at various times" from the sanctuary.

That's a surprise. In today's climate of zealous environmentalism, most of us would expect a conservation group such as the Audubon Society to reject with horror the approaches of an oil company—an *oil* company!—that wanted to put drilling rigs, with their inevitable noise and unsightliness, not to mention their possible pollution problems, into a bird sanctuary. Few things seem less likely, on a cursory glance, than Audubon's allowing the oil company in.

And yet, until 1999 when leases expired, oil and gas were extracted from the Rainey sanctuary. What do you think happened such that oil companies were admitted there?

* * * * *

Sometimes my students suppose that the oil companies got into the Rainey Sanctuary because of some government intervention, and that is a sensible guess. In this case, however, there was no government intervention; Audubon Society's property rights were completely respected. Here the public policy was laissez-faire—the parties relied upon the protection of property rights and freedom of exchange. So what happened?

Again, ask two questions:

1. What groups are primarily affected?
2. What are their incentives?

Those incentives will determine (or strongly influence) the outcomes.

One group primarily affected was the oil companies. They had a strong incentive to make oil production in the wildlife preserve advantageous to conservationists. The other primarily affected group was the Audubon Society, of course, who had a strong incentive to protect the wildlife in the Rainey Sanctuary, but also to protect other wildlife elsewhere, too. The oil companies offered the Audubon Society a deal. They would let the conservationists set the terms on which it would allow oil production in Rainey, including very substantial royalties. Baden reports that "[the] managers of Rainey found that the timing, placement, operation and structure of oil exploration could be carefully planned in conjunction with the seasonal requirements of wildlife, and adverse environmental effects could be avoided." The oil company offered to route their roads over the least sensitive lands. They had the ability to drill at an angle, so they could site their drills on unimportant land and still reach the expected oil and gas deposits. They agreed to suspend operations in nesting season. Of course they agreed to safety procedures strict enough to satisfy Audubon. And they agreed to pay Audubon very well. Over the years, Audubon earned over $25 million in royalties from their gas and oil. What did Audubon do with the revenue? It maintained Rainey with it, and also bought additional land on which to preserve still more wildlife.

As of January, 2010, the officers of Rainey were investigating further leases in hopes of earning more revenue with which to maintain and improve the sanctuary.

Rainey gives us a marvelous example of dual use of a resource. From that beautiful marshland, society gains both wildlife preservation *and* more abundant natural gas. The oil company benefits. Audubon benefits. Consumers of gasoline and heating oil benefit. There are benefits all the way around.

## The All-Important Institution of Private Ownership

Consider the contrast between the Tongass National Forest and Rainey Wildlife Sanctuary. In the former, we have serious environmental degradation at a substantial financial loss. In the latter, we have both environmental and energy benefits. In the one, the physical resource is allowed to deteriorate; in the other, it is carefully maintained.

What explains the difference? Is Tongass run by bad people and Rainey by good? No. The difference is in ownership and the corresponding incentives triggered by ownership in each case. Tongass is owned by everybody, therefore by nobody. Decisions about it are made by government bureaucrats with no ownership stake in the land. When the logging operation loses money, there is no particular owner who feels and notices that loss. Accordingly, there is no one with a compelling incentive to stop the damage and red ink.

Why is Rainey so different? Because it is privately owned. As owner, Audubon Society has a strong incentive to make the best possible use of the resource to achieve the organization's goals. The resource is a precious asset, *all* of whose value must be tapped in order for Audubon to benefit as much as possible.

In recent years a number of environmental economists, sometimes known as "free market environmentalists," have studied the consequences of private and government ownership on the stewardship of natural resources. The essence of their "new resource economics" is captured as follows: because private owners enjoy any profits and suffer any losses flowing from a resource, they have a strong incentive to use it well. As we discussed in the previous chapter on profit and loss, in a society that permits only voluntary interactions, if resource owners are to benefit from their property, they must use it in ways that satisfy the actual wants and needs of others at reasonable cost. Others communicate their wants and needs by the prices they offer. The owners notice the profit opportunities these prices present for different uses of their resources. They choose the most highly valued combination of uses because they bear the opportunity cost of the choices they make.

If Audubon Society, for example, yields to pressure from radical environmentalists today and refuses to restart gas production in Rainey, it will bear the opportunity cost of that decision—the royalties it could earn and the improvements to the sanctuary those royalties could finance. Audubon feels that opportunity cost. It notices; hence it studies the possibility.

With government ownership of resources the incentives are entirely different. The public servants charged with managing those resources, well-intentioned though they may be, do not have an ownership stake in the resource. They get paid a salary, often regardless of how well or poorly they do their jobs. If the resource is used profitably, they receive no bonus; if it is used at a loss or damaged, they suffer no personal loss or reduction in pay. Because they do not stand to profit from discovering any new and *better* uses of the resources than those the legislature dictates, they are not alert to such possibilities.

In other words, these public servants do not bear the opportunity cost of use. In the Tongass, the Forest Service does not experience the operating losses; taxpayers do. The Forest Service would not realize any savings that would accrue from stopping the waste. Indeed, the public administrators of publicly owned goods generally cannot even *know* the opportunity cost of use. The opportunity cost of any use of a resource is revealed only in competitive markets, in which an entrepreneurial owner tries out some new and different use, or where some other would-be owner offers a price for the resource, which she would try to use to serve the public better. But government-owned resources are almost never for sale, so they have no price. The administrators of Tongass cannot compare the logging companies' lease payments to, say, the purchase prices offered by logging or eco-tourism companies that would like to buy a few thousand acres. The forest is not for sale.

Because the actual uses to which the resources are put have little to no influence on the personal fortunes of the public administrators in charge of them, those public servants have little incentive to serve the public as well as possible. They have a strong incentive, however, to serve the interests that support them politically. And they have a strong incentive to protect their turf. The Forest Service has a strong incentive to serve the logging interests and their congressional overseers, and they have a very strong incentive to keep the subsidy dollars flowing, regardless of what happens to the Tongass and the taxpayers' money.

The point of these contrasting examples is to illustrate the basic principle this chapter presents:

> *Private ownership and freedom of exchange, the foundational institutions of a free market, lead people to serve others in order to benefit themselves, whereas government interventions tempt people to benefit themselves at others' expense.*

The Rainey Wildlife Sanctuary's private ownership and its owners' freedom to make exchanges with the oil companies as they see fit are free market institutions. They motivate the members of the Society to benefit themselves by serving *both* nature lovers *and* NASCAR lovers by simultaneously protecting the wetlands and supporting oil and gas production.

In the case of the Tongass National Forest, both government ownership (or non-ownership) and the compelled transfers of money from taxpayers to the logging program are government interventions. These interventions tempt the logging interests, members of Congress, and the Forest Service to benefit themselves at the expense of the citizen taxpayers.

The point made in the Tongass example merits more discussion, because so many people are accustomed to assuming that the different parts of government act in the public interest. Do they, in general?

## People are Self-Interested in Public as in Private Life

People are self-interested—they pursue their personal well-being as they see it—in both private *and* public life. And in both settings they make mistakes and sometimes behave badly.

This claim is at the heart of public choice economics. One of the founders of public choice, Nobel Laureate James Buchanan, has called it "politics without romance" because public choice rejects the tendency to contrast the imperfections of free market processes with an idealized, romantic view of government intervention. Public choice does not presume that government interventions "will accomplish the desired objectives." It compares the realities of the free market, with all its problems and imperfections, with the realities of government intervention, with all *its* problems and imperfections. Perfection is just not available to imperfect human beings. In choosing between free markets and government intervention, we must ask ourselves not which is perfect, but which is preferable, or least bad, all things considered.

Nearly everyone assumes that people in business are self-interested: Of course business people seek to maximize their profits and advance their careers. (As we saw in the last chapter, this pursuit of self-interest benefits others as long as it occurs in *free* markets.) But what about public servants— US Forest Service bureaucrats, game wardens, city politicians, zoning board members, regulators in the Food and Drug Administration, school board members, state licensing boards, politicians at various levels—are they also self-interested? Do they try to achieve their own personal well-being as they see it? Or do they strive exclusively to achieve the *public* interest, the well-being not of themselves, but of others?

It has long been assumed, in most economic theories and civics textbooks, that public employees (public "servants") act in the public interest rather than in their own personal interest. This is beginning to change. Public choice economics is beginning to persuade the economics profession that people who work in the public sector are as self-interested as people in the private sector. This assumption helps explains much of what goes on in government. By contrast, assuming that public servants aim to serve the public interest helps explains very little of their behavior. In order to understand people's choices, in both public and private life, we should assume that all people are self-interested, that they are trying to achieve their own personal goals at the lowest possible cost to themselves.

Note how this view differs from that of many people who support large, controlling government. People who believe "the government" should provide this service, regulate that activity, and subsidize the other industry implicitly believe that "the government" will do all this in the public interest, not their own personal interest. Or at least, such public-minded service is believed to be possible, if only the right people or the right party get control of government and put "good people" in charge of government agencies and policy-making.

Long experience with governments around the world shows that people in government are as self-interested as people anywhere else. All people behave according to their personal self-interest as they see it, whether they are entrepreneurs or public servants. Of course there will always be people of great integrity in both private and public life who do their duty to others even to their own detriment. There are too few such people, however, to staff a large government, and no reliable way of identifying or electing them in the first place, or persuading them to serve if they could be identified. Of necessity, then, governments will be staffed by people like the majority of those we know, who put their personal self-interest first and the public interest second.

Of course pursuit of self-interest means more than a sterile pursuit of more money, regardless of what some economics textbooks imply. People earn money to accomplish various purposes. They want to feed their families, provide music lessons for their children, strengthen their places of worship, support the United Way, help cure heart disease, and so on. And wise people understand that they promote their own self-interest when they thoughtfully consider the well-being of others. Decent people seek to live honestly and generously as well as prosperously. We know that our true, enlightened self-interest is harmed when we seek material benefit at the expense of a customer, employer, employee, co-worker, supplier, or investor. Honorable people—most, I hope—interact with others only in ways that benefit *both* themselves and others. As Mises wrote, "If honour cannot be eaten, eating can at least be foregone for honour."

In both private and public life, people's aims may be lofty or low, admirable or ugly, considerate of others or contemptibly selfish. Most people probably have a combination of aims across some range of that spectrum, as most of us are a combination of good and bad. In our actions in pursuit of those goals, we can be kind or mean, magnanimous or petty, diligent or lazy. A lot depends on our upbringing, but surely much of our actual behavior depends on the incentives we face.

Incentives are crucial.

Given the inescapable self-interestedness of human beings, the key to a productive and cooperative social order is incentives that channel human beings' pursuit of their own self-interest into actions that benefit others at the same time. To this end we need underlying institutions—basic rules of the game—that give everyone the incentive to cooperate with others and contribute to others' well-being as a way to accomplish their *own* interests. Private property and freedom of exchange are the core institutions that provide this incentive.

When society adheres closely to the underlying institutions of private ownership and freedom of exchange, people tend to establish particular-purpose institutions—organizations, religions, enterprises, associations, clubs—that give people strong incentives to serve others, because in that free setting, people *must* serve others *in order* to achieve their own ends. By contrast, on the underlying institutions of government ownership and restriction of exchange are built particular-purpose institutions—government agencies, regulations and private-sector enterprises adapted to that governmental control—that give people weaker incentives to serve others. These institutions often give people perverse incentives to use governmental power for their own benefit, at others' expense.

## The General Superiority of Free-Market Incentives

The incentives we face depend on the institutions we live and work within, because the institutions shape the way we pursue our self-interest.

Ubiquitous self-interest has profound implications for the desirability of government intervention in general, because *intervention establishes legal power to infringe on property rights and restrict freedom.* That power is dangerous. It is dangerous *because* people are self-interested. Self-interested people in both the private and public sectors will be attracted to this governmental power and use it to their personal advantage, even at others' expense. In words attributed to George Washington, "Government is not reason, it is not eloquence; it is force. Like fire, it is a dangerous servant, and a fearful master."

People interacting by governmental authority thus face incentives very different from those interacting in voluntary association. Where property must be respected and people are free to exchange with one another or not as they wish, the incentive to serve one's fellow man is much stronger than where government compulsion is in play. Accordingly, voluntary associations generally perform better in achieving human well-being. Though the same sorts of people work in both, particular-purpose institutions based on property rights and consent generally contribute far more to human well-being than those based on governmental power. Indeed, the latter often reduce human well-being.

At the core of the difference is that in the private sector—in both for-profit and non-profit voluntary associations—if you want something from someone else, you must persuade her to give it to you. Somehow you must offer her something she values more in return. (In this I exclude, of course, the closest human relationships of family and intimate friendships, which are too strong to be called just "associations." We do things for our loved ones out of love alone.) General Electric and the local supermarket, your church and the United Way all want your money, and they do not know or care about you personally (well, we hope your church does). But to get your money, they must offer you something you want—light bulbs, vegetables, an uplifting religious experience or the satisfaction of helping troubled people—at a price you are willing to pay. They must persuade you to give them your money, and they don't get a nickel without your consent. The interaction must offer mutual exchange to mutual advantage, or it does not happen. Hence in the private sector, based on underlying rules of private property and freedom of exchange, all of us have strong, systematic incentives to serve our fellows. *Serving them is the only reliable way we have to induce them to give us what we want.*

The consequence of these incentives is generally cooperative, productive outcomes. The underlying institutions of private ownership and freedom of exchange require people to cooperate if they are to interact at all—we are not permitted to force our wills on those who do not wish to cooperate. And because we may not take from others by force, we must produce goods and services they want, to exchange for those we want.

In the government sector, by contrast, people may interact by legal force. Where governments intervene in society, when you want something from somebody else, you can use that intervention to force him, legally, to give it to you. The government threatens him with punishment if he does not. Loggers in the Tongass, employees in government schools and in the US Postal Service, and bondholders of failing financial institutions all want your money also, and they don't know or care about you personally either. To get your money, however, they *don't* have to offer you something you want at a price you are willing to pay. The logging companies, the government schools, and the failing financial institutions get your money indirectly but legally, through the taxes that pay for the logging roads in the Tongass, the salaries in government schools, and the bailouts of the financial institutions. You must surrender those taxes or go to jail. The law forces you to use the Post Office for first-class mail service because the private alternatives you would use if allowed to are forbidden. (For more on this intervention see the notes to Chapter 4.) Government-supported enterprises and agencies need *not* gain your consent to interact with you; therefore they may gain at your expense, against your will. Where governments intervene in society, where private property may be legally invaded and exchange may be forbidden or compelled, all of those in positions to gain from the intervention have strong, systematic, corrupting incentives to get what they want the easy way, regardless of the desires of their fellows.

The consequence of these incentives is generally contentious, less productive or unproductive outcomes. When property and contract may be legally infringed, where people may force their wills on unwilling others, (many) human beings succumb to temptation. Rather than produce and exchange, they take. Hence, the lobbying; the manipulation of regulation;

the grasping for subsidies, corporate welfare, licensing, tariffs, and industry bailouts; and the growth of bureaucracy, taxation, and government spending.

Self-interested people, both inside and outside government, will be tempted to use government power to achieve their goals if government power is available to them. Government intervention in the economy, even when ostensibly or initially intended for good purposes, often gets used by people for their own, selfish purposes at the expense of everybody else. Both private interests and government employees, often acting in concert in crony capitalism, will be tempted.

The consequence of this insight for public policy is straightforward: No matter how good the intentions nor how important the goals of interference with private property or freedom of exchange, that interference is dangerous to the public well-being. It carries with it incentives for some people, usually in special interest groups, to use the intervention for their own selfish purposes at the expense of the general public. It is preferable—safer for society—to avoid such interventions altogether. Any net good some particular intervention might do on occasion is more than offset by the net harm most interventions do most of the time. The safest course is to free our markets, completely.

Does this mean markets should be totally unregulated? Not at all. Freedom of exchange, and the corresponding freedom to *decline* exchange, engenders very strong and effective regulation, as we shall see in Part II.

Part I

# Conclusion

The three principles we have discussed in Part I help us understand spontaneous economic order. Let's review them and give each a name for ease of reference.

We'll call the principle from Chapter 1 the Price Coordination Principle:

> *Market prices coordinate the actions of billions of people pursuing their myriad goals, by communicating the changing, particular knowledge of everyone about the availability and potential uses of everything.*

We'll call the principle from Chapter 2 the Profit-and-Loss Guidance Principle:

> *In free markets, profit and loss guide entrepreneurs to discover the most value-creating uses of scarce resources by providing those entrepreneurs feedback about how well they are serving others: profit rewards value creation; loss punishes value destruction.*

We'll call the principle from Chapter 3 the Incentive Principle:

*Private ownership and freedom of exchange, the foundational institutions of a free market, lead people to serve others in order to benefit themselves, whereas government interventions tempt people to benefit themselves at others' expense.*

The more free an economy, the better these principles will work to make it coordinated, innovative, and responsive to people's desires. On the other hand, the more governments interfere with private ownership and with peaceful, voluntary exchange, the more the operation of these principles is inhibited and economic well-being is undermined.

This is not to say that free markets work perfectly! On the contrary, for reasons of inescapable human ignorance we have discussed, in free markets we all make lots of mistakes, some of them desperately costly (remember Iridium). But we don't all make mistakes all the time. With prices to tell us what others know (or think they know), with profit and loss to guide us, and with market incentives to keep us focused on the good of others, we do pretty well for one another when we are free to interact, or not to interact, as each of us sees fit.

One implication of these principles is that free market forces can and do regulate the actions of market participants (not perfectly but) better than government regulators can. That is a hard idea for many people to accept, so we devote Part II to considering it.

Part II

# Regulation by Market Forces Outperforms Government Regulation

Readers of Part I may be ready to agree that market prices, profit-and-loss feedback, and the private ownership and freedom of exchange on which they depend are important to human well-being—even very important.

Many of those readers may nevertheless hesitate to endorse fully free markets. *Largely* free markets make sense, they may think, but don't we need government intervention *here and there* to make sure the free market works properly? People should have private ownership rights and freedom of exchange *mostly*, but suppose people misuse their property or try to take advantage of others? Don't we need *some* government regulation—restriction of property use and limits on free exchange—to make sure that markets work well?

I used to have the same misgivings. I still have a few, but they have weakened over time, almost to the vanishing point. I've come to appreciate the power of property rights and freedom of exchange to discipline human action, and I've grown increasingly uneasy about government action as I have watched it turned to private advantage.

Even though free markets don't work perfectly—nothing human is perfect—they work better than government. The basic institutions of free markets—private ownership and freedom of exchange—set in motion a dynamic *regulation by market forces* that benefits society better than government intervention can. Even when intended to further the public interest, interventions backfire. They distort prices, distort or block profit-and-loss feedback, and tempt special interest groups to use the intervention for their own sakes. In these ways government interventions damage the spontaneous economic order on which rising standards of living depend.

Part II will emphasize that government interventions tempt people to benefit themselves at others' expense, the second part of the Incentive Principle discussed in the previous chapter. Good people who support governmental intervention in the economy want "the people" to discipline "business." They want "business" controlled—lest business put its own interests ahead of the people's. So far as it goes, this concern is wise. But based on this concern they support *government* control of the economy; and this step is deeply ironic and mistaken.

The irony is that governmental power intended to restrain business is power that gets used *by* business to restrain competition and secure bailouts and subsidies. The power, once created, gets out of control. Regulated capitalism becomes crony capitalism. It doesn't work. We need free market capitalism.

The only way to make sure "the people" discipline business is to ban the use of force in the economy—to free our markets completely. *Then*, if "business" wants to further its own interest, it must offer "the people" what the people see as a beneficial exchange. "The people" do control "business" in a free economy.

I suggest that the reader put aside now forever the idea of "unregulated free markets." The conception is fundamentally misleading. In free markets each participant's actions are tightly regulated by the property rights of *others* and the freedom the parties have *not* to deal with each other.

Our choice is not between government regulation and no regulation; our choice is between regulation by centrally planned, static dictates of government and regulation by decentralized, dynamic market forces. It is between regulation handed down by a few authorities with power to coerce and regulation emerging bottom-up from the choices of market participants, none of whom may impose his will on others. It is between regulation by the edicts of monopoly agencies immune from profit and loss and regulation by the choices of consumers and businesspeople, all of whom are subject to profit and loss, as are the standards of behavior they follow.

The fundamental but limited role of government remains: there must be some organized force in society that protects property rights and enforces contracts. But doing that "is the sum of good government," in Jefferson's words. Nothing more is needed from organized force. All the other regulatory functions—assuring quality and safety, establishing industry standards and the like—are or would be handled better by market forces.

Let us see how.

# Chapter Four

# Ownership Matters

The incentives and rights of private ownership are potent regulators. Keeping in private hands the rights to use natural resources and to run enterprises of all sorts promotes good stewardship of resources and good organizational performance. Private owners have strong incentives to look after their property so that it can be a source of profits and other benefits to them year after year. Private owners also have strong incentives to perform well in their interactions with others because their income depends on the quality of that performance.

Under government ownership, things are different. Public administrators of government-owned property may care for or neglect the resources under their charge; but either way, they face no consequences of personal profit or loss from that care or neglect. Hence, their economic incentives to be good stewards of valuable resources are weaker than those of property owners. And, because government-owned enterprises are generally tax-funded, the income they receive does not depend on the quality of their performance; so their incentive for good performance is weaker than it would be if their income depended directly on satisfying customers.

Let us first consider how private ownership improves stewardship, beginning with wildlife in Africa.

# Private Ownership Leads to Good Stewardship

As we saw in the last chapter's examples of Rainey Wildlife Sanctuary and the Tongass National Forest, the institution of *ownership* matters greatly to the incentives for stewardship, because ownership rights give owners a stake in what they own. The changing fortunes of wildlife in Kenya, Zimbabwe, and Namibia illustrate the point well.

## Elephant Management in Kenya and Zimbabwe

The great threat to elephants in Africa is poachers, who kill elephants to which they have no right, cut off their tusks with a chain saw (or an axe), leave the area quickly, and then sell the ivory on the black market. Poachers indiscriminately kill young bulls as well as old. Some poachers are professionals, but some are local people whom foreign middlemen pay, often at prices far below market levels, for the stolen ivory. By 1979, poaching had endangered elephants in much of Africa.

At the other extreme is the threat posed by overpopulation. In the absence of poaching or legal hunting, elephant populations can grow at seven percent per year, a rate at which herd sizes can double in ten years. When elephants are well protected, culling of the herds is usually necessary to prevent the herds from growing too large and destroying woodlands and savannas. Elephants will push over trees just to test their strength or to get at a few high hanging seedpods, so excessive populations can turn woodlands into grasslands, with devastating consequences for browsers such as giraffes and endangered black rhinos.

In both Kenya and Zimbabwe, the elephants were (and still are) formally unowned, or owned by all the citizens, so the countries' governments are ultimately in control of them. The governments of the two nations took very different approaches to management rights and use rights to elephants, however. Below I describe the different approaches, and I ask you, reader, to estimate the changes in the numbers of elephants in each country over the decade from 1979 to 1989, before African elephants were listed as an endangered species and a world-wide ban on trade in ivory was enacted.

In Kenya the elephant population in 1979 was approximately 65,000. Most Kenyan elephants lived, then as now, on game preserves, watched over by game guards. Unfortunately, the Kenyan game guards in the 1980s were relatively few in number, poorly paid, and ill-equipped.

Significantly, Kenya permitted no hunting of elephants. Even before the worldwide trade ban went into effect in 1990, Kenya also had outlawed all trade in elephant products. (The hides, which are made into boots, wallets, and other leather goods, are as valuable as the ivory.) Thus Kenyans had no use rights to elephants of any kind, other than the benefits they might enjoy from tourism. Most rural Kenyans gained little from tourism; those gains were enjoyed by better-off Kenyans in the tourist trade. Rural Kenyans bore the costs of crop damage and personal danger presented by the large and sometimes aggressive animals.

In Zimbabwe the elephant population in 1979 was approximately 30,000, less than half than in Kenya. But Zimbabwe instituted more varied and extensive management and use rights. While Zimbabwe, like Kenya, has extensive national parks and game preserves, the Zimbabwean government also allowed and promoted hunting of elephants. In several large, state-owned areas, strictly controlled hunting was (and still is) allowed. Zimbabwe also allowed trade in elephant products until the trade ban took effect in 1990. In fact, the Zimbabwean government covered part of the expenses of its Department of National Parks and Wildlife Management by selling the ivory and hides of elephants that were culled to prevent overpopulation or killed because they posed a threat to humans. This source of market revenue helped Zimbabwe pay and equip its game guards better than was done in Kenya.

Another significant difference between Zimbabwe and Kenya is that beginning in 1975, the Zimbabwean government increasingly allowed private landowners (mostly ranchers, almost exclusively white) to manage the wildlife on their property. These use rights meant that landowners could hunt, for commercial purposes, the non-protected game on their lands or sell the hunting rights to safari outfitters. Then, in 1988, the Zimbabwean government began to extend these sorts of use rights to villagers who lived on state-owned communal land.

Based on this information, what do you suppose happened to the populations of elephants in the two countries in the ten-year period between 1979 and 1989? 1989 is significant because in that year the African elephant was placed on the list of endangered species by the Convention on International Trade in Endangered Species of Wild Fauna and Flora, to which the governments of Kenya, Zimbabwe, the United States, and some 170 other nations are signatories. That listing effectively meant that trade in elephant hides and ivory was banned worldwide. (The provisions of the treaty are so strict that it is illegal to import an antique piano into the United States, if the keys are ivory.) Again, in 1979 there were approximately 65,000 wild elephants in Kenya and 30,000 in Zimbabwe. What do you suppose the numbers were on the eve of the trade ban?

\* \* \* \* \*

By 1989, the population of elephants in Kenya had dropped from 65,000 to approximately 19,000, while in Zimbabwe the numbers had increased from 30,000 to 43,000.

The first point to jump out of these figures is that government ownership and "protection" are no guarantee of good stewardship. That approach failed badly in Kenya, where the government officials were corrupt and poaching was rampant. Indeed, evidence indicates that Ngina Kenyatta, wife of the Kenyan President Jomo Kenyatta, was a major smuggler of poached ivory. Also involved in poaching and smuggling was John K. Mutinda, Kenya's top wildlife civil servant (see the notes for Chapter 4). Consistant with the Incentive Principle from the last chapter, Kenyan government ownership of the elephants tempted those in charge to use their authority to benefit themselves at the expense of other Kenyans and all who wish for the flourishing of the species.

On the other hand, we cannot conclude that government ownership and "protection" are sure to fail, because the public officials in Zimbabwe protected well the elephants in their national parks and game preserves. It's noteworthy, however, that in Zimbabwe the elephants were a source of revenue for the Department of National Parks and Wildlife Management—the department had an ownership interest in the elephants they protected—so those in the department had a much stronger incentive to do a good job in protecting elephants from poachers than did the Kenyan game guards. (In addition, the elephant hunters represented boots on the ground and, therefore, a deterrent to would-be poachers.)

A lesson to learn is that leaving stewardship of natural resources to government is risky. It's not dependable; it relies too much on good bureaucratic management culture to overcome weak institutional incentives for stewardship.

The 1975 decision by the central government in Zimbabwe to give private landowners authority to manage the game on their lands, including commercial hunting, gave landowners an incentive to preserve the wildlife there. Up to that point, ranchers had had no ownership rights to the wildlife on their lands, so they used the land largely for raising cattle, which they could own and sell. Cattle ranching was not only permitted, but also actively subsidized by the Zimbabwean government with state-provided veterinary and marketing services. Wildlife competed with and sometimes killed cattle, so the ranchers had incentives to eliminate the wild animals which they didn't own. Because they were not allowed to hunt game commercially, they often gave hunting opportunities to their friends. According to Brian Child, one of the wildlife officials who helped implement the CAMPFIRE program discussed below, "without value to landholders, wildlife disappeared."

The improved management culture in Zimbabwe after 1975 produced a healthier environment for elephants, and other wildlife, to thrive alongside the human population. Between 1975 and 1989, even a weak dose of private ownership in the form of management and use rights, coupled with freedom of exchange of elephant products, produced incentives for people to care for what they "owned" for their own sakes, not just because it was their job. After 1975, when the subsidies for raising cattle began to be removed and the ranchers were allowed to profit from the game on their lands, incentives shifted dramatically. With use rights, if not full ownership, came stewardship. By the late 1980s hunters paid on average $25,000 for a hunt in which an elephant was the main trophy. With such money in prospect, according to Child, ranchers began to look after the game on their lands, and "[this] caused a massive increase in wildlife numbers and species, as landholders developed hunting and tourism enterprises." Some landowners added these enterprises to their cattle operations, but some got rid of their cattle entirely and let their land revert to habitat for wild animals. Once the ranchers could own them, the wild animals were often more profitable than cattle.

Given the successes on land owned free and clear by ranchers and with the urging of a few individuals who understood the economics of ownership and stewardship, in 1988 the government extended to villagers use rights over the animals in their areas. Under the Communal Areas Management Programme for Indigenous Resources (CAMPFIRE) the state retained legal ownership of wildlife, but it devolved (or perhaps more accurately from a long historical perspective, it *returned*) the right to manage and benefit from wildlife to rural district councils (local governments), and through them to local communities. (Unfortunately the communities did not hold the use rights directly, but through the rural district councils—local governments. This layer of bureaucracy reduced somewhat the effectiveness of the program; for example, in certain areas the rural district councils did not pay out to the villagers all the money they were owed. Despite this limitation, CAMPFIRE did transfer rights to villagers in substantial degree.) Ultimately there were many CAMPFIRE areas on land totaling some twenty to thirty percent of Zimbabwe.

The principles of CAMPFIRE gave the villagers partial but significant ownership rights over the animals on their lands: Of first importance is that CAMPFIRE provided the villagers with revenue from hunting and tourism on their lands and allowed them to decide how to use it. Payments from hunters and tourists were treated just like revenue from livestock or crops. Communities would decide democratically how to allocate the funds. Child reports that the first CAMPFIRE community "sat down for two days to debate how to use their money, and decided to invest in a grinding mill, provide funds to a school, and retain almost half as cash."

The right to take benefits directly in cash made a world of difference to villagers' attitudes toward wild animals. Instead of viewing them merely as dangerous pests, villagers treated the animals as assets of direct value to themselves.

Trophy hunting on their lands meant not just cash, but also food for the sometimes-hungry villagers. Child writes, "Many [villagers] were astounded that westerners would pay for horns twenty times what the meat was worth, and yet outfitters could still deliver the majority of the carcass to the community."

With these benefits of just partial ownership at stake, everyone in the community looked after the animals. Every villager became a game guard. According to wildlife economist Urs Kreuter, "In some areas villagers began to actively inform on illegal poaching in their areas (unheard of in the preceding colonial era)."

Under CAMPFIRE, community members bargained directly with the safari companies that provided tourism or hunting. As the villagers bargained, much higher, true market prices for the wildlife emerged, rewarding the villages for their stewardship.

CAMPFIRE avoided the knowledge problem of central planning. According to Child, CAMPFIRE let "communities, not outsiders, set quotas for the number of animals that could be taken each season." (Again, this authority had to be exercised through the rural district councils, the local governments.) The authority gave the villagers the opportunity—and the incentive—to manage "their" wildlife for long-run, sustainable benefit to their communities. The results were uplifting. Child again: "With time, communities began to invest in their wildlife, employing game guards, managing fire, counting animals, and fencing crops or homesteads to reduce human-wildlife conflict." And the elephants thrived: "Between 1990 and 2003, the population of elephants on communal lands doubled, even though human population doubled at the same time. Other wildlife increased fifty percent, and trophy size was maintained."

As in Rainey Wildlife Sanctuary, here we have a case of dual use—use of the land as habitation for both people and wildlife—thanks to the incentives of, in this case, quasi-private ownership.

Unfortunately we can't leave the story there; the fortunes of wildlife in Zimbabwe changed again. After the world-wide trade ban was imposed in 1990, Zimbabwe was no longer permitted to sell elephant products. Also, due to pressure from animal rights groups that opposed any killing of elephants, Zimbabwe ceased culling the elephant herds in its national parks. The result has been mixed, and potentially very sad: Elephant populations have increased too much. On parkland spanning the Zimbabwe-Botswana border, according to Kreuter, the herds that used to be maintained in sustainable numbers by Zimbabwe's culling have grown to approximately 120,000 to 180,000 (the number is hotly debated by pro- and anti-hunting groups), "which is about two to three times the previously estimated carrying capacity for this region, and the impacts on the trees in some areas, such as the Chobe River, are devastating. It is expected that with the next severe drought many of these elephants will die from starvation."

Zimbabwean elephants, villagers, and ranchers alike have also suffered from tyranny. Although CAMPFIRE was successful and celebrated, and though it spread widely through Zimbabwe for over a decade, after the year 2000, Zimbabwe's increasingly authoritarian president, Robert Mugabe, began to roll back land use reforms, seizing ranchers' lands and recentralizing control over communal lands. CAMPFIRE continues to limp along, but it has been greatly weakened by Zimbabwe's dreadful misgovernment.

Stewardship still leaves much to be desired in Kenya as well. After the international ivory ban was imposed in 1990, under the influence of animal rights groups and with pressure from its mass tourism industry, Kenya has retained its anti-hunting policies. Further, with generous financial support from western nations, Kenya greatly reduced poaching. Sadly, the consequence, according to Kreuter, has been that the exploding elephant populations "have led to the eradication of most trees in some national parks such as Amboseli [one of Kenya's most popular and magnificent parks] and, with that, the disappearance of browsers, such as black rhinos and giraffes, in these areas."

## Namibia's Stewardship through Local Ownership

Those sad developments in Kenya and Zimbabwe, however, are not all there is to the unfolding story of wildlife conservation in Africa through ownership rights. According to economist and Africa specialist Karol Boudreaux, the successes that came from granting use rights to local residents were so striking that the approach is spreading, most notably to neighboring Namibia.

Namibia has seen a resurgence of wildlife—along with a steady increase in local people's standard of living—since the government gave black Namibians rights to the wildlife on communal lands, in an approach similar to Zimbabwe's CAMPFIRE known as Community-Based Natural Resource Management. Boudreaux writes that the results of changes in ownership rights in Namibia were very similar to those in Zimbabwe:

> [Namibia's experience] was a natural experiment of sorts—in 1974 the
> South African government [which at that time was the governing entity
> in South West Africa, the former name of Namibia] ... gave white
> freehold farmers rights to fence in, manage, and use wildlife. Black
> Namibians had no such rights. Poaching was rampant throughout the
> country on non-freehold land until, in 1996, the [then independent]
> government extended similar rights to rural black Namibians. Now
> poaching on those lands is near zero and the kinds of increases in
> wildlife numbers [seen] in Zimbabwe ... have happened in Namibia.

In Namibia, the legislation enabling Community-Based Natural Resource Management allows local people to form "conservancies" of which they are the members. A significant difference from CAMPFIRE in Zimbabwe is that in Namibia the conservancies hold the rights directly rather than through local governments. Included are the rights to:

- hunt for animals for the use of conservancy members ("own-use");
- capture and sell game;
- cull game;
- manage protected game;
- become a game preserve that permits trophy hunting with a quota; and to engage in non-consumptive use. (This primarily means tourist-related activities that use game; but the definition also encompasses other recreational, educational, cultural, or aesthetic uses.)

The successes of Community-Based Natural Resource Management in Namibia have been substantial and continuing, with, as yet at least, no backsliding from the Namibian government. Boudreaux's 2007 report on community-based natural resource management in Namibia captures the importance of private ownership rights to the flourishing of both wildlife and local people. Included in the report are these and other statements from conservancy members:

"Wildlife numbers are now way up, and this makes us happy. Before, we had no say over the wildlife. Now we can say how much to harvest. This is something we're proud of. And today, we can contract with any investor. Now, we have a contract with a professional hunter, and that never happened before. We are planning for many more things."

"Wildlife numbers are really increasing. I see increases in every species. When we started, there was no wildlife. The animals were owned by the Ministry, so people poached them. Everyone was poaching. What ownership means is you have to take care of it."

"People come here to see the desert elephants, the magnificent scenery and wildlife, the black rhino, and the local people. We have stopped poaching because people value wildlife and see what tourism can do."

## Texas Ranchers Help

One other remarkable piece of the story of protection of African wildlife through private ownership deserves mention.

The scimitar-horned oryx, sadly, went extinct in Africa some time ago. And yet it is thriving under careful management and protection … in Texas. A variety of African exotic species, including the critically endangered addax and the dama gazelle, thrive today, privately owned, on sprawling ranches given over to wildlife instead of cattle. The ranchers have made the switch from cattle to African wildlife guided by profit: Hunters are willing to pay as much as $50,000 for a hunt in which those animals are the trophies.

Providing habitat for exotic animals began years ago when Texas ranchers bought surplus animals from zoos. Under the careful stewardship of their private owners, more than a quarter million such animals now range largely free in the hill country.

And yet, distressingly, these animals are now endangered. They are vulnerable to the good intentions of misguided individuals and animal rights groups who have won a judgment in federal district court for the District of Columbia under the Endangered Species Act.

The decision limits the property rights of the ranchers that own them—and that limitation is dangerous for the animals. Ranchers are now required to get permits from the U.S. Fish and Wildlife Service in order to hunt the three endangered antelope species. According to economist Terry Anderson,

> Everyone agrees that obtaining these permits will be virtually
> impossible—based on past experience, they're very hard to get, and
> they're also subject to objections by groups like the Friends of Animals.
> As a result, Charly Seale, a fourth-generation rancher and the executive
> director of the Exotic Wildlife Association, speculates that there will be
> half as many of these antelope in five years and none in 10 years.

If the ranchers cannot benefit from maintaining the antelope on their land, they lose the incentive to do so.

Elephants, antelope, and other resources, natural and otherwise, should be left in private hands or put into private hands with strong property rights. Governments should sell or give away government-owned resources to private-sector individuals, villages, or groups as the case may warrant, in order for us all to take advantage of the healthy incentives and profit-and-loss guidance of the market process.

## Private Ownership Leads to Good Performance

As the story of elephants demonstrates, private ownership rights (even partial rights) give owners strong incentives for good stewardship. Owners look after their property so that it can be a source of profits and other benefits to them year after year. There is yet another benefit of private ownership: Owners also have strong incentives to perform well in their interactions with others because their income depends on the quality of that performance. Just as owners are accountable for the protection and enhancement of what they own, in free markets they are accountable to those they interact with for fulfilling their part of a bargain. Where enterprises are government-owned, by contrast, performance of obligations tends to be more hit-or-miss. Leaving behind the exotic story of elephants, we take up the more mundane matter of package delivery. For illustration, consider the following thought experiment.

### Package Delivery

Suppose you have a package you want delivered overnight, whose safe and timely arrival matters very much to you. Suppose your choice is to pay a little less to ship it via the Post Office or to pay a little more to ship it with FedEx or UPS. How would you send it?

* * * * *

In my experience asking this question to many classes and lecture audiences, the results are always the same. A substantial majority always say they would choose FedEx or UPS even though they would have to pay a little more. The reason they give is that FedEx and UPS are more reliable. But why is that? Are the people who work for FedEx genetically more reliable, intelligent, and dedicated than those at the Post Office? Surely not. So why does FedEx outperform the Post Office so consistently?

Surely it is a matter of the different incentives facing the two enterprises. FedEx is privately owned and faces robust competition. Its funding depends on its performance. The better the people of FedEx please their customers, the more money they make; the more they disappoint, the more their customers go elsewhere. The connection between their performance and their funding is direct and tight. Hence, FedEx employees throughout the enterprise have strong incentives to perform well.

Employees of the United States Postal Service face much weaker incentives to perform well. Even though they lose billions of dollars on operations in a typical year, they don't go out of business—the government makes up the losses with taxpayers' money. There are no owners pushing managers to cut losses. In fact, there are no owners at all (apart from U.S. citizens as a whole, and are we really owners if we can't sell our shares?). This is a big part of the problem. Also, the Post Office's legal monopoly on delivery of regular mail shields a large portion of their funding from competition. Because Post Office employees are part of a bureaucracy with no owners' profits at stake and with a protected income flow, their funding is little affected by their performance; hence they have a relatively weak financial incentive to perform well.

To generalize the point, under private ownership, enterprises (e.g. FedEx) face a connection of performance and funding that gives them a strong incentive to perform well. Under government ownership, enterprises (e.g. the US Postal Service) face a disconnection of performance and funding that gives them a weaker incentive to perform well.

To improve mail delivery in the U.S., the Post Office's assets—buildings, trucks, equipment, everything—should be sold off to the private sector, and the delivery of first class mail should be opened up to free competition. I would expect a variety of companies, probably including FedEx and UPS or subsidiaries they would set up, to jump into the business. I would also expect Post Office employees in many areas to set up their own local delivery and collection companies. They might even buy the buildings where they have been working and the trucks they have been using. Entrepreneurial innovation would generate more enterprises than I am clever enough to imagine, and profit and loss would select from all those trials the companies and networks of companies that serve the public best. Wouldn't it be fascinating to watch the performance of mail delivery improve, not without some initial problems, presumably, as the incentives of private ownership and the discipline of profit and loss were applied to mail?

## Social Services

Let's look at the consequences of this connection or disconnection of performance and funding for another pair of enterprises in a very different field of endeavor—providing funds to the needy:

When I was a student in Scotland years ago, on returning to classes one September, I was greeted by my friend Donald Henry. "Howard," he said with a twinkle in his eye, "I have a story for you." I wish I could capture his wonderful accent. "After classes this summer I didn't have a job, so I signed on." (That is, he signed on to "the dole," the British unemployment compensation system.)

"Then, before I went to collect the first time, I got a job," he said. Donald went on, sheepishly, "but I kept my appointment anyway. I felt guilty about it, standin' there in line. Then, when I got up to the window and the lady started countin' out the pound notes, I couldn't stand it any longer. I said to her, 'No, I don't desairve it; I have a job.' Guess what she said to me?" Here he gave me a you-won't-believe-this look.

What do you think the lady did?

"She pushed the notes out to me and said, 'Oh, go on, dearie! Everybody does it!'"

How's that for careful husbanding of scarce resources? The purpose of the Scottish unemployment system is to get money to the unemployed, not the employed. In handing money out indiscriminately to unemployed and employed alike, the woman was performing poorly. But how strong an incentive does she have to perform well? If she performs badly, will the organization lose funding? Not at all. The British taxpayers must provide that funding or face jail for tax evasion. With the British dole, as with the US Postal Service, funding and performance are disconnected; hence the incentive for good performance is dramatically weakened.

Contrast that with privately-owned enterprises that provide funds to the needy. Consider, for example, Children's Scholarship Fund (CSF) Baltimore, on whose board I was privileged to serve for a decade. With money raised from private sources, CSF Baltimore provides tuition assistance to low-income Baltimore families, with which parents send their children to private and parochial schools of their choice. Without CSF Baltimore's support, many of these children would be trapped in dreadful government schools.

How careful do you suppose the staff at CSF Baltimore is in making sure that only eligible, low-income families get scholarships? Very careful, of course. They require families to document their income every year; they go over every tax return; when families become income-ineligible, no additional scholarship support is awarded.

Again, what's the difference? Why does the CSF staff take more care than the woman in the Scottish dole office to make sure recipients qualify for grants? They do so because CSF Baltimore's funding depends on how well the organization uses the funds it raises. The trustees and staff of CSF Baltimore understand that their donors make contributions based on the quality of the service the organization provides the community and on its operating efficiency. Those dollars are hard to raise. CSF Baltimore has a strong incentive to be very careful with them. If they don't perform well, they lose their funding, as they should. Not so the tax-supported unemployment office.

The principle here is that the close connection of performance and funding in private-sector institutions gives them a strong incentive to perform well. The funding of privately-owned institutions depends on their performance because they cannot force their funders to pay or contribute. This is true for both for-profit and non-profit enterprises. FedEx must earn its funds by pleasing its customers; CSF Baltimore must earn its funds by pleasing its donors. They must perform well or go out of business. In short, market forces—in the broad sense of forces at work on voluntary exchange —regulate strictly the performance of these privately-owned enterprises.

By contrast, the US Postal Service has a government-enforced monopoly on first-class mail; its customers are trapped. And when it doesn't earn enough to cover its expenses, Congress gives it taxpayers' money. The Scottish dole office, like all government-provided unemployment compensation, raises funds through taxes. If the taxpayers who fund it are dissatisfied with its performance, tough. They must keep paying regardless. In the public sector, performance and funding are largely disconnected; hence public-sector institutions have a far weaker incentive to perform well. With no market forces to regulate them, these institutions perform poorly. (Of course there are other layers of government that are supposed to regulate the USPS and the Scottish unemployment system. But *those government regulators are also publically owned and tax-supported*, so they perform badly, too. We discuss the need for private-sector regulation in Chapter 6.)

Private ownership is not a flawless institution—nothing human is flawless. Owners often use bad judgment, make mistakes, neglect their property or even abuse it. But one of the great things about the system of private ownership is that, in such cases, ownership tends to change hands: The market value of the property tends to drop, and others who know better how to use and care for the property buy out the incompetent owner. Market forces tend to move property into the hands of the careful and competent.

How much better is this situation than one of government ownership! Public officials *also* use bad judgment just as often; they are people, too. They make mistakes, neglect or even abuse the public property under their charge, just as private owners do. But in a system of government ownership and bureaucratic management, the forces that tend to correct this situation are weak. Think of the Tongass, of the Post Office, of the Scottish dole office.

Government ownership surely must be well-intended most of the time, but it does not work well. Neither does interference with freedom of exchange. To that we turn in the next chapter.

Chapter Five

# Government Regulation Gets Captured by Special Interests

How you would answer the following question, and how do you think most others would answer it?

> *Should competent adults be allowed to exchange freely with one another? That is, should we be legally permitted to exchange our property and services with one another on mutually agreeable terms?*

Most of us answer yes to the question when it's asked this way. In principle and in general, we believe in freedom of exchange—people should be allowed to do as they see fit with their own as long as they don't harm anyone else, and they should be allowed to decide the terms on which they interact with others. Of course.

But though most of us support freedom of exchange in principle, many reject it in practice: they support particular restrictions on exchange. They support occupational licensing to protect people from incompetent practitioners, zoning restrictions to foster better-planned communities, minimum wage laws to raise incomes, anti-trust regulation to prevent monopolies, Food and Drug Administration restrictions on the sale of pharmaceuticals to assure their safety and effectiveness, and so on. All of these restrict freedom of exchange. They prevent competent adults from exchanging their property and services on mutually agreeable terms.

Most people, I find, when they hedge their commitment to freedom of exchange by supporting some restriction of it, do so because they believe the restriction will make people better off; they believe unrestricted freedom of exchange would harm people.

This chapter and the next argue that this belief has it exactly backward. In practice, given the principles we discussed in Part I, restrictions on freedom, even when well-intended, almost always make people worse off; that's the subject of this chapter. And unrestricted freedom of exchange—so long as it's peaceful and not fraudulent—unleashes powerful market forces that regulate very effectively in the public interest; that's the subject of the next chapter.

Please note at the outset the important distinction between regulation and restriction. To regulate means to make regular. In the present context it also means to control or assure the quality of a good or service. To restrict means to limit one's freedom of action. As we will see, governments can and do restrict without regulating (in the sense of assuring quality); free markets can and do regulate without restricting.

Let us begin with an illustrative example, government restrictions on our freedom to exchange money for a haircut.

## Hairdresser Licensing

In every state in the U.S., in order to cut or dress somebody's hair for pay a person must first obtain a license (a "cosmetology" license) from that state. Generally one must go to beauty school or serve an apprenticeship and then take a qualifying test. Once one has the license, one may practice; without it, one may not. Consider two questions before reading on:

What is the purpose of hairdresser licensing? Do you suppose there is a difference between the avowed, official purpose and some other actual purpose?

\* \* \* \* \*

The avowed purpose of hairdresser regulation is "to protect the public health and safety." Although hairdressing is not a particularly dangerous business, I am told that sometimes misused chemicals can burn the scalp or even make people's hair fall out. And of course, hairdressers use scissors and curling irons which can cause cuts or burns.

Hairdresser licensing interferes with freedom of exchange. It is not enforced by invitation and polite request. Like all regulations, it is enforced by the police. If someone is caught dressing hair (in the licensing-law jargon, "practicing beauty culture") without a license, or in an unapproved location such as a home, the practitioner can be fined and have her license suspended or revoked. This is so even if the hairdresser and the customer both desire the transaction. They are not free, under the law, to exchange money and hairdressing services as they see fit.

Now apply our quick public-choice analysis (from Chapter 3) to hairdresser licensing. What groups are most affected by licensing? And what are their incentives? Hairdressers themselves are the group most affected, of course. Let's illuminate their incentives with a story.

In the mid '80s I was invited to speak at Bryn Mawr School, a fine prep school for girls in Baltimore. To an eighth grade history class I had been describing some of the problems with occupational licensing that Walter Williams describes in *The State Against Blacks*. As I was explaining Williams's claim that hairdresser licensing is often stacked against low-income people, a black student in the third row raised her hand and thoughtfully shared, "That happened to me."

Her name was Sharissa. She told us that one of the five-year-olds in her neighborhood was having a birthday party, and the girls going to the party wanted their hair done in gold braid. That involves braiding the hair close to the scalp, weaving gold thread through the braids in decorative patterns, and then curling the bangs in front. Sharissa was good at it, and there was a new outfit she wanted to buy, so she dressed the hair of some of the little girls for five dollars each. In all, she did the hair of about ten children, some at her house and some at the children's houses. She estimated her income at about $50.00 and her expenses, for gold twine and styling gel, at about $6.75. Her net was enough to buy her new outfit.

But that's not the end of the story.

A neighbor stopped six-year-old Devin, one of Sharissa's clients, on the sidewalk one day and asked, "Who did your hair for you?"

"Rissy did it," said Devin. That night, Sharissa's mother received a call from a neighbor. The neighbor said she had heard through the grapevine that Sharissa was doing hair without a license. That was illegal, and she should stop. Sharissa's mother reluctantly told Sharissa to cancel her other appointments. "We don't want any trouble."

Sharissa found out later that the woman who had stopped the child and asked, "Who did your hair for you?" has a niece ... who is a licensed hairdresser, who had had a thirty-two dollar appointment canceled by the mother of one of Sharissa's five-year-old clients.

Based on this story, what would you say is the actual purpose of hairdresser regulation, as opposed to its official purpose, if in fact there is a difference?

* * * * *

In trying to understand the effects of government regulations that interfere with free exchange, concentrate on the incentives those regulations generate. Ask yourself,

> *Where hairdressers must get a license from the state in order to practice, what are the incentives for* licensed *hairdressers with respect to the licensing?*

In the case of Sharissa and her little neighbors, at least, the actual effect of the licensing was to hinder competition. It blocked Sharissa from earning some income, it forced the five-year-olds' parents to pay six-fold higher prices, and it protected the income of the licensed hairdresser. This effect in Sharissa's Baltimore neighborhood generalizes to all licensing everywhere. Licensing blocks competition and thereby supports the incomes of the already-licensed practitioners. Accordingly—and this is crucial—the existence of licensing gives licensed practitioners a strong incentive to support licensing requirements that are strict and strictly enforced, regardless of their effect on the public health and safety.

The actual purpose of hairdresser licensing is to block competition to raise the prices licensed hairdressers can charge.

The general public believes that licensing protects their health and safety, and licensed hairdressers encourage this belief. But the public has been bamboozled in this; they are ignorant—"rationally ignorant" (we discuss this phenomenon in Chapter 7)—of what is really going on. In the crude vernacular, hairdresser licensing lets licensed hairdressers rip off consumers by squashing their competition. A thoughtful look into the details of the regulations makes this plain. In the description that follows, keep asking yourself, how does this protect the public health and safety? And, notice the systematic effect of restricting entry into the profession in a wide variety of ways that have nothing whatever to do with public health and safety.

Sharissa's story inspired me to do some investigation of Maryland's hairdresser licensing laws. I visited the offices of the Maryland State Board of Cosmetologists, which regulates the work of hairdressers, manicurists, and cosmeticians. Naively, I asked to see a copy of the licensing examination, because I wanted to confirm Walter Williams's assertion that the written part of the examination was often irrelevantly difficult—designed to exclude those who have had poor schooling. The clerk whom I asked for the test looked at me with astonishment: no one gets to see the examination except those taking the test.

All right, then, could I please see the regulations? Of course. The clerk handed me The Annotated Code of Maryland, Article 566, Sections 479-507, with Code of Maryland Regulations 09.22.01, 09.22.02, 09.01.03, and 09.22.12. Of the booklet's fifty-six pages, slightly less than four deal directly with health and safety, in two virtually identical passages, one for beauty salons and one for beauty schools. The requirements related to health and safety are either so obvious as to go without saying, or so petty as to be more a nuisance than anything else.

It is required, for example, that salon employees wear clean clothes, wash their hands, and keep their curling irons "free from rust, grease, and dirt." Is this a necessary regulation? Can we imagine a hairdresser staying in business using rusty, greasy, or dirty curling irons? Some other important rules:

- "A minimum of 12 combs and 4 brushes shall be available for each on-premises employee licensed to perform beauty culture."
- "Implements to be used for pressing and thermal waving shall be adequate in quantity and variety to perform the complete service."
- "Protective neck bands shall be used on each patron."
- "Fluids and powders shall be applied to patrons from a bottle or shaker dispenser."

If such regulations do improve safety, the effect is surely miniscule, because any beauty shop must stay clean and sanitary enough to keep its customers coming back and to convince the insurance inspector that lawsuits are unlikely. In any case, the other ninety-three percent of the regulations make clear that protecting health and safety is a minor goal at best—a cover for the real work regulations do.

To begin with, only those who practice cosmetology "for compensation" are covered by the statutes; this is stated three times on the first page. But if hairdressing is dangerous and if the law is meant to protect the public safety, shouldn't any practice, whether for compensation or for free, be covered?

Anyone under seventeen is excluded from the business. Sharissa, no matter how competent, would not have been allowed to offer her services for pay for three more years.

The regulations define and control various job categories and access to them. For example, a beauty shop "owner" (distinct from "owner-operator") may not simply promote a capable employee from "junior manager" to "senior manager." That employee must first take a test, but not until "such person has had twelve months' experience working as a junior manager."

Entry into the profession at the lowest level (as an "operator") is tightly controlled. All would-be operators must pass the board's examination.

Though I'll argue below that even an examination is unnecessary, a test of basic competence does not seem unreasonable on its face. But being competent to pass the examination is not legally sufficient. No one may take the examination until having already put in 1500 hours training or served as an apprentice in an approved beauty shop for at least two years. That's right; even if one is already competent enough to *pass* the examination, it does not matter; he must nevertheless get (more) extensive training before getting permission to *take* the examination.

Beauty school is expensive. In 1988 the total price of beauty school in Maryland (enrollment fee, kit, tax, insurance, and tuition) ran about $3,300, not counting foregone income from a job. Today tuition, fees, books and supplies run about $16,150.

Beauty schools are regulated also, with the same effect—and purpose—of limiting access to the profession. Each school must be licensed, and each must hire the right number of duly trained and licensed teachers, as well as a licensed physician "as a consultant." School terms may not run less than nine consecutive months nor give more than forty hours of training per week (for day school; for night school it is eighteen months and twenty hours per week).

Would-be hairdressers can avoid beauty school by going the apprenticeship route, but similar restrictions apply to apprentices. They must be licensed as such and "shall be required to work at least 40 hours per week, for a period of 24 months." Part-time work is out. "Apprenticeship training shall be completed in not less than 24 months, nor more than 30 months." (Why the six-month window?) Beauty shops may take on only a limited number of apprentices. (Why?) They "may not charge for operations performed completely by an apprentice," and these operations must in any case have the "complete and constant supervision of the designated operator or the junior-manager."

The evident purpose of this maze of regulations is to restrict entry into hairdressing. If competence were the object, a suitable examination would do the trick. The suitability of the examination we cannot judge, but the regulations are clearly designed to reduce dramatically the number of people who ever get to take that exam.

Once licensed, a hairdresser faces still more restrictions. One that indirectly but potently reduces competition is number 09.22.01.11 B: "Operations may not be performed at the dwelling house of the licensee, or at any other premises other than the dwelling place of the patron, without the permission of the Board, which shall be received in advance of the operation, in writing." No dressing hair in one's own house is permitted—no saving the cost of a separate facility, no saving the cost of travel there, no keeping an eye on one's children in one's own house while one earns money to provide for them. All these are forbidden, for the sake of the public health and safety, of course.

Not only do the licensing regulations themselves suggest that licensing aims to restrict competition; so does the manner in which they are enforced. Eunice Alper, executive director of the Maryland Board of Cosmetologists, explained to me that most illegal hairdressing is performed not by unlicensed people but by licensees operating outside the rules. It can be difficult for the Board to track down such miscreants, because the consuming public virtually never complains about such violations. Sometimes a neighbor, but usually "some other cosmetologist makes the complaint." See who's protected by the regulations?

The public's attitude is well illustrated by Alper's account of one basement beauty shop that the board shut down with the help of a ruling on the particular meaning of "compensation." The shop was just that: a full-fledged beauty salon, with people waiting in line and a closet full of supplies. But the hairdresser and her patrons all insisted that this was not a beauty shop under the law, because the service was not provided "for compensation." No cash changed hands. The patrons, in exchange for having their hair done, would do favors for the hairdresser: bake cakes, do laundry, make clothes, baby-sit, and so on.

The ruling was: that's compensation. For three patrons at $500 per violation, the hairdresser was slapped with a $1,500 fine. The board closed down her salon, thereby denying her customers a convenient service they valued. Those actions were to protect the public?

Alper added that money probably did change hands. "But why wouldn't the customers have said so?" I innocently asked. "Some people are protecting their hairdressers," replied Alper, "so they lie." The irony is delicious, isn't it? The board pretends to protect the health and safety of customers from improper hairdressers, while the customers protect those hairdressers from the board.

## Regulatory Capture

Hairdresser licensing illustrates what economists call the capture of regulation. The basic idea is as follows: Whenever governments regulate a particular industry, the dominant enterprises within that industry are strongly affected by the regulations. Accordingly, they have a strong incentive to influence those regulations in their own favor. They respond to this incentive. They strive to influence the regulators and regulations, acting through their industry associations and lobbyists. Eventually they come to direct the regulatory process more or less.

The influence of the regulated group results in part from the necessities of regulation: Who knows enough about an industry to craft appropriate regulations? The members of that industry do, of course. For this reason, industry representatives are almost inevitably in a position to influence the regulations, if not to write them directly.

When representatives of the dominant groups in an industry control the regulatory process, we say that the regulation has been captured by the regulated group. They direct the regulation not in the public interest, but in their own particular interest, usually at the expense of their politically weaker competitors and the general public.

In our current example, established beauty salons and already licensed hairdressers dominate the hairdressing industry. As long as the salons can keep themselves satisfactorily staffed, they benefit from keeping newcomers out of hairdressing altogether. They also benefit by restricting the number of places where licensed hairdressers may work, and by preventing them from working anywhere they and their customers might choose, such as in the hairdresser's home. If that were allowed, every hairdresser's basement would become a potential competing salon. The regulations do not protect the public; they protect the established salons, which have captured the regulatory process. In effect, licensing gives established hairdressing salons a legal cartel.

Members of the hairdressing industry want the regulation. They fight for it. So I was informed by Thomas Berger, the cheerful executive director of the National Cosmetology Association, headquartered in St. Louis. He told me proudly of the association's successful lobbying against some states' efforts to "sunset" their licensing boards (let their licensing laws expire), and he sent me a copy of the model bill the association was sending state legislatures. Among its recommended provisions were increasing the schooling minimum from eighth grade to high school graduation, and boosting the training-time requirement from 1,500 to 2,100 hours. What would be the purpose of this increased restriction, I asked Mr. Berger. He replied, "No reason other than consumer protection."

There are many, many examples of regulatory capture. Occupational licensing alone has been spreading across the United States at a great rate as established practitioners in various fields use it, or try to use it, to block competition. Here are some examples from the web pages of the Institute for Justice, a public-interest law firm that, among other things, litigates on behalf of ordinary people trying to earn an honest living providing a valued service, who are being obstructed from doing so by captured regulators. Notice how in each case the regulated group is trying to use the licensing process to their own advantage, to the detriment of their (would-be) competitors and the general public.

## Massaging Horses

On behalf of veterinarians and chiropractors, Maryland restricts who may massage horses. The effort is being challenged in the case of Clemens v. Maryland State Board of Veterinary Medical Examiners, et. al.:

Mercedes Clemens is a Maryland entrepreneur with a thriving massage practice in Rockville that, until recently, offered both human and animal massage. In addition to being a licensed massage therapist, Mercedes has more than 30 years of practical experience as a horse owner and rider, has been certified in equine massage—a growing practice that can alleviate physical discomfort and calms horses, making them easier to handle—and has even taught animal massage to others.

Despite these qualifications, Mercedes has found herself whipsawed by two licensing boards intent on protecting a veterinary cartel from competition. According to the Maryland State Board of Veterinary Medical Examiners, Mercedes cannot practice animal massage without spending a fortune on four years of veterinary school. Further, in February of 2008, the Maryland Board of Chiropractic Examiners ordered Mercedes to stop practicing equine massage and take down her website or else lose her license to massage humans, which now makes up the bulk of her practice.

## Owning Funeral Homes

On behalf of funeral home owners, Maryland restricts who may own (not work in, own) a funeral home. This restriction is being challenged in the case of Brown v. Hovatter:

> All Charles S. Brown wants is the chance to offer consumers the best service a funeral home can at the best price. But the State of Maryland is standing in his way.

> Brown owns Rest Haven Cemetery in Hagerstown, Maryland, and runs it with his wife Pat and their son Eric. Charles wants to own the funeral home he built in order to provide additional revenue to care for the gravesites in his cemetery when the cemetery itself is full.

The State of Maryland arbitrarily restricts who can own a funeral home. In Maryland, only licensed funeral directors and a handful of politically favored corporations and individuals may own a funeral home. Becoming a licensed funeral director takes two years of study and thousands of dollars. Among the many requirements of a mortuary science degree is learning how to embalm corpses. As a result, consumers pay more than they otherwise would, and opportunities for would-be entrepreneurs are blocked.

## Interior Design

Connecticut does not (yet) require interior designers to get a state license, but on behalf of state licensees it restricts unlicensed interior designers from advertising themselves as designers. The Institute for Justice is challenging this restriction in the case of Susan Roberts v. Jerry Farrell:

> Susan Roberts is an interior designer, but the state of Connecticut will not allow her to tell anyone that. This is because Connecticut has a law that allows anyone to perform interior design services, but dictates that only those with government-issued licenses may call themselves "interior designers." Besides unconstitutionally censoring truthful commercial speech, "titling laws" like Connecticut's serve as precursors to full-blown occupational licensure, which is the ultimate goal of a small faction within the interior design industry led by the American Society of Interior Designers (ASID).

> In November 2007, the Institute for Justice (IJ) released an updated case study, "Designing Cartels," which documents a long-running campaign by ASID and its affiliates to increase regulation of interior designers in order to thwart competition and impose a one-size-fits-all set of credentials for the entire interior design industry. Not surprisingly, the nationwide push for more regulation of interior designers has come not from the public or the government, but from

a small cartel of industry insiders seeking government protection from competition.

Only three other states besides Connecticut license the use of the term "interior designer" without regulating the work itself. The anti-competitive intent behind such title acts is clear: anyone who goes looking for an "interior designer" on the Internet or in the Yellow Pages in those states will find only government-licensed cartel members, while overlooking scores of capable designers like Susan Roberts.

## Hairdressing, Again

And bringing us back to hairdressing, Utah protects hairdressers by making it illegal to braid hair without a cosmetology license. Jestina Clayton is challenging this restriction in the case of Clayton v. Steinagel:

> The Constitution protects the right to earn an honest living without arbitrary and unreasonable government interference.

> But if you want to braid hair for a living in Utah, you must submit yourself to a completely irrational licensing scheme to get permission from the government before you are allowed to work.

> Jestina Clayton, a college graduate, wife, mother of two and refugee from Sierra Leone's civil war has been braiding hair for most of her life. Now she wants to use her considerable skills to help provide for her family while her husband finishes his education. But the state of Utah says she may not be paid to braid unless she first spends thousands of dollars on 2,000 hours of government-mandated cosmetology training—not one hour of which actually teaches her how to braid hair. In the same number of class hours, a person also could qualify to be an armed security guard, mortgage loan originator, real estate sales agent, EMT and lawyer—*combined.*

By the way, I checked with the Institute for Justice about what looks like a misprint in this last sentence, but those numbers are accurate.

## Increased Harm from Stricter Electrician Licensing

As these examples show, the capture of occupational licensing by established members of a regulated industry allows the privileged insiders to exclude would-be competitors. That denies those would-be competitors their right to earn an honest living, it forces customers to pay more, and it restricts their choices. These ill effects are substantial on their own, but sometimes there are additional, more insidiously harmful effects. Ironically, licensing can *reduce* the public health and safety it is supposed to promote. Economists Sidney Carroll and Robert Gaston did a study of the effect of licensing of electricians. The strictness of electrician licensing requirements differs substantially from state to state. In some states the requirements are quite strict, so it costs a would-be electrician a lot of time, effort, and money to gain a license. In other states the requirements are less strict, so qualifying is much less costly. To judge the effect of licensing on public health and safety, the authors correlated the strictness of licensing requirements in various states with the states' rates of death by electrocution. They found a significant relationship. Before reading on, try to figure out what they found and try to explain the findings you expect in terms of the incentives of the affected groups. Remember that in all fields subject to licensing, those already licensed have an incentive to keep others out, so they can charge more for their services.

* * * * *

If we don't take incentives into account, and consider only the apparent intention of the regulation, we might expect to find that rates of death by electrocution are lower in states where electricians are very strictly licensed and vice versa. After all, the more strictly licensed electricians are, the more competent electricians should be and consequently the fewer problems we should have with bad wiring and electrocutions. At the other extreme, where it is so easy to get an electrician's license that almost anyone can do so, we might expect incompetents to practice, wiring buildings badly and causing more deaths by electrocution. But that is not what Carroll and Gaston found.

They found rates of death by electrocution to be significantly higher in states with stricter licensing of electricians. A large portion of those electrocuted were amateurs—homeowners—trying to do their electrical work for themselves. In their inexperience, they made fatal mistakes. Why do such fatalities occur at higher rates in states where electrician licensing is more strict? Because in those states the comparatively fewer electricians don't have to compete as hard on price, so their services are more expensive, and hence incompetent homeowners have a stronger incentive to do the work themselves.

*The intentions of regulation don't determine its outcomes; incentives do.*

Occupational licensing is spreading. According to the Institute for Justice, "Fifty years ago, one in 20 Americans needed a government license to work in their occupation. Today that number is close to one in three. In 1981, there were roughly 80 occupations that required a license in at least one state. Today there are 1,100."

## Capture of Other Kinds of Regulation

Not just occupational licensing but all kinds of government regulation are liable to be captured by special interest groups. The coercion that backs government regulation always offers special interest groups the possibility of a short cut to higher profits. If they can just find a way to use that legal coercion to advantage, they can bypass the free market's relentless requirement that they actually serve their customers as well or better than their competitors do. Humans are resourceful beings. When regulatory authority offers us the possibility of getting what we want by force rather than by creating value, many of us fall prey to the temptation. Here are two more examples.

## Airline Routes and Fares

Before air travel was largely deregulated, the Civil Aeronautics Board (CAB) controlled which airlines could operate, the routes that airlines could fly, and the prices they could charge. The special interest group most immediately affected was the established airlines themselves; they had a strong incentive to influence that regulation to their own advantage. They did so, at great expense to consumers. The CAB held airfares high enough to keep the existing airlines in business and denied would-be airlines the freedom to compete. What little competition occurred among existing carriers was along such lines as the quality of meals. Under this regulation, consumers paid high prices for a limited choice of carriers and routes.

Airline deregulation was long opposed by the major airlines, but it improved air travel dramatically for most consumers. By allowing new entrants to compete, and to do so by offering lower fares, deregulation spawned a variety of new airlines, new service to more destinations, and substantially lower fares on routes between major cities. "Deregulation also allowed existing airlines to enter new routes without having to get the government's permission. [For example], Southwest started as an intrastate airline in Texas and could only expand because of deregulation." The profit-and-loss feedback that resulted from deregulation drove into bankruptcy many of the airlines that regulation had kept artificially profitable, such as Eastern, TWA, and Pan Am. It rewarded lower-cost, more efficient carriers such as Southwest.

## Mexican Trucking Companies in the U.S.

The Teamsters' Union and other American trucking interests have largely captured safety and environmental regulations as applied to trucking, using regulations to block competition from Mexican trucking companies and their Mexican drivers. The consequence is higher wages for U.S. truckers and trucking companies, higher shipping costs in both the U.S. and Mexico, and increased pollution.

Under the North American Free Trade Agreement (NAFTA), trucks and drivers that met both nations' safety and licensing requirements were to be free to operate on both sides of the border. There was to be no discrimination based on national origin. The resulting competition would be good for everyone in either country who buys goods that have been shipped by truck. (That's all of us.)

NAFTA went into effect in 1994. Dan Griswold, former director of the Herbert A. Stiefel Center for Trade Policy Studies at the Cato Institute, reports that President Clinton "unilaterally suspended implementation of [its U.S.-Mexico] trucking provisions in 1995, citing safety concerns." Mexican trucks already had to meet all the safety requirements of American trucks to operate in the U.S., but nevertheless Clinton treated Mexican trucks as unsafe. Mexico officially objected in 1998, claiming correctly that the U.S. was violating NAFTA by discriminating against Mexican trucking firms. In 2001 a NAFTA dispute-resolution panel unanimously agreed, and forbade the U.S. to assume that all Mexican trucks and drivers are unsafe.

Nevertheless, the American trucking interests kept using "safety" restrictions to block the Mexican competition. They persuaded Congress to pass twenty-two new safety requirements that Mexican trucks must meet in addition to the safety requirements for all trucks on American roads, before they would be allowed to go outside "commercial zones" near the border. The U.S. Department of Transportation duly implemented the twenty-two new requirements in 2002 and prepared to issue licenses to complying Mexican trucks.

To prevent that, the American trucking interests then turned to environmental restrictions. With the help of environmental activists they complained in court that the new trucking regulations violated environmental laws. (This argument looks particularly insincere because forbidding Mexican trucks from delivering cargo directly to destinations in the U.S. means diverting cargo to warehouses in "commercial zones" near the border, where it is reloaded onto American trucks. The extra truck mileage and delays result in needless air pollution.) The 9th U.S. Circuit Court of Appeals upheld the American truckers' complaint in 2003 (thereby banning Mexican trucks from the U.S.), but the Supreme Court unanimously rejected it in 2004 (thereby allowing the Mexican trucks into the U.S.).

Denied the use of environmental regulation to block Mexican competition, the American trucking interests fell back on licensing, which they have held captive with Congress's help. As of 2007, the Federal Motor Carrier Safety Administration had developed a "pilot program" under which (only) fifty-five Mexican trucks were allowed to deliver goods deeper than twenty miles into the U.S. (and fifty-five American trucks were allowed to deliver goods deeper than twenty miles into Mexico). In a world not manipulated by special interests, this pilot would have been expanded to allow all safe Mexican trucks to operate in the U.S. But Mexican trucks need licenses to operate on American roads, and safety inspections cost money. So what did Congress do, at the behest of American trucking interests? They simply declined to fund the pilot program any longer, or to appropriate any money for licensing and inspecting Mexican trucks.

To risk belaboring the point lest it be missed: Licensing trucks to operate on American roads is supposed to protect Americans from unsafe trucks and untrained drivers, but it is not used that way. According to Dan Griswold, "the Mexican trucks that have been allowed to operate in the United States under the pilot program have actually had a better safety record than U.S. trucks." Instead of protecting the American public's safety, the licensing protects American trucking interests from competition. The consequence for the American public is less choice and higher prices.

## Regulations Captured by Indirectly Affected Groups

In the standard theory, as in the examples we have considered so far in this chapter, capture of regulation occurs by the regulated group. But the regulatory process can be captured by groups other than those regulated. Often some group that is affected only indirectly will have strong interests at stake in the regulation. In such cases that group usually tries to gain control of the regulation, or at least influence it to their advantage. The general principle is the same as in capture of regulation by the regulated group: Wherever governments intervene in the economy, using force to restrict people's freedom or use of their property, special interest groups will have an incentive to use that governmental force to their own advantage, even to the detriment of others. In this section we consider two such cases.

## Minimum Wage Laws

Here is a quick refresher on the effects of minimum wage laws:

In a free market for labor services of any sort, the wages or salaries paid will be determined, as all market prices are determined, by the interaction of suppliers and demanders in that market. Employers who need ("demand") workers will try to outbid one another to the extent they must, in order to attract the number of workers they would like. This competition among employers holds wages up. Workers who want jobs ("suppliers" of labor services) will try to underbid one another to the extent they must, in order to win the available positions. This competition among workers holds wages down. The market wage is determined "at the margin": It will be right around the level negotiated by the last (or "marginal") employer willing to pay at least that much and the last (marginal) worker willing to accept that little. To put it another way, the wage will be in the narrow range in which the number of workers employers are willing to hire (at that wage) just equals the number of workers who are willing to work (at that wage). The crucial point about the going market wage at any time is that if it were any higher, some employers would not be willing to pay that much and would lay off workers or hire fewer in the first place.

It follows, sadly, that when legislatures set a legal minimum wage high enough to make a difference—higher than the freely-negotiated market wage—they cause unemployment. For the marginal employers—the ones barely able to pay so much—that higher wage they are required to pay means they'll make losses instead of profits, so they don't hire them. The immediate consequences of minimum wage laws are therefore twofold: 1) some low-skilled workers—those who keep their jobs—earn higher wages and higher incomes, and 2) some other low-skilled workers—those who lose their jobs—earn no wages at all and thus lower incomes. How much lower depends on their other options, including relying on family, public or private charity, or work in the black market.

Thus, while minimum wage laws are intended by their well-intentioned supporters to hold up wages and hence incomes for all low-skilled workers, the laws must have the opposite consequence for *some* low-skilled workers, usually the lowest-skilled, if they have any effect at all.

With that refresher of price theory in mind, let us return to an investigation of why certain groups try to capture the process of setting minimum wages. Use the public-choice framework for analysis as we have in earlier examples:

Of any policy, ask two questions:
1. What groups are primarily affected?
2. What are their incentives?

Those incentives will determine (or strongly influence) the outcomes.

What groups are significantly affected by the minimum wage? What are their incentives? Of course low-skilled workers whose market-determined wages would be at or below the legal minimum are affected (for better or worse, depending on whether they keep or lose their jobs). And we have also discussed the incentive for employers: When forced by law to pay higher wages, they have an incentive to lay off workers who earn for the enterprise less than what paying them costs the employer *in total*. (In addition to wages, that includes unemployment insurance tax, Social Security tax, workmen's compensation tax, and any other contractual or mandated benefits.) With minimum wage regulation, there is one other broadly-defined group with a significant financial interest. Before reading on, try to figure out what group that is and what incentive they have with respect to the minimum wage.

If you don't see it right away, try a much more cynical approach: Who benefits when the low-skilled and disadvantaged become too expensive to hire? Be warned: Public choice analysis of public policy can be disillusioning.

\* \* \* \* \*

Lower-skilled workers compete with higher-skilled workers who can accomplish the same results. Accordingly, higher-skilled workers who can accomplish results now achieved by lower-skilled workers have an interest in minimum wage laws. Why? When minimum wage laws make lower-skilled workers more expensive, employers have an incentive to turn to higher-skilled workers whose services have now become a relatively better bargain.

What are the organized associations of higher-skilled workers? Unions. Even unions whose members earn far more than minimum wage have a financial interest in higher minimum wages because their higher-paid members compete with lower-skilled workers. Thus it should be no surprise that unions frequently back higher minimum wages.

A thought experiment will clarify the arithmetic of the minimum wage: Suppose you are a general contractor on a construction site and among the many tasks to be done, you need to get a ditch dug. You have two options for digging it. One is a group of five men with strong backs, picks and shovels, and little education. They are willing (and we'll assume legally allowed) to work for five dollars an hour each; together, the five will get the ditch dug in one hour. Your other option is a single backhoe operator with his own backhoe and the training to use it well. He is prepared to work for union wage of twenty-seven dollars an hour; he, too, will get the ditch dug in one hour.

Whom will you hire? On what reasoning?

If you hire the five unskilled workers, the cost of getting the ditch dug is

*5 men x $5/hour x 1 hour = $25.*

If you hire the backhoe operator, the cost is

*1 man x $27/hour x 1 hour = $27.*

Probably you'll hire the unskilled workers if you and they are free to deal with one another on those terms, because they will accomplish the same results for less.

But suppose, with union support, the government imposes a minimum wage of six dollars an hour. Now whom will you hire?

If you hire the five unskilled workers, your cost is no longer $25, but

$$5 \text{ men} \times \cancel{\$5} \ \$6/hour \times 1 \ hour = \cancel{\$25} \ \$30.$$

If you hire the backhoe operator, your cost is

$$1 \text{ man} \times \cancel{\$27} \ \$29/hour \times 1 \ hour = \cancel{\$27} \ \$29.$$

You'll hire the unionized backhoe operator, even if the unions have taken this favorable opportunity to increase the wages they demand, because the union worker will do the job for less. In this case, the minimum wage would mean that the five unskilled workers would lose a job they otherwise would have had, the union worker would be able to charge more than he previously could, and your customers would have to pay more for their building.

This conclusion applies to unions and minimum wages generally. By pricing low-skilled labor services out of the market, minimum wages increase employers' demand for the services of higher-skilled (often unionized) labor services that are the alternative. Though union workers earn far more than minimum wage, higher minimum wages can benefit union workers.

Based on unions' incentive to achieve higher minimum wages, the outcome we observe is understandable—steady pressure by unions, and year after year, bills introduced in Congress by the unions' politicians to raise the minimum.

Of course the unions never say their intention is to increase their own incomes at the expense of the lower-skilled. In fact, they say the opposite: They claim that they are working for the well-being, even the rights, of their laboring brethren. They express outrage at the injustice of working people being paid so little. Nevertheless, the consequence of their policy is that some people who would otherwise be working receive no pay at all.

On the ethical issue here, no one has been more eloquent than Adam Smith, writing over two and quarter centuries ago:

> The property which every man has in his own labour, as it is the
> original foundation of all other property, so it is the most sacred and
> inviolable. The patrimony of a poor man lies in the strength and
> dexterity of his hands; and to hinder him from employing this strength
> and dexterity in what manner he thinks proper without injury to
> his neighbor, is a plain violation of this most sacred property. It is a
> manifest encroachment upon the just liberty both of the workman, and
> of those who might be disposed to employ him. As it hinders the one
> from working at what he thinks proper, so it hinders the others from
> employing whom they think proper.

Whether or not one supports minimum wage laws, everyone must concede that minimum wage laws infringe on property and restrict freedom of exchange. In preventing people from offering their labor services for wages below the legal minimum, they prevent people from disposing of this "most sacred property" as they see fit. At the same time, minimum wage laws abridge freedom of exchange by making illegal any contracts specifying wages below the legal minimum. They deny the unskilled the freedom to compete with the higher-skilled in the only way available to them—on price. Those who have learned to evaluate public policy by the approach recommended in this book will immediately be wary of such laws, not just on account of their interference with the price system discussed in Chapter 1, but also on account of their abridgment of property rights and freedom of exchange. Whenever these occur, the analyst should look for incentive problems and efforts by special interest groups to turn the government power to personal, selfish advantage.

Union influence over minimum wage policy is another instance of regulation being captured by special interest groups and used not in the general interest, but in their private interest, at the expense of their (would-be) competitors and of the general public.

## Pollution Controls and the Coal Interests

The 1977 Amendments to the Clean Air Act are the starting point of another clear, and painful, illustration of how special interest groups can capture regulation and use it to their private advantage while harming the general public. This example is particularly interesting because the economic relationships are so complex that the benefit to the special interest group seems entirely unrelated to the regulation they pushed through the legislature.

The Amendments required all newly constructed electricity generating plants in the eastern half of the U.S. that burn coal to clean the smoke coming from their stacks with a *particular* technology—a gigantic piece of equipment called a scrubber, which removes sulfur dioxide from the smoke. Much coal contains sulfur, which turns into sulfur dioxide when the coal is burned. Sulfur dioxide is a nasty pollutant, so we want to keep it out of the atmosphere. But is using a scrubber the best way to reduce sulfur dioxide emissions?

As we discussed in Chapter 2, human beings can never know for certain ahead of time the best ways of achieving any purpose. We need freedom for entrepreneurs continually to try out new approaches, and we need profit and loss to select the innovations that perform best at low cost. That goes for reducing sulfur dioxide emissions. Environmental regulation by government, if any, should never specify what technology to use; rather it should specify the standard to be met and leave it up to plants' owners to achieve that emission level as cheaply as possible. But the 1977 Amendments specified scrubbers. As long as a plant used a scrubber, it was in compliance regardless of the emissions it produced. Hence plants' owners had no incentive to experiment with other ways of reducing those emissions.

Why did the 1977 Amendments to the Clean Air Act specify the use of scrubbers rather than a particular target for sulfur dioxide emissions? The answer lies in capture of the regulatory process by a special interest group. In this case, the capture came early, in the very process of drafting the regulatory legislation.

I'll lay out the most relevant information below. My challenge to the reader is to deduce from this information the special interest group behind the scrubber requirement for plants that burn coal. Who had a financial incentive to push it through? How does that requirement benefit the special interest group?

Not all coal has sulfur in it; there is low-sulfur coal that burns very clean of sulfur dioxide, and there is high-sulfur coal that burns filthy with sulfur dioxide. Coal mined in the eastern states, in the Appalachians, generally contains a lot of sulfur, whereas coal mined in the western states is generally quite low in sulfur. Indeed—and this is crucial—the untreated smoke from some clean western coal contains less sulfur dioxide than remains in the smoke from some eastern coal after it has gone through a scrubber.

Western coal is more expensive than eastern, however. Whereas eastern coal lies close to the surface where it can be extracted at relatively low cost, western coal lies deep underground and can be extracted only at greater expense.

Now consider what the incentives of coal-burning power-plant operators would be if the Clean Air Act were simply to require that the plants reduce their emissions of sulfur dioxide to some particular levels by any means they choose. They would try to do that at the lowest possible cost. (Remember, low cost in a free economy would mean that a power plant is able to abate pollution while using fewer valuable resources, so those resources may be used to produce other goods and services that consumers want.) That cost includes both the cost of the coal they burn *and* the cost of the scrubber, if they install one. For some plants, especially large ones close to the eastern coal mines, eastern coal is so much cheaper on account of both its extraction and its transportation costs that the least expensive means of achieving target levels of sulfur dioxide would be to install a scrubber and continue burning dirty but cheap eastern coal.

For others, however, perhaps smaller plants in the West, it would be cheaper in the long run to avoid the huge up-front costs of a scrubber altogether, and meet emissions targets by burning more expensive but cleaner western coal.

As the 1977 Amendments to the Clean Air Act were being drafted, what were the respective incentives of the eastern and western coal producers? Who would have benefited from a Clean Air Act that left technologies to the discretion of individual plants? Who would have benefited from a law that required every plant to install a scrubber, regardless of what sort of coal they burn?

One more piece of information will be helpful in completing this picture of special interest group action: the eastern coal interests were unionized and the western were not. Of course the eastern interests, including the United Mine Workers, would have lost a lot of business to the western coal companies if the law had allowed power plants to keep emissions down simply by burning cleaner coal. For many companies, the least expensive approach to pollution abatement would have been to switch from cheaper eastern coal to more expensive western coal, because by burning western coal they could avoid the huge expense of a scrubber. That would have meant less business for eastern coal interests and the United Mine Workers.

Offsetting that harm to eastern coal interests would have been the benefit to western coal interests, and, crucially, the benefit to society in general of having sulfur dioxide emissions abated at the lowest possible cost, as determined by the various plant owners, each in a position to judge the least costly course in his particular situation.

But the eastern coal interests had the political muscle to force the scrubber requirement into law. Being unionized, they had the political organization necessary to put pressure on those drafting the legislation, and when the 1977 Amendments to the Clean Air Act became law, they required scrubbers on *all* newly constructed coal-fired electricity generating plants in the eastern half of the U.S. Plant owners, in compliance with the law once they installed a scrubber, had every incentive to burn the cheapest coal they could find, even if the resulting sulfur dioxide emissions were greater than they would have been if the plants had burned western coal with no scrubber.

## Summary

Any government intervention in any area of human relationships carries a serious risk of capture by special interest groups because it introduces force into those relationships. Thereby intervention makes it possible for special interest groups to get what they want from others without the others' consent. The sheer availability of legal force creates a nearly irresistible incentive for people to use that force to personal advantage. They organize, they lobby, they manipulate the governmental force for personal gain, disregarding harm to others.

The *intentions* of those who support and implement the interventions don't matter. The *incentives* of affected interest groups trump good intentions. Whenever governments intervene in the mutually consensual activities of people using their own property, even when the intervention is well-intended, they introduce power—force and compulsion, policemen, jails—into human relationships. People don't handle such power well. We get tempted to use it to our advantage, even at the expense of others, especially when we can hide in a large group and thereby evade individual responsibility. The power to license hairdressing in order to exclude incompetents is also the power to raise established hairdressers' incomes by excluding the competent. The power to regulate wages in order to protect low-wage workers is also the power to raise union wages by eliminating low-wage workers' jobs. The power to require power plants to clean up their pollution in particular ways is also the power to increase the profits of eastern coal interests.

It does not matter that in each of these cases—and in thousands of others like them—it might be possible, in theory, to make the intervention cause net social benefit. It does not matter that *if* we could find legislators immune from political pressure (angels, perhaps?) to draft the legislation, and *if* we could find truly public-interested bureaucrats (more angels?) to administer the programs, and *if* we could somehow insulate the legislative and regulatory process from the constant pressure of the interest groups affected, that *then* the interventions might have the good effects we intend.

None of these *ifs* apply to real human affairs. Legislators and bureaucrats are self-interested human beings, inevitably influenced by the special interest groups that pressure them. The governmental force is wielded not only or mostly in the public interest, but also on behalf of private interests. The unavoidable danger with every government restriction of freedom of exchange is that on the whole, the private interests will prevail over the public interest, so that the intervention will result in net harm to society.

This chapter addresses the incentive problems of restrictions on freedom of exchange, but we should note also that even if there were no incentive problems, regulators would still face problems of incomplete knowledge and lack of innovation addressed in Chapters 1 and 2. Government regulators presume to override the judgments of the distributed market process, but why should we suppose that regulators, however well-intentioned and well-educated, *know* enough to draft regulation that will cause net benefit? No one even knows how to make a pencil. Is it likely that legislators and regulators will know enough about the industries they restrict to make a good job of it? As for innovation, government regulation blocks it. Government regulations are static and free of competition from other, maybe better, regulations. Government agencies that cause harm and loss have no competing agencies offering competing rules for market participants to turn to. There is no profit-and-loss discovery process sorting out good rules from bad. There are no forces assuring that the regulations evolve as technologies and industries change. For these reasons, too, we should doubt that centrally planned restrictions benefit society when all their costs and limitations are accounted for.

Jefferson was right that government should leave men "free to regulate their own pursuits of industry and improvement," and the framers of the Constitution were right to give Congress no power to restrict the freedom of economic enterprise.

I recommend to the reader, for cautionary inoculation against naïve trust in government restrictions, the skepticism in this passage from the great Chicago economist George Stigler, originator of the capture theory:

Suppose you want to figure out why a particular regulation passes and the way that it's written. Imagine the Legislature putting that regulation up for auction. Suppose people could bid on the terms of the regulation and the outcome went to the highest bidder.

Under those rules it would be clear whose interest is served by a government restriction on freedom of exchange.

I doubt that actual government regulation comes about, in most cases, by such a corrupt process. But Stigler's thought experiment is close enough to reality that we should altogether shun government restrictions on freedom of exchange. Instead, we should rely on market forces for the regulation of safety and quality we all desire.

We next discuss the way regulation by market forces could work, indeed, the way it already it does work to a great extent in our partially free economy.

# Chapter Six

# Market Forces Regulate

How does the decentralized market process regulate goods and services? What are the elements of such regulation? Through which market participants does it operate? How might this process work (how does it, in some cases) in the absence of any government regulation at all? We return to hairdressing to start looking for answers to these questions.

## Elements of Regulation by Market Forces

Let's approach this with a thought experiment: Suppose there were no hairdresser licensing. Suppose state legislatures repealed or "sunsetted" their hairdresser licensing laws, relying thereafter only on freedom of exchange and regulation by market forces—what would happen? In a true free market for hairdressing, with no state license on the wall to assure the customer of a hairdresser's competence, what reasons, if any, would a person have to trust a hairdresser or barber? What institutions and incentives would we expect to arise to pressure hairdressers and salons toward safety and competence?

Please think this question through for a few moments before reading on. What's the best the market could do to make you safe when you go for a haircut?

\* \* \* \* \*

One way to begin is to consider how people choose their hairdressers now, in the presence of licensing. How many base their choices on their hairdressers' license? Probably not many. Most of us rely primarily on experience. We try a hairdresser or barber, and if we like the results, we go back. If not, we go elsewhere. Hairdressers' need for repeat business, along with customers' freedom to go elsewhere, is enough by itself to enforce pretty high standards of quality.

The most important regulator in the market is thus competition itself, which subjects every business to the continuous judgment of the consuming public, who are free at every moment to give their business to a competitor. One main reason we trust the stores we go to and the electricians and plumbers we hire is our understanding of competition. We know that because they need repeat business and because their customers are free to go elsewhere, they must do a decent job or go broke. Businesses that stay in business in relatively free markets are probably doing a decent job. It is not always or perfectly so, but competition is a good regulator.

Note that the essential requirements for meaningful competition are *freedom of sellers* to enter into a business, if they can find a willing buyer, and *freedom of buyers* to take their business where they will. Consumers must have others to turn to and be free to turn to them in order for markets to punish businesses that offer shabby service or shoddy goods. Government licensing in hairdressing—and a host of other occupations—reduces competition by excluding many who would be able to find willing buyers, as it excluded Sharissa in our story of the last chapter. Market discipline grows stronger as freedom of exchange is expanded.

Working together with customer experience are reputation and word of mouth, which give customers the benefit of experiences others have had with a particular hairdresser. I remember a conversation between my wife and cousin at a family party: "Kathy," asked my wife, "who did your highlights for you?" On hearing Kathy's enthusiastic reply, I knew the market was about to cost my wife's hairdresser a customer. It did; my wife switched to Kathy's hairdresser.  Salons and salon franchises, such as the Hair Cuttery, work hard to establish and maintain a good reputation by giving good service.

Suppose a customer *is* injured while getting a hairdo—perhaps the stylist burns the customer's scalp or cuts her ear. Most salons would go to great lengths to make it up to the customer with free hairdos and the like to preserve their reputations, but perhaps not all would. What could the customer do then? In such cases—rare, we would hope and expect—the customer can sue for damages under the legal institution of tort liability. "Tort" means injury; holding people accountable for injury they do to another's property or person is one of the foundational legal institutions— along with private property and freedom of exchange—on which a free market in a free society is based.

While customers' bad experiences with incompetent hairdressers would of course tend to drive such hairdressers from the market eventually, and while it is possible to sue a hairdresser who actually harms a customer, we would far prefer that customers not have such bad experiences to begin with. State licensing of hairdressers aims to restrict poor hairdressers from practicing in the first place. Are there incentives in an unhampered market that do the same?

Certainly there are: Salons themselves have a strong financial incentive to establish and strengthen their reputations by hiring only hairdressers they expect to please their customers. Accordingly, they are likely to require some assurance of quality and competence *before* hiring. They might get that by observing apprentices' work or giving their own tests to applicants. More commonly, many salons might require some third-party certification of the hairdressers they hire, such as a diploma from a reputable beauty school. Not only is such a diploma some assurance of quality to the salon, but also, hung on the wall, it is good marketing to customers.

Salons are not the only business enterprises with a financial stake in their stylists' competence. To return to the case where an injured customer sues a negligent salon for harm she has suffered there, suppose the judge rules in favor of the customer, ordering the salon to pay damages. Who would probably write the check for the damages? Probably not by the salon itself, but the salon's insurance company. And what is the insurance company's incentive with respect to the competence of the hairdressers in salons it insures? The more competently and safely the hairdressers work, the lower will be the payments the insurance company has to make to injured parties; therefore, the insurers of hairdressers also have an incentive to require reasonable standards of hairdresser competence and training. Possibly insurance companies would refuse to insure salons that hire hairdressers with no recognized diploma or certification of competence, or charge those salons higher premiums.

Notice that all the market-regulating factors mentioned here are regulating hairdressing now, alongside the state governments' licensing requirements. Which is more effective in assuring the public health and safety, not to mention good haircuts? When you go for a haircut, reader, which do you rely on more?

I believe market forces are so effective that licensing is entirely superfluous in assuring health and safety. The only meaningful effect of hairdresser licensing is to reduce consumer choice and raise prices, as we discussed in the last chapter.

Let us generalize from the hairdressing thought experiment above: The elements of regulation by market forces that we have identified are:

- Freedom among service and goods providers to enter the market and compete for buyers
- Freedom of buyers to take their business where they will
- Reputation of sellers, and customer experience spread by word-of-mouth
- Tort liability, a legal means by which people can recover damages if they are harmed
- Requirements imposed by insurance companies as conditions of insurance
- Third-party certification of product quality and service competence

In a free market, these market forces would regulate the provision of virtually every good and service. Like other aspects of the free market, they wouldn't work perfectly because human beings are imperfect. But they would work well.

The last element in the list, third-party certification, is important enough to deserve extra treatment.

## The Role of Competitive, Third-Party Certification

In any business with freedom of entry, competition and reputation by themselves do a great deal to assure customers of the quality of the goods and services they purchase; because when a provider does not perform well, dissatisfied customers leave and the word gets out.

But that does not and should not satisfy most of us. We want protection from unsafe, defective, or otherwise poor quality goods and services *before* they go on the market. Unfortunately, many people believe that only government regulation can provide that protection. They make a tragic mistake in this, because in supporting government regulation they open the door to all the abuses of regulatory capture we discussed in the last chapter. There is a superior free-market alternative: voluntary, third-party certification.

In free and competitive markets, goods and service providers have a strong profit-and-loss incentive to provide assurance of the quality of their products. Their customers want such assurance. Their insurance companies are eager to have it. And the companies themselves are eager to provide it. To do so, they often turn to independent third parties in the business of testing for and certifying quality, safety, or competence as the case may be. Under freedom of exchange, of course, goods and service providers would not be *required* to secure such certification, but market forces would motivate them to do so. A variety of enterprises would arise that set standards, test for quality, and provide consumers with information.

In hairdressing, various beauty schools provide certifications of different kinds of competence. Another private-sector incentive for hairdressers to receive training comes from the manufacturers of hair care products. I learned about this from one of my students some years ago. A licensed hairdresser himself, he explained that the makers of certain hair-coloring and styling products will not permit a salon to sell those products unless and until the salon's employees have been trained in how to instruct customers in their use. Hair care product makers don't want their reputations damaged by customers' getting poor results because they misuse the products. Accordingly, salons that want permission to sell these products have a profit-based incentive to insist that their stylists receive the required training.

Consider the business of servicing automobiles. In Maryland, where I live, no license is required for auto mechanics. Service stations are legally permitted to hire as mechanics people with no training or credentials whatever. The Exxon service station near my house, however, has two signs advertising that its mechanics are all "ASE certified." ASE is the National Institute for Automotive Service Excellence. Its website declares:

> The independent, non-profit National Institute for Automotive Service
> Excellence (ASE) was established in 1972 to improve the quality of
> vehicle repair and service through the *voluntary* testing and certification
> of technicians and other automotive service professionals. [my
> emphasis]

Why would profit-seeking service stations pay to have their technicians tested and certified by ASE when no regulation compels them? They do so, of course, to improve the quality of their technicians' work, enhance their reputations, and thereby attract more business. For the technicians themselves, the ASE courses are an investment in their own skills and earning power. ASE offers a wide variety of certifications in specialties such as alternative fuels, medium/heavy trucks, school buses, undercar, damage analysis and estimating, and many others. Customers benefit.

Another illustration of how incentives in the free market lead to voluntary, third-party certification of product quality comes from a recent *New York Times* article:

> With huge losses from food-poisoning recalls and little oversight
> from the federal Food and Drug Administration, some sectors of the
> food industry are cobbling together their own form of regulation in
> an attempt to reassure consumers. They are paying other government
> agencies to do what the FDA rarely does: muck through fields and pore
> over records to make sure food is handled properly.

Even though government officials are supposed to check on and assure food quality, they don't, at least not to the satisfaction of the California lettuce and spinach growers discussed in the article. But the profits of the growers depend on their producing safe and healthy food and assuring their customers that it is safe and healthy. Providing that assurance requires independent inspections, so the California growers formed the Leafy Green Products Handler Marketing Agreement which pays for their own inspection system. Driven by profit-and-loss incentives, the growers are regulating their own products and processes because they have found their official FDA regulation to be ineffective and insufficient.

> Participation in marketing agreements is voluntary, but in California,
> more than 95 percent of the leafy greens industry signed up, in part
> because major processors like Dole and Fresh Express agreed to
> participate. Produce growers had little choice but to follow.

Consumers benefit.

Because nearly all enterprises in an advanced economy carry liability insurance, insurance companies are a powerful regulating force in free markets. Insured companies prefer to pay lower premiums rather than higher, and insurance companies prefer to pay fewer and smaller claims rather than more and higher claims. Accordingly, insurance carries with it strong incentives to keep goods and services safe.

Indeed, insurance companies have a strong incentive to regulate—set appropriate standards for—the quality and safety of the products of companies they insure. This incentive led to the creation of perhaps the largest and foremost of third-party certifiers, Underwriters Laboratories (UL). "Underwriter" means "insurer" in this context.

Underwriters Laboratories is an international organization that "evaluates more than 19,000 types of products, components, materials and systems annually with 20 billion UL Marks appearing on 72,000 manufacturers' products each year." UL originated at the 1893 World's Columbian Exposition in Chicago, where newly-invented electrical power was both dazzling attendees and causing fires. Fire insurance companies needed guidance as to the safety of electrical appliances and the resistance of different materials to fire, so they provided the funding for what became Underwriters Laboratories in 1901. Let us emphasize that bit of history: Private, for-profit insurance companies, responding to market incentives, created an independent standard-setting and certifying organization. UL has no authority to require manufacturers to obtain its certification (the now-famous UL product safety mark). Nevertheless, thousands of companies voluntarily seek UL approval and design their products to UL standards. Though created to serve insurance companies by certifying for them the safety of products they insure, UL serves manufacturers at the same time by helping them improve their product designs. The benefit to consumers is obvious.

A crucial element of quality and safety regulation by market forces is competition among *certifiers*, not just among service providers or goods producers. This competition, or even the potential for such competition, tends to hold certifiers to meaningful standards at reasonable cost to their customers. The process is another instance of how profit and loss guide discovery of the enterprises, products, and processes that create the most value for the public. Competition among certifiers spurs innovation in the standards themselves and in techniques for assessing quality. UL does not have a legal monopoly on product-safety certification; rather it faces numerous competitors including ETL SEMKO, The Canadian Standards

Association, and a variety of specialized certifiers of products in particular fields. ASE competes with a wide variety of technical schools that offer their own diplomas in auto repair and maintenance. Other competitors are automobile manufacturers, such as Audi, Mercedes, and Volvo, which offer their own training programs for mechanics who want to specialize in servicing their brands. This competition drives UL and ASE to hold their standards reasonably high, but not so high as to be burdensome, and to develop a variety of different categories of certification in response to their customers' needs.

I experienced competition among certifiers directly, once, when shopping for a present for my wife. One jeweler I stopped in on (on word-of-mouth recommendation from a friend) showed me a pair of what he said were very good diamonds that could be made into earrings. They were pretty. They were also expensive. Trying to persuade me to buy them, the jeweler brought out certificates vouching for their high quality. As I looked over the certificates, he pointedly said, "You see these are *not* from the Gemological Institute of America." He said that, in the industry, that organization was suspected of grading diamonds too generously in order to please some jewelers willing to overstate the quality of their stones; he did not want any suspicion on the grading of the diamonds he was showing me. Accordingly, he had paid extra to have them certified by the European Gemological Laboratory, a more reputable institution, according to him.

Two years later I read in the newspapers of allegations that graders in the New York laboratory of the Gemological Institue of America (GIA) had taken bribes in exchange for higher-than-deserved ratings. GIA had already acted to protect its reputation with an internal investigation, and it fired four New York employees. The episode bore out the jeweler's suspicions about the GIA.

Two lessons emerge from this story: One is that regulation by third-party certification will not work perfectly. No kind of regulation can work perfectly, because human beings are imperfect; we are prone to both honest error and dishonest dealing. That, of course, applies to both private-sector certifiers and government regulators.

The other lesson is that free competition *among certifiers* pushes them to offer a good product at a reasonable price just as free competition among goods and service providers pushes them to do the same. When customers have a choice among certifiers, malfeasance or shabby work tends to be discovered and corrected. This is the main reason public policy should not grant any government regulatory body a monopoly on licensing or certification. When certifiers compete, those that do a better job over time tend to gain business and those that do worse tend to lose business. The greater reliability of regulation by market forces comes not from the trustworthiness of any particular certifier, but from the *process of competition* among certifiers. That process tends, through profit-and-loss selection (discussed in Chapter 2), to reveal the certifiers and certification standards that really create value for the general public.

Just as no business person knows for sure what products or processes will provide the most value for customers at the least cost, no regulator or certifier knows that either. That goes for all the many regulatory agencies that burden markets in the U.S. today: the Fed, the SEC, FDA, USDA, FTC, FCC, FINRA, CFTC, or any of the regulatory agencies now being created under the (remarkably named) Patient Protection and Affordable Care Act or the (Dodd-Frank) Wall Street Reform and Consumer Protection Act. Just as entrepreneurial innovation and profit-and-loss feedback are necessary to guide business people to discover ever more value-creating products and processes, so they are necessary to guide certifiers and regulators to discover ever more value-creating kinds of standards and better ways of testing and analyzing quality.

With respect to the strictness or laxity of standards, as the diamond-certification story shows, third-party certifiers who must compete with others cannot afford to set their standards too low. Their certification would begin to lose its value if, say, ASE, the Gemological Institute of America, or Underwriters Laboratories were to become careless in their testing, or if they tried to attract more business (in the short run) by certifying substandard performance or products. Service stations would turn from ASE, jewelers would turn from the Gemological Institute of America, manufacturers would turn from UL. They would turn to some other certifier or some other kind of quality assurance. This is precisely what happened with the California spinach and lettuce growers. When their existing monitoring system, FDA inspection, showed itself to be insufficient, they created their own.

At the other extreme, if a certifier were to set its standards unreasonably high or charge excessively for its services, its potential customers would find that meeting the standard costs more than the value of the certification, so they would go without certification or turn to a more reasonable alternative. Or create one for themselves.

For market forces to regulate a particular market well, businesses that want certification of their products and services must be free to go without if they cannot find a certifier that offers them the value they want. Only this freedom can reliably keep a spontaneously-ordered system of certification under constant pressure to improve. If the law permits only one certifier to operate (e.g. a government regulator or licensing body), or if businesses are required to obtain certification from only one or a few specified certifiers, society loses the dynamic process through which better standards and methods can be discovered and used.

The FDA's legal monopoly on certifying drugs and medical devices provides a useful illustration of this principle. Its "customers" are not legally permitted to market their goods without FDA approval, nor are they permitted to turn to alternative certifiers. This restriction on freedom of exchange leads to serious problems, as we shall see below.

Which works better, all things considered? Regulation by free market forces or regulation by government bureaucracy? I have made the strongest case I can for the former—for complete freedom of peaceful exchange— and I hope some readers are persuaded that market forces might regulate hairdressing better than state licensing laws do, that auto mechanics should need no license, and that market competition adequately protects us from overpaying for diamonds.

But perhaps those are easy cases with little at stake and small danger of tragic errors. What about services or products where people's lives are at stake? What about pharmaceuticals and medical devices?

With these a regulatory error can mean death or disfigurement. Remember Thalidomide? Isn't government regulation necessary, some readers are undoubtedly asking at this point, for *drugs*? Can we safely tolerate freedom of exchange between pharmaceutical companies and drug stores, doctors, and hospitals, before the FDA has certified the safety and effectiveness of drugs and medical devices to be exchanged?

The logic of the argument I'm presenting actually cuts the other way: the more there is at stake—here human lives and safety—the more important it is to take advantage of market feedback and the healthy incentives of free exchange, because they get *better* results than restrictions imposed by legislators and bureaucrats, all of whom face the problem of incomplete knowledge as well as perverse incentives. Let's consider pharmaceutical regulation.

## Regulating Pharmaceuticals

Here's an exercise similar to the one we did at the opening of this chapter with hairdressing: Suppose Congress were to repeal the FDA's legal authority to block the purchase and sale of drugs and medical devices, relying thereafter on freedom of exchange and regulation by market forces—what would happen? What institutions and incentives would we expect to arise to pressure drug companies to make their drugs appropriately safe and effective? What's the best the free market could do?

\* \* \* \* \*

All of the elements of regulation by market forces that operate with hairdressers would operate in this case as well. Surely the strongest incentive at work would be the profit incentive of the drug companies. Their profitability over the long term depends not only on getting a lot of drugs to market, but also on the safety and effectiveness—and reputation for safety and effectiveness—of those drugs.

Other market actors with a strong financial incentive to give the public good information about drug safety, and to administer only safe and effective drugs, are doctors, pharmacies, and hospitals. The profitability of each of these (or the economic health of non-profit hospitals) depends on the quality of care they give their patients and customers, and on their reputation for that quality.

With tort liability always in the background—and with everyone aware of the high damages courts award for medical malpractice or negligence—doctors, pharmacies, clinics and hospitals all have strong incentives to make sensible judgments about the potential risks and benefits of different therapies and to give patients good information. And behind them stand their insurance companies, which pay damage claims. Just as insurance companies have a strong incentive to finance testing and certification of dangerous products such as electrical appliances, they also would have a strong incentive to finance the testing and certification of pharmaceuticals in a free market. In a world without an FDA monopoly on drug certification, insurance companies that insure drug companies would almost certainly require a robust third-party certification process as a requirement for insurance. Indeed, were the FDA's monopoly to be revoked, Underwriters Laboratories seems a good candidate for one of the first institutions to set up a division for drug testing.

So market forces would regulate, but would it be good enough? When I take my students through this thought process, often one asks if it is not too dangerous to try out market regulation of drugs. What if it didn't work? Wouldn't the cost of the experiment in human lives and suffering be too high? It's a fair and important question.

But behind that question lies the unchallenged assumption that the current system of FDA regulation itself works pretty well and does so at relatively low cost in human lives and suffering. That assumption does not turn out to be valid.

In deciding whether it is preferable to regulate pharmaceuticals by market forces or by the FDA, we need to contrast the *reality* of market regulation with the *reality* of FDA regulation. We need to resist the inclination to contrast the reality of market regulation, with all the imperfections it would surely have, with some idealized notion of regulation by the FDA. Economists who advocate revoking the FDA's power do not claim that regulation by market forces would be perfect—of course it wouldn't, because in a world where people are inescapably ignorant and biochemistry is fantastically complex, it is impossible for any person or group to forecast perfectly the effects of different compounds on different patients. We claim rather that regulation by market forces would produce much *better* (though still imperfect) results than FDA regulation. To understand why, we have to understand the problem of incentives in the FDA.

What are the incentives for people who work in the FDA? In the words of Professors Dan Klein and Alexander Tabarrok, "Is the FDA safe and effective?"

There are two kinds of mistakes that regulators such as the FDA can make, Type I and Type II error. Type I error is to allow a harmful drug onto the market. Type II error is to keep a beneficial drug off the market. It is not possible to eliminate both kinds of errors. In a world of inescapable uncertainty and human ignorance, to decrease the likelihood of one type of error does, necessarily, increase the likelihood of the other. The only way to eliminate *all* chance of letting a bad drug go through (Type I error) is to ban all drugs. After all, somebody somewhere might have an adverse reaction to almost any medicine, however beneficial it might be to the vast majority. Conversely, the only way to eliminate *all* chance of blocking from the market a drug that might do someone some good (Type II error) would be to ban nothing at all. While the FDA has the authority to ban drugs, it should strike a sensible balance between the two kinds of error, minimizing both together as much as possible.

Now another question for the reader: Are FDA regulators more likely to make Type I or Type II errors? Why? Consider the personal consequences to individuals working in the FDA of making each type of error. Please think it through before reading on, and consider the consequences of that kind of behavior for how well the FDA serves the public interest. When FDA personnel commit a Type I error and allow onto the market a drug that has harmful side effects, *what are the consequences for them personally?* On the other hand, when they commit a Type II error and keep a useful or even life-saving drug off the market for a number of months or years, *what are the consequences for them personally?*

\* \* \* \* \*

Unless you are very unusual, you have answered that people in the FDA more carefully avoid Type I error than Type II. Letting a harmful drug out onto the market has serious, public consequences for FDA officials, especially if the drug causes actual harm. The media publicize any harm done, and the public rebukes the FDA for failing to do their duty. Politicians in Congress get involved, sometimes appointing a commission to investigate a failure to protect the public health and safety. If the harm caused by the drug is horrible enough, some of those responsible for letting it through would undoubtedly be wracked with guilt and self-reproach. In short, for those in the FDA, making a Type I error has strong, unpleasant, public consequences. Henry I. Miller, an important critic of the FDA who worked there from 1979-1994, describes the incentives in colorful language:

> This kind of mistake is highly visible and has immediate consequences—the media pounces, the public denounces, and Congress pronounces. Both the developers of the product and the regulators who allowed it to be marketed are excoriated and punished in modern-day pillories: congressional hearings, television news magazines, and newspaper editorials. Because a regulatory official's career might be damaged irreparably by his good faith but mistaken approval of a high-profile product, decisions are often made defensively—in other words, to avoid Type I errors at any cost....

The consequences for FDA personnel of a Type II error are entirely different. There are no substantial public consequences because such errors result in things not happening—medicines not prescribed, diseases not treated with them (but with some other drugs instead), and patients not cured who might have been cured. Such non-events do not attract attention. The families of patients who have suffered or died because the FDA has not (yet) authorized an effective treatment rarely blame their loved ones' suffering on the FDA; they believe the patients are receiving the best available care and don't stop to think that there might be effective treatments that their doctors are forbidden to use.

In brief, then, regulators in the FDA have a strong personal incentive to avoid Type I errors, whose consequences for themselves are severe. They therefore commit a lot of Type II errors, for which the consequences to themselves are negligible. These incentives are disastrous for the American public, however.

One aspect of the problem is very long delays, known as the "drug lag," in getting a new drug to market. During this delay, patients go untreated who might have been treated; they suffer or die when they might have thrived or lived. Another aspect of the problem is that the FDA approval process is so long and expensive that only drugs that promise to sell to a large population can possibly recoup their development costs. Accordingly, drug companies tend not to research and develop drugs for more rare illnesses. In consequence, there are many diseases for which we might have treatments in a free market, for which we do not have treatments. All the research expense also means higher prices for the drugs once approved, of course, because revenue from selling the drugs must cover the costs of the approval process.

The immediate and shocking problem is thousands of avoidable illnesses and deaths every year because of FDA delays in approving effective drugs. Figure 6.1 summarizes some examples.

These figures are staggering, aren't they? And they document only five well-understood cases among hundreds. Extrapolate to the hundreds of other medicines delayed by the FDA—taxotere, vasoseal, ancrod, glucophage, navelbine, and many others—all denied for months or years to real patients with real families, and the horrifying magnitude of the damage suggests itself. Estimates are that, every year, tens of thousands of preventable deaths are attributable to the FDA's over-caution.

**Figure 6.1 Examples of Type II Errors by the FDA**

| Drug or Device | Length of Approval Delay | Estimated Consequences |
|---|---|---|
| Thrombolytic Therapy dissolves blood clots | 2 years | up to 22,000 deaths |
| Interleukin-2* treats kidney cancer | 3 ½ years | 3,500 deaths |
| Misoprotol prevents bleeding ulcers | 9 ½ months | 8,000-15,000 deaths |
| AmbuCardioPump** | not approved | 7,000 deaths annually |
| Home HIV test | 5 years | 10,000 infections |

\* Already available in Europe

\*\* Available in most industrialized countries

The thoughtful reader will wonder about the countervailing benefits: Granted that lives are lost to Type II error, how many lives are saved by the avoidance of Type I error? Do the benefits of the caution exceed the costs? No. According to Klein and Tabarrok, "There is no evidence that the U.S. drug lag brings greater safety."

The disaster is a consequence of the perverse incentives of the FDA. The individuals working there are good people, trying to do their best, like all of us. But in that institutional setting, the incentives they face are dreadful. FDA critic Sam Kazman puts it this way:

> From FDA commissioners to the bureau heads to the individual
> NDA [New Drug Application] reviewers, the message is clear: if you
> approve a drug with unanticipated side effects, both you and the
> agency will face the heat of newspaper headlines, television coverage
> and congressional hearings. On the other hand, if FDA insists on more
> and more data from a manufacturer, and finally approves a drug which
> should have been on the market months or years before, there is no
> such price to pay. Drug lag's victims and their families will hardly be
> complaining, because they won't know what hit them. ... They only

know that there is nothing their doctors can do for them. From the standpoint of ... politics, they are invisible.

## Summary

In a free market, pharmaceuticals would not be regulated by the FDA, UL, or any particular certifier. They would be regulated by the market-imposed requirement for pharmaceutical companies to meet the standards of drug testing that would evolve as doctors, hospitals, pharmacies, and insurance companies choose among the different standards and certifications in their own efforts to please their patients and customers. Rather than the FDA—a government monopoly restricting what drugs may be sold, shielded from competition, lacking profit-and-loss feedback, sure of its customers no matter how little it innovates or how many innocents die waiting, sure of its funding no matter how badly it controls costs—we would have a dynamic process in which any organization might offer its testing and certification services. At any time among these service providers would be those who earn a good reputation for reliable processes and meaningful evaluation standards. Some might advertise the speediness of their process and others the comprehensiveness of their testing, but none could ignore one for the other and survive in the market. Doctors, hospitals, pharmacies, and insurance companies would draw on all of these certifiers and information providers, and standards would evolve with experience.

Of course, all the drug certifiers would make mistakes in their testing or their judgments (as the FDA does now). Sometimes they would certify the safety of a drug that turns out to have harmful side effects; sometimes they would withhold certification from a safe and effective drug. The importance and size of those mistakes would be judged by the doctors, hospitals, and pharmacies, as well as the drug manufacturers, insurers, and knowledgeable people (including bloggers) in the general public. Those certifiers that perform better would gain business; those that perform worse would lose it. No certifier could rest on its laurels nor ignore the tradeoffs among speed, accuracy, and low cost in coming to their decisions, because neither drug companies nor patients could be required to use their services. Best practices would tend to spread to all the different certifiers; certifiers that did not adopt best practices would tend to make losses and go out of business. Steady innovation in testing and disseminating useful information would occur.

Drug manufacturers would have a strong incentive to get evaluations from at least one, and perhaps more, of the certifiers, depending on the cost and the value of second opinions to doctors, hospitals, and pharmacies. Insurance companies would have a strong incentive to cover only therapies whose certifications they trust. Costs driven down by competition, dramatically lower than those imposed by the FDA, would allow for more drugs and therapies to be developed and tested.

As with drugs, so with all other goods and services. Market forces are not perfect regulators, but they are the best available.

Many idealize government regulation. They imagine it to be clean and effective. They imagine that government regulators have the knowledge they need to make good decisions, the wisdom to use knowledge well, and the incentive to serve the public interest rather than their own. But, in fact, all regulators are people—human beings with all their various strengths and weaknesses and inescapable ignorance.

Like everyone else, government regulators tend to put themselves first—they are self-interested. Often their main concerns, like those of their fellows in the private sector, are their career advancement, job security, or next pay raise. Some people won't stand up to a superior who is clearly making a mistake. Some of us are corruptible, willing to take a payment or promotion for looking the other way. Some of us have simply been promoted beyond our competence.

Because of the natural, inescapable limitations of human beings, there can be no perfectly effective system of regulation. There is no way to "get it right." Every approach will have flaws. Our goal should be the more modest one of achieving the least-flawed institutional setting—of minimizing the problems inherent in human limitations.

The least-flawed, best available approach to regulation is one that:

- generates an on-going discovery of new and better knowledge and invention of new and better processes, and
- gives those involved a strong incentive to create value for other people in order to benefit themselves.

A healthy process of regulation will not confer a legal monopoly on one regulatory body. Doing so insulates that regulator from the feedback it needs about how well it is performing. Healthy regulation needs profit-and-loss feedback that rewards good regulating and punishes bad. It needs a close connection of performance and funding. The criteria of good or bad performance must be criteria used by the people the regulation is meant to serve, not those of a bureaucracy with monopoly power.

A healthy process of regulation must be a market process with consumers ultimately in control, with profit-and-loss feedback flowing to both the providers of goods and services *and to their certifiers*, and with freedom of exchange that allows any enterprise to try its hand at providing information about the safety and efficacy of a product.

The actual regulator in this setting is not some regulatory body. It's the *process* whereby 1) different certifiers strive to create valuable information and standards, 2) goods and services providers select from among the different standards, information, and certifications offered—or refuse them all—and 3) customers, at each level, reward with profit those that serve them well and punish with loss those that serve them badly.

# Chapter Seven

# Special Interests versus Democracy

In reading of the undesirable consequences of government intervention, some readers have undoubtedly wondered why our democratic political processes can't solve these kinds of problems. For example, if hairdresser licensing laws really do hurt the general public by restricting our hairdressing choices and thereby making us all pay more for a haircut, then the public can simply vote out of office those who support such excessive restrictions, and vote in those who will repeal them or make them sensible. In a democracy the voters ultimately control legislation, don't we? So why should we abandon government intervention altogether? Why not rely on the democratic process to make it work in the public interest?

This is a question studied at length in public choice economics, and at least two answers are pretty clear. One is that special interest groups tend to dominate the political processes of economic intervention because of *the concentration of benefits and the diffusion of costs*, a phenomenon I'll refer to here as "the special interest effect." The special interest effect is well understood as an elaboration of the second part of the Incentive Principle, that "government interventions tempt people to benefit themselves at others' expense." The other answer is that voting for particular legislators is just too indirect a way for the citizen voter to affect particular policies.

As usual, let's begin with an example.

# Federal Dairy Programs

The federal dairy programs are a tangle of laws that benefit dairy farmers at the expense of taxpayers and consumers. There are three major programs:

- The Milk Income Loss Contract program "compensates dairy producers [with taxpayers' money] when domestic milk prices fall below a specified level."
- By Federal Milk Marketing Orders the federal government sets the prices farmers will receive for their milk, thereby eliminating price competition among dairies and raising milk prices above market levels.
- The Dairy Product Price Support Program "support[s] the price of cheddar cheese, butter and nonfat dry milk through the purchase of such products," with taxpayers' money, again.

These programs vary in their effects from year to year as the weather and other market conditions change, but on average, the first two programs are estimated to cost taxpayers about $1.3 billion a year. A lot of that money goes to pay the salaries of the USDA bureaucrats and general expenses of the programs, but the rest, about $900 million annually, goes to dairy companies in payments for milk, cheese, and butter, and as compensation for low milk prices. The third program, which supports prices, costs consumers about $420 million per year while it increases farm income by about $293 million per year.

The total estimated costs to taxpayers and consumers, then, come to about $1.72 billion per year. The total estimated benefits to dairy farmers come to about $1.19 billion per year. Because there are about nine million dairy cows in the country, we can say that each cow is subsidized about $132 on average.

For taxpayers and consumers, these dairy programs are a bad deal. Taxpayers have to foot the bill not only for the payments to dairies, but also for the storage of the excess cheese and nonfat dry milk, as well as the salaries and expenses of the USDA bureaucracy that administers the programs. The payoff of the program for taxpayers is that when we get to the store we pay more than we otherwise would for milk, butter, yogurt, ice cream, and cheese. It really is quite remarkable: taxpayers are taxed so that we will have to pay more for milk at the store.

The programs yield no net benefits; they are as wasteful as they seem. The artificially high prices foul up the operation of the Price Communication Principle, so that dairy farmers invest more scarce resources in milk production than they should. Other goods and services that would have made the public better off go unproduced.

The key question for this chapter is:

*How can these programs last in a democracy?*

The majority are supposed to rule in democracy. There are about 310 million Americans now, most of whom pay taxes of one kind or another, and a majority of whom consume dairy products. Each of us suffers from this program, which takes money from our pockets and puts it in the pockets of those in the dairy business. But there are fewer than seventy-five thousand dairies in the U.S. now, so across the country, only a few hundred thousand people own or work in dairies. Why don't the many outvote the few? How could the dairy programs last when they harm two hundred million or more and benefit only a half million or so? If democratic processes are adequate to guide policies toward accomplishing the public good, then certainly these farm programs should never have been started, or, once started, immediately eliminated.

But the dairy programs last and last. Like thousands of other economically damaging public policies that harm far more people than they benefit—like logging in the Tongass and hairdresser licensing—they last because of the special interest effect. The key to the special interest effect is the perverse incentives that arise when Congress is allowed to intervene in the economy: incentives for taxpayer-consumers, for people in the affected industry, and for members of Congress.

In order to clarify the incentives at work, let us imagine a representative taxpayer-consumer and a representative dairy owner. Our taxpayer-consumer we'll call Vince, a young athlete trying to build up his size, who drinks a lot of milk. Our dairy owner is Mrs. Watson, who owns a medium-sized dairy with 200 cows.

Let's consider Vince's incentives first. What does the program cost him? Suppose the price support program increases the retail price of milk by a representative 20 cents a gallon. Suppose further that Vince drinks a lot of milk, a couple of gallons a week. In extra money he pays for milk, the program costs Vince:

*20 cents/gallon x 2 gallons/week x 52 weeks/year = $20.80/year.*

We estimate what Vince pays in taxes toward the dairy programs at the per person average of $4.19 (about $1.3 billion in total cost to taxpayers, averaged over the approximately 310 million Americans). Hence the dairy programs cost Vince about $25 per year in higher prices and taxes. Note that we have set up the example so that that figure is probably higher than the cost would actually be to most consumers, who drink less milk.

Now the crucial question: how strong an incentive does Vince have to do something about it? Ponder that while we consider Mrs. Watson's situation.

What is the benefit of the dairy price support program to someone like Mrs. Watson? She has 200 cows at her dairy, and we have seen that the average subsidy per cow over the last decade has been on the order of $132. In extra revenue to her dairy, then, the program pays to Mrs. Watson:

*$132/cow/year x 200 cows = $26,400/year.*

Note that we have set up the example so that the subsidy is substantially lower than it would be to a larger dairy (large dairies in the U.S. have more than 15,000 cows, and most of the country's milk is produced on farms with more than 500 cows).

Now the same crucial question: how strong an incentive to do something about it does this $26,400 a year give Mrs. Watson?

Back to Vince's incentives: how energetically will Vince object to this transfer of $25 a year from "the poor" (him, a college student accumulating debts) to "the rich" (established businesspeople such as Mrs. Watson)? Is it likely that Vince even knows about these programs?

Let us suppose that Vince does know about the programs—perhaps he learned about them in an economics class. How strong an incentive does he have to do something about them, to object, to write or call his congressman, or to organize other victims of the programs into a lobbying group to oppose it? Clearly his incentive is weak because the programs cost him only $25 a year. Vince would not spend much more than $25 worth of time and effort to oppose the program, even if he thought he could defeat it by his efforts. But of course he knows that any effort he personally makes is likely to have a tiny effect on national dairy policy, even if he visits his congressman and both senators. And it might cost him more just to *park* in Washington, D.C., for a day than the price support program costs him in a year.

Under these circumstances it makes sense for Vince simply to ignore federal dairy policy. And what is true for Vince is true for every other milk-drinker taxpayer in the country. The $1.72 billion total cost is *so widely diffused* over all consumers and taxpayers that each of us bears only a very small individual cost. Therefore each of us individually has only a very weak incentive to do anything about it. The effort is not worth the $25 it would save a milk-guzzler like Vince, even on the vanishingly small chance that his individual efforts should get the program repealed.

Indeed, the $25 cost to Vince is so small that, like almost every other milk-drinker taxpayer in the country, he probably never learns of the program at all. Most Americans quite reasonably do not even know that the dairy programs exist. Public choice economists call this "rational voter ignorance." It is rational—it makes sense—for Vince and most taxpayer-consumer-voters to remain ignorant about the federal dairy programs because the value of the time it would take them to learn and keep informed about them is greater than what the programs cost them.

(We should note here that another kind of ignorance surely contributes to the survival and even the flourishing of these destructive dairy programs: plain economic ignorance of the kind this book aims to reduce. Undoubtedly many Americans support measures to "save America's dairy farmers" because they do not understand how prosperous most of those farmers are or how much harm the programs cause.)

What about Mrs. Watson and other dairy farmers? The program benefits Mrs. Watson to the tune of about $26,400 a year. How strong an incentive does that give her to support it? Is it likely that she knows about the program? What percentage of American dairy farmers, do you suppose, know about the program?

Clearly, all dairy farmers have a strong incentive to keep informed about the program and to support it politically. Offsetting this incentive, for the principled and honorable among them, is the incentive to earn income only by free exchange, to refuse this corporate welfare, to oppose these redistributive dairy programs, even though they lose financially by doing so. Unfortunately, in many dairy farmers the former incentive prevails. The second part of the Incentive Principle is in play: They are tempted to use this intervention to benefit themselves at others' expense. So they write their congressional representatives; they support lobbying efforts; they organize with other dairy owners, generally through some already-established industry group such as the National Milk Producers Federation. Because the program benefits her by $26,400 a year, Mrs. Watson is willing to spend up to nearly that amount in time and money to support the program. Even if she spends $26,000 a year, she will come out ahead. She knows that her contributions will have an impact in Washington, because they will be used by the experienced lobbyists the Dairymen's Association hire.

Because the number of dairy farmers is small relative to the millions of dollars spent in the program, the *benefits of the program are concentrated* on a relatively small group. Each dairy farmer therefore receives a substantial benefit from the program. Accordingly, each has a strong incentive to stay informed about the program and to give it substantial political support.

The consequences for dairy policy follow logically from the different levels of lobbying and political activity of taxpayer-consumers and dairy farmers. When it comes time to vote on reauthorizing the dairy programs, whose voices will be heard in Congress? Would you say it is the voice of taxpayer-consumers, who would like to pay less for milk, or the voice of dairy farmers, who would like to keep being subsidized for producing it? Hardly any voices are raised for taxpayer-consumers, while the voices of the dairy farmers are loud, clear, and insistent.

What are the politicians' incentives? Though they would like to do the right thing (we hope)—support sound policies that respect property rights and keep food prices down for poor families—they definitely want to be reelected. Accordingly we can count on most of them, most of the time, to do what will help them get reelected. In the case of dairy programs, politicians know that supporting the programs is the clear winner. If they back dairy price supports and subsidies, they will lose hardly any votes from the taxpayer-consumers who are harmed: those taxpayer-consumers don't even know about the programs. At the same time, backing the programs will win them both votes and campaign contributions from the dairy interests. Consequently, the politicians have a strong financial and career incentive to vote for the dairy programs. In most of them, this incentive is stronger than their incentive to do the right thing. In keeping with the Incentive Principle, the politicians' ability to intervene in dairy markets tempts them to do so, to benefit themselves at the expense of the general public. What is really in the *public* interest, sadly, has not (yet?) been able to stand up against the special interest incentives generated by government intervention in the dairy industry.

## The Special Interest Effect

Let us generalize to the special interest effect that the federal dairy programs illustrate: Bad public policy tends to last and even flourish when the policy concentrates benefits on a special interest group and diffuses costs over the general public. The concentrated and therefore large benefits enjoyed by each individual member of the special interest group give them a strong incentive to support the policy politically. By contrast, the diffused and therefore small costs borne by each taxpayer-consumer give them only a small incentive to oppose the policy politically, or even to find out about it. The consequence of these incentives is lively political pressure on politicians from the special interest group and little to no political pressure from the general public. Accordingly, when it comes time for a legislature to vote on the policy, the politicians tend to support it.

The greater ease of organizing a smaller group helps special interests pass legislation that benefits them at others' expense. Whereas large groups of consumer-taxpayers are difficult to identify and contact, concentrated special interest group members are relatively easy to identify and contact. Indeed, as in the case of the Dairymen's Association, many special interest groups are already organized in industry associations formed initially for non-political purposes such as networking and sharing information.

We can see in Figure 7.1 the operation of the special interest effect in five of the examples we have considered in these first seven chapters.

The special interest effect goes a long way toward explaining why democratic political processes often cannot improve bad economic policy. Because of the special interest effect, the incentives that drive political processes tend to perpetuate bad policy. The public cannot vote out of office those who support economically destructive legislation when the public does not and will not know such legislation exists. Indeed, there is so much special interest policy on the books that even professional policy analysts cannot keep track of it all. No average citizen can be expected to do so while holding down a job.

## The Bluntness of the Ballot Box

Another reason why democratic political processes cannot be relied on to protect the public from bad policy is that control through the ballot box is far too indirect and imprecise to be effective. How well are you able, reader,

**Figure 7.1 The Special Interest Effect: Concentration of Benefits and Diffusion of Costs**

| Institution | Recipients of Concentrated Benefits | Those Bearing Diffused Costs |
|---|---|---|
| Forest Service's logging program in the Tongass | Loggers and logging companies | Taxpayers and wilderness lovers |
| Hairdresser licensing | Established hairdressers and salons | Consumers |
| Minimum wage laws | Unions and other higher-skilled workers | Low-skilled workers; consumers (who pay higher prices) |
| Scrubber requirement on coal-fired electricity-generating plants | Eastern coal interests; United Mine Workers | Consumers of electricity; (some) breathers of air |
| FDA's excessive caution | FDA employees | Drug consumers |

to register your objection to, say, the logging program in the Tongass or to the hairdresser licensing in your state by your votes for your representatives in Congress and your state legislature? Not very. In the first place, all available candidates might support the policies you object to. More important, when one votes for a representative, one votes for a package—*all* the various policy positions that politician takes. When we agree with some and disagree with other policy positions a representative takes, there is no way for us to communicate that when we vote. Still another problem is that we have no guarantee or even much likelihood that politicians will do what they have promised. And how, by voting for one candidate or another, might a voter register her discontent with the *details* of a particular policy? If, for example, she supports hairdresser licensing in principle, but believes the requirements are far too strict and expensive, can she express that preference by voting? No.

The democratic process cannot be relied on to regulate economic intervention in the public interest. Special interest groups can and will control that intervention in large measure. Politicians and bureaucrats will act largely in their own private interest, even when doing so hurts the public interest. The citizens, as voters, can do little to prevent them.

The idea that intervention will serve the public interest if we get "the right people" into office is an illusion. People are people, whether Republicans or Democrats. In Lord Acton's famous words, "All power tends to corrupt." The solution is not to get "the right people" into power, but to *do away with the power*. There should be no power to interfere in the peaceful, rights-respecting interactions of competent adults. Nobody can handle that power well. Nobody.

Part II

# Conclusion

The solution to the problem of special interests is to limit government to the role Jefferson identifies in his first inaugural address, quoted in this book's introduction. Governments should "restrain men from injuring one another" and nothing more. Policy should "leave them otherwise free to regulate their own pursuits of industry and improvement." Take away the governmental power for some to impose their wishes on peaceful others, and the problem of special interests will evaporate.

Imagine American society supporting freedom of exchange as strongly as we support freedom of speech and freedom of religion. No lobbyist for a newspaper chain or a religion goes to Washington today to insist that any new newspaper or religion first get a license assuring the quality of their news or doctrine. If members of Congress were asked to institute such licensing, they would shrug, bemused, and say, "Well, I'm sorry, but the Constitution does not permit us to interfere with the press or religion."

That's the way it should be with the rest of the economy as well! No special interest group, such as loggers or hairdressers or dairy farmers, should even think of going to Washington—or state capitals—for licensing, subsidies, tariffs, bailouts, or other special treatment. They should know that their legislators would have to say, "Well, I'm sorry, but the Constitution does not permit us to subsidize businesses or interfere with commerce."

If politicians had no favors to hand out, special interests would seek no favors from politicians.

Government regulation tempts special interests to use government power to benefit themselves at others' expense. The special interests regularly fall into temptation. The economy works for the benefit of all to the extent that resources are privately owned, exchange is free, and regulation is by market forces.

"Yeah, right!" will come a retort from some. "That's the kind of free market fundamentalism that caused the housing bubble and the financial crisis of 2008!"

Really? Let's take a close look.

# Part III

# The Housing Boom and Financial Crisis

Housing prices stopped their dramatic, decade-long ascent in 2006. They declined slowly in 2007; they fell fast in 2008. Lots of home owners fell behind on their mortgage payments. The Wall Street investment bank Bear Stearns was holding a huge inventory of shaky mortgages it planned to bundle into mortgage-backed securities (MBSs); but with mortgage delinquency rising sharply, suddenly no investors would buy mortgage-backed securities. In March, 2008, Bear Stearns failed.

A shudder went through the financial world. The New York Federal Reserve bank bailed out Bear Stearns' creditors by marrying the company off in a shotgun wedding to JP Morgan Chase—on the condition that the New York Fed put taxpayers on the hook for thirty billion dollars' worth of bad assets that JP Morgan Chase would not accept.

In September, Wall Street investment bank Lehman Brothers, also deep in mortgage-backed securities, failed. But this time, against expectations, no bailout occurred. In the words of Peter Wallison,

> [I]nvestors panicked. They withdrew their funds from the institutions that held large amounts of privately issued MBSs, causing banks and others, such as investment banks, finance companies and insurers—to hoard cash against the risk of further withdrawals. Their refusal to lend

to one another in these conditions froze credit markets, bringing on what we now call the financial crisis.

Thousands of healthy small businesses suddenly could not get routine loans for normal operations. Business fell off, employees got laid off. The "Great Recession of 2008," which had officially begun in December of 2007, deepened. Unemployment shot up, rising to ten percent by mid-2009. Economic distress made it still harder for many homeowners to pay their mortgages; delinquencies and foreclosures mounted. Millions watched their main asset, their house, lose value. The stock market plummeted, falling twenty-four percent in a two-week period, taking families' retirement and college funds down with it.

Why? What caused the turmoil? Who or what is to blame?

Two widely held answers are: 1) human greed and 2) lack of regulation. On the first of these, economist Lawrence H. White has quipped that blaming the financial mess on greed is like blaming an airplane crash on gravity. Greed (or at least, in a gentler term, *self-interest*) is always present in human affairs, else how would we ever get pencils? What we need to figure out is why in this case the spontaneous order that channels self-interest into the creation of pencils, houses, mortgages, and other valuable goods and services got so fouled up.

A strong statement of the second answer was offered by economist Paul Samuelson in 2009 (at one time Samuelson, an advocate of government intervention, wrote a *Newsweek* column every other week, alternating with noted free market advocate Milton Friedman):

And today we see how utterly mistaken was the Milton Friedman notion that a market system can regulate itself. We see how silly the Ronald Reagan slogan was that government is the problem, not the solution. This prevailing ideology of the last few decades has now been reversed. Everyone understands now, on the contrary, that there can be no solution without government.

Professor Samuelson is entirely mistaken. As I argued in Part II, a *free* market system does regulate itself. The financial turmoil we have been going through results from restrictions on, not the presence of, economic freedom. In this case, as in most, Reagan's slogan does apply: government privileges, mandates, monopolies, bailouts, and restrictions *were* the problem. But readers must not take my judgment on this; they must use their own.

In this Part III, I offer arguments and evidence to help readers make up their own minds as to whether economic liberty or economic restrictions are to blame for the housing boom and bust and the financial turmoil that followed. This powerful, painful case study shows how interference with the Price Coordination Principle, the Profit-and-Loss Guidance Principle, and the Incentive Principle makes everyone poorer.

It is gravely important that we understand whether too much freedom or too little caused the financial and economic mess America got itself into in the first decade of the 21st century. If we misunderstand, we'll make the same kinds of mistakes, perpetuate our difficulties, and bring more problems on ourselves in the future. I fear this is, in fact, what we are doing.

The first goal of Part III is easy: to make clear that the housing boom and bust and the financial mess that followed were not caused by free markets. There is no proof here that interventions caused the mess; it is conceivable, as some have argued, that the problem was not too much intervention, but too little. But the problems cannot have been a consequence of free markets, because the markets were *not* free: there was extensive government intervention in housing, mortgage, and banking markets.

A second goal is to explain in terms of the three principles laid out in Part I how these interventions disturbed or obstructed the spontaneous ordering processes of the economy. We'll see how special tax treatment and subsidization of housing distorted housing prices away from their free-market levels, so that prices "told a lie" about housing values. We'll see how the Federal Reserve's creation of new money and Congress's implicit guarantee of the debts of Fannie Mae and Freddie Mac distorted interest rates away from their free-market levels, so that interest rates "told a lie" about resource availability and the risks of housing. We'll see that government guaranteed not just Fannie Mae and Freddie Mac's debts, but also bank deposits and loans to large financial institutions. These guarantees shielded investors from the possibility of losses, and thereby blocked profit and loss from rewarding value-creating investments and punishing unwise investments. We'll see how government regulators' lack of profit-and-loss feedback blocked discovery of better standards and practices for reducing risk in banking and insurance. And we'll see how the incentives of most participants in the system, from house buyers to lenders, investors, and regulators, were distorted by the pervasive intervention.

A third goal is to introduce free-market alternatives to these interventions, and explain how free-market institutions, processes, and incentives would have spared us all the loss and turmoil by fostering balanced, sustainable improvements in our standard of living.

Chapter Eight

# Mortgage-Making in a Free Market

W hat went wrong? How did the housing market get so out of control, and why did the problems in housing spill over into banking and lending?

In order to understand how government intervention caused the housing boom and bust and the resulting financial fiasco, we'll first identify the elements of American housing finance that are market-based, that we would expect to see in a truly free market. Having done that, we'll see more clearly in the following chapters that the housing boom and bust occurred in a far from free market. A wide variety of government interventions—we'll focus on the main culprits—interfered with the principles of spontaneous economic order, fouling up price signaling, distorting profit-and-loss feedback, and creating perverse incentives.

## Direct Mortgage Financing

In the great majority of cases, a buyer finances the purchase of a home by getting a mortgage from a bank (or a savings-and-loan association [S&L]— when we speak of banks, we'll mean S&L's, too). The bank, of course, gets that money from depositors who put their money in the bank in savings accounts, checking accounts, certificates of deposit (CDs) and the like. In exchange for giving the homebuyer the money for the purchase, the bank gets the homebuyer's promise to pay that money back and pay interest on the borrowed sum. Importantly, the mortgage contract also specifies that the bank becomes legal owner of the house if the homebuyer does not keep his part of the bargain by paying back the principal and interest as promised.

Three types of actors play different roles in the process: Before there can be any money to lend, someone has to save that money. First, then, are the *saver/lenders*. These are individuals and organizations of all sorts—businesses, churches, foundations, clubs, etc.—that save some of their money in savings and checking accounts and CDs. At the other end of the process are the *borrower/spenders*, in this case those who want to borrow money to buy a house. Acting as *intermediaries* are the banks. A bank's role is intermediation; the bank saves borrower/spenders the hassle of finding people willing to lend them money, and spares saver/lenders the hassle of finding creditworthy people to borrow their money. Banks specialize in bringing together borrower/spenders and saver/lenders. They make money by charging homebuyers and other borrower/spenders a slightly higher rate of interest than they pay the lender/savers who put their money in the bank.

These three basic roles—borrower/spenders, intermediaries, and saver/lenders—are played in most borrowing and lending. Note that as banks earn profits and accumulate their own wealth, they can and do become saver/lenders in their own right, lending directly for themselves without any other intermediary.

The mortgage itself is essentially an IOU; it's a record of the agreement between the bank and the homebuyer. Figure 8.1 gives a fictitious example, stripped to essentials.

Mortgages may be of either the fixed rate or adjustable rate variety. In a fixed rate mortgage, the rate of interest is fixed at the outset. Fixing the rate has the advantage of making the size of the mortgage payments completely predictable for both the homebuyer and the bank. Most mortgages are fixed-rate—virtually all of them were until the late 1970s when high inflation spurred the development of adjustable rate mortgages.

**Figure 8.1 A Basic Mortgage Contract**

> ### MORTGAGE CONTRACT
>
> I, <u>Howard Baetjer Jr.</u> owe
> <u>Columbia Bank</u>
> $<u>100,000</u> at an annual interest rate of 7%.
> I promise to pay $<u>665.30</u> each month
> in principal and interest for <u>30</u> years
> or the bank gets the house.
>
> Signed *Howard Baetjer Jr.*

An adjustable rate mortgage (ARM), as the name suggests, has an interest rate that changes or "resets" at specified intervals (often once a year) to keep it in line with other interest rates. The purpose of the adjustment is to protect the homebuyer from having to keep paying a relatively high mortgage payment if interest rates in general fall, and to protect the bank from having to keep accepting a relatively low mortgage payment if interest rates in general rise. The interest rate adjusts so that borrowers pay and lenders receive something close to the going rate of interest.

There is a danger to borrowers in adjustable rate mortgages. That is, the monthly payment generally rises after the initial period; the initial interest rate is set relatively low to make the ARM attractive in comparison with a fixed rate mortgage. But the interest rate (and hence the mortgage payment) usually increases after the initial period, and it may increase further at subsequent resets. Some people get carried away by the attractiveness of the initial low monthly rate (sometimes called a "teaser rate") and don't seriously consider their ability to pay the higher rates that may come later; they commit themselves to paying what they may not be able to afford. (Sad to say, many people made this mistake during the housing boom.)

When borrowers fall behind on the interest and principal payments agreed to in their mortgage contracts, they are said to be in default. The default rate is the proportion of mortgages of a given category on which their borrowers are behind in their payments.

When a borrower is in default deeply enough or long enough, the bank that holds the mortgage may foreclose on the mortgage; that is, the bank exercises its right to take over ownership of the house. Banks generally don't like to foreclose because they are in the business of lending money, not managing and selling houses; but they do it when they must. Normally on foreclosure, the bank sells the house at auction; after auction expenses and legal costs, the bank may end up with a loss on the mortgage overall.

A sound mortgage loan is one that is likely to be paid off as agreed. Various factors reduce the risk of default and increase the soundness of a mortgage loan. Among these soundness factors are:

- The ratio of the monthly mortgage payment to the borrower's monthly income: The less a mortgage payment takes out of a borrower's monthly income, the less trouble the borrower may have paying.

- Having less other debt: The less other debt a borrower has to pay off, the more income will be left over to pay the mortgage.

- Having good credit history: This speaks for itself. Those with good credit history are "prime" borrowers.

- Completeness of documentation: The more documentation a borrower can and will provide of her income, job, assets, and other debt, the less likelihood of fraud and the more sound the loan.

- Living in the house: People generally care more about paying their mortgage on a house they live in than on a house they rent to others or intend to resell soon.

- Ratio of loan amount to value of the house (LTV): As the bust following the housing boom progressed, this factor showed itself to be very important. The lower the ratio, the more sound the loan. Until the early 1990s, banks traditionally loaned homebuyers no more than eighty percent of the purchase price. Home buyers were required

to put twenty percent down—to pay twenty percent of
the price of the house out of their own resources. Under
these circumstances, homeowners try hard to keep up with
their mortgage payments lest they lose their equity—their
ownership stake—in the house.

For example, a couple that puts $20,000 down and borrows $80,000
to buy a $100,000 house would lose the house and their $20,000 if the
bank were to foreclose. Furthermore—and this is crucial to understanding
the housing boom and bust—until and unless the price of the house were to
fall by 20 percent (by historical standards a very large decrease), the couple
would be able to sell their house for more than they owe on it. Hence they
would want to stay current on their payments and avoid foreclosure.

By contrast, if a bank loans a homebuyer a very large portion of the
purchase price, say, ninety-seven or even one hundred percent (not uncom-
mon in the housing boom), then the homebuyer has little or nothing of
his own to lose if he can't make his payments and the bank forecloses—he
has little "skin in the game." For example, suppose a bank lends a buyer
$98,000 for the purchase of a $100,000 house. On such a loan, it takes a
decrease in the market value of the house of only a little over two percent
for the homebuyer to owe more than the house is worth. In such cases the
homebuyer is said to be "under water," and he has an incentive to "walk
away" from the house—to stop making payments and let the bank foreclose. (Of course doing so means he breaks his promise to pay; this will hurt
his credit. Most people, admirably, keep their promises to pay even when
they do go "underwater.")

Soundness factors are used to identify borrowers with good credit. A
prime mortgage is one made to a prime borrower, that is, someone with
good credit. A subprime mortgage is one made to a subprime borrower,
someone whose credit is not so good. For banks, making subprime loans is
not necessarily unwise, even though they recognize that a greater proportion of subprime borrowers than prime borrowers will probably be unable
to make their payments. Banks compensate for this by charging a higher

interest rate to subprime borrowers, so that the larger interest payments from subprime borrowers who do make their payments compensate for the expected losses from those who don't.

There are degrees of mortgage riskiness that are not captured by the distinction of prime v. subprime. A mortgage loan made to a borrower with a credit history that puts her in the prime category may still be a risky or foolish loan if it is below standard in one or more of the other soundness factors in the list above. The term "Alt-A" is used to categorize mortgages that meet some but not all the criteria of a sound, high-quality loan.

## Indirect Mortgage Financing

The bank or S&L that makes a mortgage loan can hold onto that loan and keep the interest and principal payments for itself. Many banks, especially S&L's, do this, accumulating "portfolios" of mortgages. Out of the mortgage payments they receive they pay the interest they owe their depositors. If mortgage-making were no more complex than this, then only banks would hold mortgages, and the only investment money available to lend to house buyers would be the deposits small saver/lenders put in their bank checking accounts, savings accounts, and CDs.

Like pencil-making, however, mortgage-making can become very complex, and the increased complexity allows large sums of investment money to flow to house buyers. The key is that a bank can *sell* some or all of the mortgages it originates, thereby selling the right to the interest and principal payments on those loans. Banks often do sell mortgages—the loan on the first house I ever bought was sold within a month—on what is known as the secondary market for mortgages. Banks use the proceeds to make other investments, perhaps more mortgage loans or loans of other kinds. As long as a bank can keep selling the mortgages it receives from the house buyers it lends to, it can keep lending to more house buyers with the proceeds.

This secondary market for mortgages has become very large; indeed most mortgages are now sold after they are originated. The secondary market in mortgages allows savers/lenders much larger than the average bank depositor to loan their funds (indirectly) to homebuyers. These large savers/ lenders we'll call *institutional investors*; they are organizations with a lot of wealth that they need to keep invested. Examples include university endowments, insurance companies, pension funds, mutual funds and the like.

Big institutional investors could conceivably lend to homebuyers directly by issuing new mortgage loans themselves, but it makes no sense for insurance companies, college endowments and the like to develop the skills and facilities necessary to do mortgage lending. Less directly, they might buy individual mortgages on the secondary market, but again, they would need to go outside their own specialties to identify, purchase, and keep track of many individual mortgages. Accordingly, big institutional investors who invest in housing almost always do so through a different set of intermediaries that buy the mortgages for them. These intermediaries are non-depository financial institutions. Investment banks and hedge funds are "non-depository" because they do not take deposits into checking and savings accounts.

Investment banks and other non-depository financial institutions play their role of intermediating between large institutional investors and homebuyers in one of two ways. The first is analogous to the commercial banking most of us are familiar with; that is, the investment banks borrow from the institutional investors and use those borrowings to buy and hold mortgages. With the principal and interest payments they receive from the mortgages, they pay the interest they owe the institutional investors. (Investment banks do not usually originate mortgages themselves; usually they buy them from commercial banks, S&L's, and other mortgage originators.)

Here a word might be useful on borrowing by selling bonds, which is what investment banks generally do in this kind of situation. A bond is best understood as an IOU. Suppose the investment bank Goldman Sachs wants to buy, say, $10 million worth of mortgages. It might borrow the money it needs for that purpose from a big institutional investor such as, say, Yale University's endowment fund. When Yale lends Goldman the $10 million, Goldman gives Yale a formal document, called a bond, in which it promises to pay back to Yale—or, more likely, to the "bearer" of the bond so that Yale can sell it to someone else if it chooses—the $10 million on a specified date (ten years in the future, perhaps), and also pay Yale interest on the loan of a specified amount on a specified schedule. Figure 8.2 gives a simplified version of a ten-year bond we imagine Goldman Sachs to issue to the Yale endowment on October 17 of 2013, paying 6 percent interest, on receiving a loan of $10 million from Yale.

**Figure 8.2 A Basic Bond**

### BOND

Goldman Sachs Inc.

promises to pay the bearer

$10,000,000, on October 17, 2023

and interest of $600,000

on October 17 of every year until then.

Signed *Irving G. Eyeshade*, Treasurer

Notice that to say that Goldman Sachs sells a $10 million bond means that Goldman Sachs borrows $10 million from whoever buys the bond. The bond is the contract, the formal record of the loan, entitling its holder to the interest and principal repayment from Goldman Sachs.

Returning to investment banks and the two ways in which they intermediate between large institutional investors and homebuyers, the first way is to borrow from institutional investors by selling them bonds and then to use that money to buy mortgages from the commercial banks that originated them. (The banks that originated and sold those mortgages then can use the proceeds to make new mortgage loans to additional homebuyers.) In this first kind of intermediation, the investment bank would hold the mortgages in its own account. It would collect the mortgage payments, use as much of that revenue as required to pay interest and principal on its bonds, and keep what remains (if anything) as profit. To flesh out our simple example, Goldman Sachs might use the ten million dollars it borrows from Yale's endowment to buy a hundred mortgages that average $100,000 in size and pay interest rates of 7 percent on average. If all goes well for Goldman Sachs, it will collect 7 percent interest on the $10 million in mortgages, pay 6 percent on the $10 million bond it used to finance its purchase of the mortgages, and have the 1 percent difference, or $100,000 per year, to cover its costs and leave something for profit. In such a case it is said that the bond Goldman Sachs sold Yale is "backed by" the hundred mortgages it has bought with the money.

The second way in which an investment bank intermediates between large institutional investors and homebuyers is to act as a broker, not buying mortgages itself, but helping the investors to buy mortgages—or, as we shall see, to buy pieces of a large number of mortgages. Altering our example to fit this second way, Goldman Sachs could initially buy those one hundred mortgages but then compose them into a bundle or a pool. The pool itself becomes an independent legal entity. Goldman Sachs would then sell *the pool* of mortgages to the Yale endowment. Yale would pay a one-time commission to Goldman for arranging the deal; that's how Goldman would make its money. Yale then owns the mortgage pool and receives (if all goes well) the 7 percent average interest payments. (It would also pay an annual fee to some service company hired to collect all the individual mortgage payments and send Yale a check for the remaining income.)

A pool of mortgages such as we have described here is called a "mortgage-backed security" (MBS); these were very important in the housing boom and bust and the financial turmoil that followed. Mortgage-backed securities usually have one other important feature: they can have multiple owners, each of whom owns just a portion of the pool. In our example, Yale University's endowment might want to buy only $1 million worth of the $10 million mortgage-backed security. In that case, Goldman Sachs might arrange with nine additional institutional investors—such as, say, The Hartford Insurance Company, a T. Rowe Price mutual fund, a Proctor and Gamble employee pension fund and others—each to buy $1 million worth of that same MBS. In this example, we imagine only ten investors with equal shares of a $10 million MBS; in practice many MBSs had scores of investors owning different sized shares, and there were often hundreds of mortgages worth many millions of dollars in the pool.

Over time, depending on how well they create value for their customers, some commercial banks and investment banks earn profits with which to expand, while others suffer losses and have to contract or be taken over. Those that do well, becoming not just intermediaries but large institutional investors in their own right, purchase for themselves mortgage-backed securities and the bonds of various major enterprises.

As the secondary market for mortgages took off and it became commonplace for mortgages to be sold shortly after origination, another kind of business arose whose role was simply to originate mortgages for immediate sale to a big enterprise that would bundle the mortgages into MBSs. These businesses are called *mortgage originators*.

Mortgage-making is complex, isn't it? Like pencil-making it involves many different skills and processes carried out by many different people, all of them self-interested and each of whom knows only his or her tiny portion of the whole. And no one is in charge; no one could possibly manage such a far-flung network of activities. Yet, when the principles of spontaneous economic order are allowed to operate, like pencil-making, the process of mortgage-making is smooth and dependable.

## Coordination via the Principles of Spontaneous Economic Order

As complex and extensive as it is, mortgage-making accounts for just a portion of a fantastically extensive network that finances projects and enterprises of all kinds. Banks are approached for loans not just by house buyers but by an endless variety of businesses, too: a farmer needs a better tractor; a restaurant owner wants to expand her pizzeria; an inventor wants to put a new gadget into production, pencils must be made, and so on. Banks have limited funds to lend, of course, so they must decide who gets a loan and who doesn't. How do they decide? How *should* they decide in order that people's well-being will be best served?

Similarly, a host of large enterprises want to borrow money for a wide variety of major projects. An airport, say, Hartford, Connecticut's Bradley International Airport, might like to borrow money with which to build a new runway; Hospital Corp. of America might want to build a new hospital building; Dow Chemical Corp. might want to establish a new research center, and so on. The major enterprises wishing to carry out these big projects can either seek loans from banks or try to borrow money by selling bonds to big institutional investors. Typically, if they sell bonds, investment banks act as intermediaries that underwrite the bonds and solicit big institutional investors to buy them. Thus, the same kinds of large institutional investors that might be interested in buying mortgage-backed securities—we have considered The Hartford Insurance Company, a T. Rowe Price mutual fund and a Proctor and Gamble employee pension fund, for example—might be interested in buying bonds from Bradley International, Hospital Corp. of America, or Dow Chemical Co. instead. How does a large institutional investor decide whether to invest in a share of a thousand home mortgages bundled in a mortgage-backed security or a bond for Bradley International's new runways, or in some other project? How *should* the investor decide in order that people's well-being will be best served?

At any time, there are only limited quantities of investable resources available to devote to all these potential projects. There are not enough carpenters, electricians, accountants, engineers, machinists, software engineers, two-by-fours, steel beams, tons of concrete, pickup trucks, dump trucks, tanker trucks, PVC pipes, watts of electricity, forklifts, rolls of insulation, tons of paving material or any of the great variety of other productive resources needed to carry out all projects at once. If more investable resources are devoted to building a new house, then fewer resources are available for expanding a pizzeria or developing a research center. The tradeoff is like that faced by the Commissar of Railroads in our thought experiment in Chapter 1: the more steel is used to build the rail line, the less steel is available for vehicles and pots and pans.

Corresponding to the limited supply of investable resources available at any time is a limited supply of loanable funds—money that banks, investment banks, and other intermediaries lend to those who wish to buy new tractors, build new homes, pizzerias, runways, hospitals, or research centers, or engage in any of the infinity of other projects human beings conceive. It is important to remember that ultimately what is needed to build a house or tractor or runway is not money, but the intellectual and physical resources the money can purchase. (As Duquesne University's Antony Davies says, "Money is just the conveyor belt.")

This means that when borrower/spenders compete with one another for access to the limited loanable funds which saver/lenders offer to lend, they are ultimately competing for access to some of the limited investable resources available for use. Correspondingly, when saver/lenders and intermediaries choose the borrower/spenders to whom they will lend, they are ultimately deciding which projects get these precious resources and which don't.

For example, if a bank chooses to make a $100,000 mortgage loan to a new home buyer instead of a $100,000 small-business loan to a restaurateur for expanding her pizzeria, then $100,000 worth of two-by-fours, pipes, carpentry work, painting and other construction resources are drawn into housing rather than into pizza-eating space. If the bank chooses to lend the $100,000 to a farmer for a new tractor instead of either the house or the pizzeria, productive resources are drawn into making steel and tires and tractor engines instead of into two-by-fours, pipes, carpentry and other construction resources.

All these zillions of investment decisions, taken as a whole, are critically important to society, because our standard of living depends on how well we use our scarce productive resources. If we use carpentry, pipes, and two-by-fours to refurbish pizzerias nobody wants to go to, or to build houses that people cannot afford to buy (because their incomes won't cover the cost of construction)—in short, if we waste valuable resources—our standard of living will decrease or grow more slowly than it could. It is critically important to social well-being that resources go where they are most valuable, as far as that can be determined.

In a free market, what determines which projects get funded, and how many get funded? How can entrepreneurs learn if there are enough investable resources available to carry a certain project through to completion? How might they find out if and when more investable resources become available, so that a project that couldn't have been accomplished last year when there was less saving can be accomplished this year when there is more? How do people decide whether it's more appropriate for them to save their money now and lend it to others, or to borrow money from others now and invest it in enterprises of their own? In general, how are the zillions of decisions to save and lend coordinated with the zillions of decisions to borrow and spend, so that the number and sizes of projects undertaken are appropriate to the quantities of investable resources available? How do we avoid having investable resources sitting idle and wasted, or having so many projects undertaken that there aren't enough resources available to finish them?

*What provides the coordination* among the millions of people who save, lend, borrow, and invest, for innumerable different purposes? Note that this is almost exactly the same question we asked in Chapter 1 about what provides the coordination that makes the production of pencils so marvelously orderly. The answer ... is exactly the same. What provides the coordination?

Prices do. Of course.

In this case, the relevant prices are interest rates—the prices of time. Based on interest rates—*as long as those interest rates emerge in free and voluntary market exchange and therefore are telling the truth*—people can answer all the questions asked three paragraphs back.

The particular levels of market interest rates at any time emerge from the ongoing negotiations among all the saver/lenders and borrower/spenders in various overlapping markets for various kinds of loans. Competition among the various saver/lenders tends to push interest rates downward, because each one must appeal to borrower/spenders to borrow from him rather than others by offering to lend at a lower interest rate than others offer. At the same time, competition among borrower/spenders tends to push interest rates upward, because they must appeal to saver/lenders to lend to them rather than others by offering to borrow at a higher interest rate.

---

### Interest Rates: The Prices of Time

Interest rates may be the most important prices of all because they coordinate the exchange of goods and services *across time*. Interest is what the saver/lender is paid for waiting to use her buying power on herself. Instead of using it now by purchasing, say, a nice meal or nice car or nice house, she decides to wait some years to enjoy that kind of consumption, and let some borrower/spender use her money in the interim to purchase or hire investable resources. In the other direction, interest is what the borrower/spender pays to make use of more goods and services today than he can purchase or hire out of his own wealth. Interest is the payment for moving access to goods across time.

Because the future is uncertain, interest rates also have a "risk premium," or additional payment that rises with risk: lenders must be paid a higher interest rate on a riskier loan.

While we often speak of "*the* interest rate" as a kind of convenient shorthand, it is important to remember that in practice there are many different interest rates for different kinds of loans.

---

Like all prices, interest rates serve as "knowledge surrogates." The Price Coordination Principle of spontaneous economic order applies. Interest rates are continually communicating the significance of the changing knowledge of saver/lenders, borrower/spenders, and intermediaries all around the economy. A relatively strong or increasing desire for investable resources on the part of borrower/spenders will cause high or rising interest rates as borrower/spenders bid against one another for loanable funds. High or rising interest rates might be caused instead, or also, by a relatively high or rising reluctance of lender/savers to lend—they require a higher rate to persuade them to lend away their buying power.

These high or rising interest rates have an important story to tell. They tell all concerned that for some reasons or other—the precise reasons are not important—investable resources are less available than before. The message to borrowers is to conserve, to undertake only those projects that create a lot of value for their customers and hence promise returns high enough to cover high loan payments and still leave some over for profit. The message to saver/lenders is that now is a good time to save and to lend more, because investable resources are urgently needed.

The reasoning works in the other direction for low or falling interest rates. These tell borrower/spenders that investable resources are relatively abundant, so they may borrow more freely and undertake projects that create less value for customers or require more resources or take longer to complete. Low or falling rates tell saver/lenders that there is relatively less need now for investable resources.

In a free market, interest rates determine which projects get funded. In general, projects receive loans as long as the value they are expected to create is large enough to cover the interest and principal payments; otherwise not.

Let's illustrate this with another thought experiment: Suppose you are a banker approached by a homebuyer, a farmer, and a pizzeria proprietor, each asking for a $100,000 loan. How would you decide how many of these would-be borrowers, and which ones, to lend to?

On the other side of the possible exchange, suppose you are one of the would-be borrowers and the bank offers you a loan. Under what circumstances would you take the loan offered? Under what circumstances would you refuse it? Suppose a loan of $100,000 would mean that:

- the homebuyer could purchase additional housing space worth $6,000 a year to her family—a 6 percent return,
- the farmer could buy a new tractor that would help him grow an estimated $5,000 worth of additional crops each year— a 5 percent return, and
- the restaurateur could refurbish her pizzeria in a way she expects to generate at least $7,000 worth of additional business each year—a 7 percent return.

Suppose you, the banker, and the would-be borrowers agree on these estimates of return and you believe in the borrowers' creditworthiness. And suppose market interest rates at the time are relatively low, say, 4 percent. To whom would you lend? Presumably you would offer all three a loan (if you had enough funds; perhaps one would have to go to a different bank if you run short) and all three would be willing to accept it. The relatively low interest rate would mean that investable resources are abundant—there are enough to support all three projects. All three create enough new value to cover the $4,000 annual interest.

But what if interest rates are high, say, 6.5 percent? That would mean that investable resources are significantly less abundant relative to borrower/ spenders' desire for funds. Perhaps saver/lenders have not been willing to save as much, or perhaps available funds are being bid away for projects that promise to generate a return of over 6.5 percent. Either way, the higher interest rate signals that there are insufficient investable resources with which to complete all three projects. In that case, you would offer a loan only to the restaurateur, and only she would be willing to accept it, because only the refurbishment of the pizzeria is expected to create enough value (for its patrons, in this case) to cover the $6,500 annual interest on the loan. The house purchase and the tractor purchase, which would create less value, are screened out by the higher interest rate. Interest rates provide the price signals used in the profit-and-loss calculations made by you and your would-be borrowers. With those calculations, you and they discover where your loanable funds should go.

And so it is in all the lending and borrowing that occur in a free economy. In the manner illustrated here, repeated countless times daily all around the world, in an immense, uncontrollable, imperfect, but marvelous and indispensable process, the people of society continually discover what quantity of investable resources is available at any point and what projects deserve to get some of those resources. The order that spontaneously emerges is well-coordinated *over time*. Saver/lenders, intermediaries, and borrower/spenders alike all frequently make mistakes, of course—in an uncertain world it is never clear ahead of time which projects will succeed or which intermediaries will identify the winners most of the time. But losses persuade us to give up on the mistakes, and profits and interest earned encourage us to pursue the successes. Borrower/spenders go bust when their projects ultimately do not create enough new customer value to cover their costs. Saver/lenders and intermediaries who make bad loans make losses on them, and go bust if they make too many for too long. Interest rates and profit-and-loss feedback keep us mostly on the right track.

This completes our simple sketch of how house buying is financed, including just the major private-sector elements consistent with a free market and leaving out the government interventions we'll describe below. To summarize, saver/lenders lend to house-buyers through intermediaries, mainly commercial banks, that turn their depositors' money into mortgage loans. The mortgages are often sold to non-depository financial institutions such as investment banks. The investment banks can retain ownership of the mortgages, paying for them with money they have received from large institutional investors to whom they have sold bonds. Alternatively, the investment banks can pool large numbers of the mortgages into mortgage-backed securities (MBSs) and sell shares of those MBSs to the large institutional investors. To the extent that there is a ready market for mortgages to be bundled into MBSs, mortgage originators arise that originate mortgages and immediately sell them to investment banks and others that create and sell MBSs. A huge variety of possible projects compete with housing for investable resources, and market interest rates allocate those resources to whatever projects are expected to serve people's well-being best by creating the most value for them.

Now a very important point for understanding the housing boom and bust: In this process *in a free market*, how many mortgages are made, of what kinds, and at what interest rates, would be determined as part of a much larger process that determines how many of all different kinds of investments are made. Housing would receive no special treatment. Banks don't care whether they lend a given amount to a house buyer, farmer, or restaurateur; they care about getting paid back with interest. Big institutional investors similarly don't care whether they lend for housing, hospitals, or runways; they care that the bonds they buy (mortgage-backed or otherwise) pay off. In a free market, therefore, all the different projects in all the different sectors of the economy would compete for loans on an equal basis; again, housing would receive no special treatment.

Likewise, in a free market, no bank would be granted a special monopoly on some aspect of banking. And all banks would be free to decide what kinds and sizes of loans to make in each category.

Also in a free market, saver/lenders would receive no special protections of their investments, whether deposits or bond purchases.

As we will see in the chapters to follow, in our actual, only partly-free market, housing *did* receive special treatment of various kinds; one bank *did* have a crucial monopoly over one part of banking; all other banks *were* restricted in the kinds of loans they could make; and certain saver/lenders *did* receive special protection of their investments.

What were the consequences of these interventions, which interfered with price coordination, blocked profit-and-loss feedback, and distorted incentives? They were not pretty, as we shall see next.

Chapter Nine

# Boom, Bust, and Turmoil

An unsustainable housing boom started around 1997. The ruinous housing bust that followed it in 2007 set off the wrenching financial turmoil of 2008 and began the Great Recession. Before we investigate why it all happened, here is an overview of what happened.

## The Housing Boom and Bust

The housing boom began around 1997, when house prices began a remarkable rise. People increasingly, if foolishly, came to believe that housing prices would always rise. For a whole decade they did rise, and much faster than consumer prices in general. The run-up in housing prices—as in previous bubbles in tulips, tech stocks, and real estate—fed itself. Many people who otherwise would have been content to rent sought to buy a house instead. Speculators, seeing the above-normal increases in prices and profits, got into the action. People with little or no experience in buying and selling real estate got flipping fever. Johan Norberg captures the fever for flipping houses in his very useful book, *Financial Fiasco*:

> On June 23, 2005, the TLC television network first aired a reality
> series called *Property Ladder*, where viewers get to follow a person or
> group who has the idea of buying a home, fixing it up, and then trying

to sell it for more. Three weeks later, the Discovery Home Channel launched *Flip That House*, which is about someone who has just bought a house, often in southern California, and does what it takes to sell it quickly at a good profit. And 10 days after that, on July 24, 2005, the A&E Network premiered a new TV series with a not entirely dissimilar name, *Flip This House*, whose subject is a company based in Charleston, South Carolina, that is in the business of buying, fixing, and selling.

As more of these new investors sought to buy houses in the expectation that housing prices would increase, they bid up the prices of housing further and thereby fulfilled their own prophecy. As shown in Figure 9.1, for a quarter century leading up to 1997, housing prices had risen at about the same rate as overall inflation; the price of a home had been about three and a half times the household income of the home owner. Not so between 1997 and 2007. Throughout that decade (shaded in Figure 9.1) housing prices consistently rose faster than inflation on a consistent basis. They climbed far above their normal range of about three and a half times average household income; by 2007, on average, the price of a house was over five times the household income of the home owner.

**Figure 9.1 Housing Prices Rose Faster than Consumer Prices**

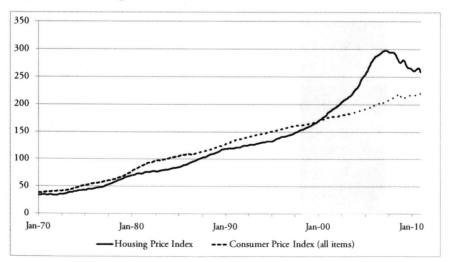

But then, in 2007, prices leveled out and began to fall, and the whole process of price changes and expectations went into reverse. That was the bust; as of this writing in 2013 the housing market has still not recovered.

As home prices increased between 1997 and 2007, the rate of home ownership also rose, to higher levels than ever before. Indeed, such increases were the goal of government policies; and as we'll see below, those policies were fueling the boom. From the 1960s to 1998, the rate of homeownership in the U.S. had fluctuated between 63 and 66 percent. But in 2000, it rose above 66 percent for the first time, on its way to 69 percent in 2007. The bust erased that increase; by April of 2012, the homeownership rate was back down to 65.4 percent, where it had stood in the spring of 1997.

Helping to finance all this new housing was a great deal of mortgage lending and a dramatic increase in the number of loans that did not meet traditional standards of soundness. Figure 9.2 illustrates the trends. The proportion of risky loans originated increased from 14% in 2001 to 50% in 2006.

In 2006, more money—more than an additional *trillion* dollars—was loaned in overtly shaky subprime and Alt-A mortgages than in sound, conventional prime mortgages. In 2008, after the bust, far fewer home loans were made and lenders returned to traditional standards of soundness.

During the boom, one of the most important ways in which traditional standards were eroded was by allowing house buyers to take out a loan without making a substantial down payment. While twenty percent down used to be the standard, loans were made to borrowers who put only ten percent, or three percent, or even zero percent down. The result for such loans was a high loan-to-value ratio; home buyers had little "skin in the game"—little actual ownership of the houses they bought. In hard times such borrowers, owning little, have an unhealthy incentive to "walk away"—default on their obligation to pay and let the bank take the house.

**Figure 9.2 Sound and Shaky Mortgages Originated in the Boom and Bust**

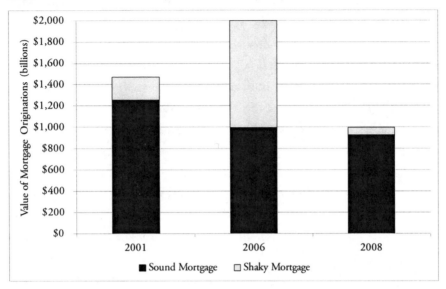

Along with making low to no down payments, many borrowers had taken out adjustable rate mortgages (ARMs) at low introductory rates, hoping to refinance later when the prices of the houses had risen. But as house prices began to fall in 2007 and to fall even faster in 2008 and 2009, they were unable to refinance. And when their adjustable interest rates reset to a higher level, many were simply unable to pay what they owed. Many were "under water"—they owed more on their loans than their houses were worth. Defaults on mortgage payments consequentially surged to levels never seen in America before, resulting, as shown in Figure 9.3, in an alarming increase in the rate of foreclosures.

As more and more homeowners defaulted on their mortgages, the holders of mortgage-backed securities containing those mortgages saw their income streams and the value of their investments shrink rapidly. And this takes us to the financial crisis because, strangely, a very large portion of those mortgage-backed securities were owned by banks.

**Figure 9.3 Foreclosure Rates on Sound and Shaky Mortgages**

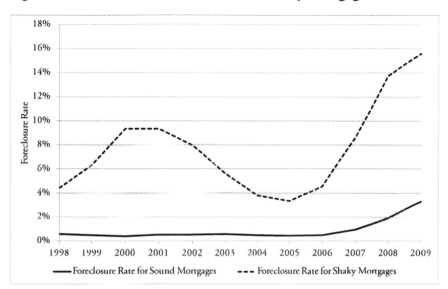

## The Spillover from Housing to Financial Institutions

The housing bust was not confined to housing. A crucial aspect of the financial troubles of 2008 and thereafter is that the big problems in the *housing* sector of the economy got transmitted to the *financial* sector and from there to the rest of the economy. That did not have to be. After the bursting of the dot-com stock bubble in 2000, a bust that wiped out trillions of dollars' worth of stock value, there was no financial turmoil; banks and banking continued unruffled.

This time, however, for reasons we'll investigate, many banks and other financial institutions had invested a tremendous amount in mortgage-backed securities (MBSs), so that when people came to suspect that those securities were worth much less than had been believed, the banks' financial security and ability to lend was badly hurt. Furthermore, because of the complexity of the MBSs and other securities derived from them, it was difficult to tell who owned a lot of "toxic" mortgage-backed securities that contained the failing mortgages. For this reason, too, financial institutions hesitated to lend to one another, worrying that if they did, they might not get paid back.

Losses in the financial sector were gigantic. Many banks around the country failed. The famous Wall Street firm Lehman Brothers failed entirely. Bear Stearns and Merrill Lynch survived by marrying themselves off hurriedly to others. As shown in Figure 9.4, bank stocks plummeted, losing on average 83 percent of their value between May, 2007, and February, 2009 (shaded area in Figure 9.4).

**Figure 9.4 Average Bank Stock Value**

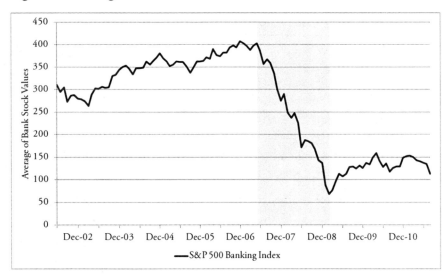

Surviving banks grew cautious, hoarded cash and cut lending, so the normal flows of credit in the economy dried up. Companies that had never missed a loan payment found they could not get financing for shipments of materials or for upgrading their equipment; shops couldn't finance routine renovations; start-ups couldn't get seed money. So orders for materials and equipment dropped off; renovators were idled; new businesses did not open up; hiring sputtered; unemployment turned upward toward heights not seen in decades, as shown in Figure 9.5. Thus the problems in the financial services industry spilled over into the rest of the economy. The Financial Crisis and the Great Recession of 2008 had begun.

**Figure 9.5 Unemployment Rate in the U.S.**

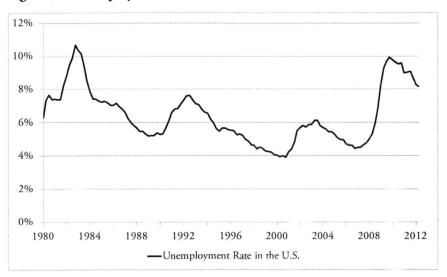

—Unemployment Rate in the U.S.

# What Was Really Lost in the Housing Boom and Bust

Before we look in detail at the causes of the whole mess, let us focus a moment on what, fundamentally, went wrong in the home mortgage boom and bust. What is the core problem reflected in all the gory statistics of prices soaring and plunging, foreclosures, delinquencies, bankruptcies, and the rest? What is the problem society got into?

The problem is that scarce, precious resources were not flowing to the different parts of the economy in appropriate proportions. The signaling system of market prices and profit-and-loss feedback that society needs to maintain good coordination got fouled up. Too many resources went into producing two-by-fours, PVC pipe, siding, wiring, and insulation for housing. Too much human talent went into architecture, carpentry, plumbing, roofing, and bricklaying for housing. Too much of the time of bankers, mortgage brokers, and investment bankers went into financing for housing.

Scarce resources were wasted there. They would have created far more value for people in other types of projects, in other pursuits.

What caused this massive discoordination? As the chapters to follow will explain, all those resources were misdirected because the market process was not permitted to guide them aright. Government intervention into the economy, well-intentioned perhaps, but wrong-headed for sure, fouled up prices—housing prices and interest rates especially—and distorted the profit-and-loss feedback that would have produced well-balanced, sustainable investments across the economy. There were market prices on all these resources, of course, but they were not *free* market prices; they were hampered market prices distorted by special tax treatment, subsidies, money creation, government guarantees, and banking regulations. Therefore the profit-and-loss calculations and feedback based on these prices could not tell entrepreneurs which projects promised to create the most value.

We turn now to seven main interventions by government that combined to cause the housing boom and bust and trigger the financial crisis that followed.

# Chapter Ten

# Why Housing Boomed

W hat caused the housing boom? There was a lot of money in the
economy to be invested (for reasons we'll examine in the next chapter). But why did that money go into housing, rather than tech stocks,
or commodities, or tulips? Three main government interventions into the
economy provide the answer: special tax treatment of housing, government guarantees of the debts of the "government-sponsored enterprises"
(GSEs) Fannie Mae and Freddie Mac, and the so-called "affordable housing" policies, which both Republicans and Democrats in Washington,
D.C., supported.

## Intervention #1 - Special Tax Treatment for Housing

The first culprit we'll consider, though probably not one of the main causes
of the housing boom and bust, may well have *started* the boom. The Taxpayer Relief Act of 1997 excludes from taxation all capital gains on a personal residence, up to $250,000 for an individual or $500,000 for a couple,
while leaving in place the twenty percent capital gains tax on all other
investments. The measure diverts the flow of resources in the economy from
higher value uses to lower value uses by fouling up profit-and-loss feedback

to investors. It does so by artificially increasing the *after-tax* profitability of investments in housing relative to investments in everything else.

In criticizing this special treatment of housing, I do not mean to oppose tax reductions as such! In a free society, taxes should be no greater than necessary to protect lives and property and to enforce contracts. The capital gains tax should probably be eliminated altogether. Accordingly, exempting up to $250,000 or $500,000 in capital gains on any and all kinds of investment would be a step in the right direction. But the special treatment of gains on housing *alone* distorts markets badly.

To understand why, consider a thought experiment: Suppose you, the reader, have a choice between two investment opportunities. The first is a pizzeria; you can buy it for $300,000, and you believe that if you invest another $100,000 in improvements, you'll be able to resell for $600,000 and net a profit of $200,000. This profit would come in the form of a gain in the capital value of the business, a "capital gain." The second opportunity is a house; you can buy it for the same $300,000, and you believe that if you invest the same $100,000 in improvements, you'll be able to resell the house ("flip" it!) for $580,000, for a net profit (via capital gain) of $180,000. In the absence of any tax, which would you choose?

### Investment Opportunities

|  | Pizzeria | House |
|---|---|---|
| Expected future sale price | $600,000 | $580,000 |
| Less purchase price + renovations | $400,000 | $400,000 |
| Profit = Capital gain | $200,000 | $180,000 |

Certainly you would choose to invest in the pizzeria, because doing so would yield you $200,000 in profit (capital gain) as opposed to only $180,000 for the house. Significantly, *this decision would be best for other people, too*, if your projections are correct. That is because the $400,000 invested in the pizzeria would create at least $200,000 in new value for others, as judged by the $600,000 price you expect the purchaser to pay for it. But the same $400,000 invested in the house would create only

$180,000 in new value for others, as judged by the best price you expect a house purchaser to be willing to pay. Here is a simple instance of the Profit-and-Loss Guidance Principle at work.

Before the Taxpayer Relief Act of 1997 was passed, capital gains on the pizzeria and the house would be taxed at the same rate of 20%. In that case, which option would give you the most profit, after taxes are taken from you?

### Before Taxpayer Relief Act of 1997

|  | Pizzeria | House |
|---|---|---|
| Profit = Capital Gain | $200,000 | $180,000 |
| Less capital gains tax (20%) | $40,000 | $36,000 |
| After-tax profit | $160,000 | $144,000 |

After a 20% tax on your anticipated $200,000 gain on the pizzeria, you would be left with $160,000; after the same 20% tax on the gain of $180,000 you anticipate from investing in the house, however, you would be left with only $144,000. Your calculations of expected profits would still lead you to invest in the pizzeria, the option that creates the most value for others. Profit-and-loss feedback is doing its job.

How about after the passage of the Taxpayer Relief Act of 1997? Now you pay no tax on any capital gains on the house (up to $250,000, or $500,000 for a couple).

### After Taxpayer Relief Act of 1997

|  | Pizzeria | House |
|---|---|---|
| Profit = Capital Gain | $200,000 | $180,000 |
| Less capital gains tax (20%) | $40,000 | $0 |
| After-tax profit | $160,000 | $180,000 |

Now the privileged tax treatment of housing would reverse your incentives. Investing in the pizzeria would yield you $160,000 after capital gains tax, while investing in the house would yield you the full $180,000 gain, untaxed. Now your profit-and-loss calculations, distorted by the differential tax treatment, would lead you to invest in housing, even though doing so would create less new value for others than the alternative. The Profit-and-Loss Guidance Principle is interfered with; the signal is distorted; the incentives are fouled up.

So it was for thousands of people after 1997. Not by chance, housing prices started their remarkable long rise around 1997, as is visible in Figure 9.1. The special treatment of capital gains on residences drew additional buyers into the bidding for houses, so prices rose. These prices were no longer free-market prices communicating the relative scarcity or abundance of productive resources; they were prices also communicating politicians' desire to take credit for expanding home ownership. As prices increased, people noticed and began to invest in housing. These distorted housing prices fouled up coordination of the economy.

Again, this intervention was not likely a major cause of the housing boom and bust, but it seems likely to have kicked off the boom and it certainly fed the boom's intensity.

## Intervention #2 - Subsidizing Housing via Fannie Mae and Freddie Mac

Undoubtedly a major cause of the housing boom and bust was the government's deep intervention into housing markets via Fannie Mae and Freddie Mac. These two "government-sponsored enterprises" (GSEs), these "housing giants," had various privileges, but we will consider just the most significant: They could borrow huge amounts of money because the government guaranteed their debts. In combination with the "affordable housing" goals Congress set for them (we'll discuss those next), this privilege sucked vast amounts of money—and the investable resources that money represents—into housing. Those resources would have been better used on other things. The consequence was too many houses at prices too high and too many mortgages at interest rates too low.

## Some Background on Fannie Mae and Freddie Mac

Founded by Congress in 1938 and 1970, respectively, to promote housing by creating a nationwide secondary market for mortgages, Fannie Mae (properly the Federal National Mortgage Association) and Freddie Mac (the Federal Home Loan Mortgage Corporation) are large—huge—intermediaries that channel the wealth of institutional investors into housing in the ways we discussed in Chapter 8.

They sell bonds to (meaning, borrow money from) large institutional investors and use that money to invest in mortgages in three different ways. First, they buy mortgages from banks and other mortgage originators and hold those mortgages themselves, earning the principal and interest payments. Second, they buy mortgages from banks and other mortgage originators and bundle those mortgages into mortgage-backed securities which they sell to institutional investors, charging a fee for collecting the mortgage payments and passing them through. Third, they buy mortgage-backed securities created and sold by private-sector intermediaries such as Bear Stearns or Bank of America, earning the principal and interest payments from the mortgages in the bundle.

One other way in which Fannie and Freddie promote housing in the U.S. is by guaranteeing mortgages. In exchange for a payment, they guarantee to the banks (or other mortgage originators) the mortgage payments they are owed. As long as Fannie and Freddie guaranteed mostly sound mortgages, they earned money on these guarantees, because relatively few well-qualified borrowers defaulted on their mortgages.

Fannie and Freddie's special privileges (described below) allowed them to grow way beyond the size any private firm without such privileges could reach. By the first decade of the 2000s they had a hand in more than 40 percent of the residential mortgages in the country, because they either owned them outright or had bundled them into mortgage-backed securities they had issued.

The government's guarantee of Fannie's and Freddie's obligations was only implicit until September 7, 2008. That is, it was nowhere a legal commitment in writing. Rather, everyone involved understood and expected that if Fannie and Freddie got into trouble by buying and guaranteeing a lot of mortgages on which the house buyers did not make their scheduled payments, and if that trouble got so bad that their income should fall short of what they needed to pay their bondholders and the holders of their mortgage-backed securities, the federal government would step in, take from taxpayers as much as needed, and pay the creditors.

As things turned out when the housing boom turned to bust, Fannie and Freddie *had* made many bad decisions, their income was *not* sufficient to pay what they owed, and the federal government *did* cover the shortfall with taxpayer money. As we'll soon see, Fannie and Freddie had been positively *directed* by Congress to guarantee and buy shaky loans.

Figure 10.1 gives a picture of the long rise and sudden fall in Fannie and Freddie's financial health.

**Figure 10.1 Net Worth of Fannie Mae and Freddie Mac**

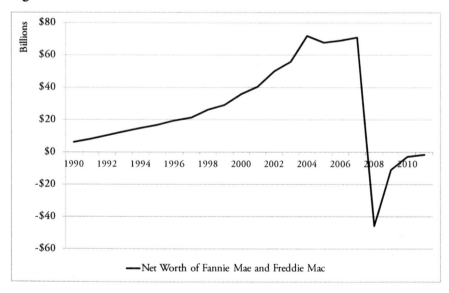

By September 7, 2008, Fannie and Freddie were bankrupt, so the federal government took them into "conservatorship." (This is a euphemism for government takeover, nationalization; the two largest companies in the

U.S. housing finance industry are now government-run.) That day Fannie and Freddie's "implicit guarantee" became explicit. Since then the federal government has paid out taxpayers' money to the large institutional investors that bought Fannie and Freddie's bonds or mortgage-backed securities. The total amount transferred from taxpayers to those investors won't be clear for many years, if ever, but as of July 2011, Standard and Poor's estimated "the total taxpayer cost to keep the GSEs [government-sponsored enterprises] solvent at about $280 billion."

As we have emphasized, in a free market regulated by the discipline of profit and loss, enterprises that destroy value long enough disappear from the economic landscape for want of customers and investors. A truly private intermediary in the mortgage-financing business that had done as bad a job of investing as Fannie and Freddie would have disappeared by 2008. Loss in a free market is the great terminator of unsound investment. But housing in the U.S. is not a free market, and government intervention continues today to spare Fannie and Freddie from the termination they deserve. As of this writing, Fannie and Freddie are still borrowing money at low rates and they continue to buy and guarantee most new mortgages.

## Consequences of Fannie's and Freddie's Non-Market Status

The consequences of Fannie's and Freddie's government guarantees are dire. The guarantees distort the interest rates—a crucial price—that Fannie and Freddie have to pay their borrowers. That distortion leads in turn to distortions in mortgage interest rates, the demand for housing, and housing prices. These distorted prices foul up the profit and loss calculations of investors and home buyers. Altogether these interferences with the operation of the Price Coordination Principle and the Profit-and-Loss Guidance Principle helped cause the tremendous overbuilding of houses and overinvestment in mortgages of the housing boom.

As we saw in Chapter 8, in a free market the return to saver/lenders (and the intermediaries they employ) depends ultimately on the profitability of the borrower/spenders to whom they lend. Loans tend to go to those projects, whether new homes, new tractors, new hospitals, or new runways, that investors expect to create enough new value to cover the principal and interest payments that must be paid at market-determined interest rates.

But in the presence of Fannie and Freddie's guarantee, investors are eager to make loans (indirectly) to house buyers even when the investors *do not* expect the new homes to create enough value for buyers to cover principal and interest payments. Indeed, many lenders to Fannie and Freddie, and buyers of their mortgage-backed securities, don't even bother to check on the quality of the mortgages Fannie and Freddie buy or guarantee. Rather, their profit and loss calculations depend heavily on their expectation that the government will pay them with taxpayers' money if the mortgages go bad.

Let's do a thought experiment to show how Fannie and Freddie's guarantee affects the decisions of saver/lenders: Suppose you are the manager of your college's endowment fund, and you have $100,000 to invest. You are eager to get the best possible deal for your college, taking both risk and return into account. To keep it simple, suppose you have two options to choose from: Hospital Corporation of America (HCA) is selling $100,000 bonds paying 5.5 percent interest to finance a new hospital. Fannie Mae is selling $100,000 bonds to finance new mortgage purchases. Now, what interest rate would Fannie Mae have to offer to induce you to buy their bonds instead of the bonds of HCA?

It would depend on the riskiness of each, of course. So to simplify the thought experiment, suppose somehow or other you determine that the hospital and the mortgages are equally likely to pay off, so HCA and Fannie Mae are equally likely to pay you your principal and interest. The key difference is that if HCA can't pay you, you might not get paid at all, because they are a private company with no government guarantee. If Fannie Mae can't pay you, however, the government will, with taxpayers' money. How much would that guarantee be worth to you (again, the guarantee was implicit until September, 2008, and explicit thereafter)?

\* \* \* \* \*

Different people would value that guarantee differently of course; the key point is that Fannie and Freddie's government guarantees let them borrow at lower interest rates than they otherwise would have to pay. If you said you'd lend to Fannie Mae instead of HCA if they offered you as much as 5 percent interest, you would be in the ballpark with actual institutional investors during the housing boom. Typically, Fannie and Freddie could sell their bonds paying interest rates a bit less than half a percentage point lower than their private-sector counterparts did.

Notice how price communication is being blocked here. In a free market, saver/lenders would in effect say to Fannie Mae and Freddie Mac, "If you want to borrow my money you are going to have to pay me a higher interest rate to compensate me for the risk that those mortgages won't all pay off." The interest rate—the price of borrowing—would communicate what people know about the riskiness of housing. But in the presence of the government guarantee, saver/lenders say in effect, "Nearly zero risk that I won't get paid? Great! I'll accept a lower rate and still lend you the money."

Free market prices communicate what everybody knows about the value of a good. A free market interest rate on Fannie and Freddie's bonds would communicate what people know about the risk that Fannie and Freddie might not be able to pay them back. But in the presence of the government's guarantee, that knowledge disappears from the interest rate. (The only risk represented in the interest rates Fannie and Freddie had to pay before September, 2008, was the risk that maybe, just maybe, the government would not bail them out if they got in trouble. Even that risk has now disappeared.)

Because of the government guarantee, the profit and loss calculations of Fannie, Freddie, and their investors are all based on a wrong price, because the price—the interest rate the investors charge and Fannie and Freddie pay—"tells a lie" about the underlying risk. With the operation of the Profit-and-Loss Guidance Principle fouled up by the faulty price, all involved are eager to devote resources to housing, even when those resources could be used to create more value in other areas of the economy instead.

What about mortgage interest rates, the most important prices in the housing market? Fannie's and Freddie's low borrowing costs distort those in turn. We can see why as we continue our thought experiment.

Let's imagine again that Hospital Corporation of America (HCA) and other large enterprises like them are selling bonds paying 5.5 percent interest to finance their various projects. This time, however, we exclude Fannie and Freddie from the thought experiment entirely. Instead, this time, you, the reader, represent the private-sector investment bank Bear Stearns. Suppose that you are buying mortgages and packaging them into mortgage-backed securities (MBSs), which you sell to large saver/lenders. (Of course your MBSs have no government guarantee.) Suppose also that you are buying these mortgages from mortgage originators who only originate and sell; they do not hold onto any mortgages they originate. Suppose as well that you have found that you need one percentage point out of the principal and interest payments coming in from the mortgages to cover your expenses (of bundling those mortgages into MBSs, selling them to investors, handling collections of principal and interest payments, making payments out to investors, and so on) and leave a little for your own profit. For example, if the mortgages in a particular bundle pay interest of about 8 percent, after you deduct the one percentage point from that to cover your expenses, the highest interest rate you could pay on a MBS made up of those mortgages (and still break even) would be 7 percent. Finally, suppose that the large saver/lenders who are in the market for the bonds consider your MBSs and HCA's bonds to be equally risky.

Once you have digested the implications of those conditions, consider this question: Under those conditions, what is the lowest mortgage interest rate the mortgage originators you work with would be able to offer?

\* \* \* \* \*

In a free-market setting, you, representing Bear Stearns, along with other "private-label" mortgage securitizers, must offer at least 5.5 percent interest on your *non-guaranteed* MBSs in order to make them competitive with the bonds of HCA and other enterprises outside the housing sector. Accordingly, 5.5 percent is the lowest interest rate you can offer on your

MBS and still sell it. You require one percentage point of the income from the mortgages to cover expenses. That means the mortgages must pay you a minimum of 6.5 percent for you to make any money. And that in turn means that you won't buy any mortgages that pay appreciably less than 6.5 percent (the pool must average at least 6.5 percent). If you won't buy mortgages for less than 6.5 percent, the mortgage originators won't originate them for less, so 6.5 percent (or very nearly) is the lowest that mortgage interest rates can go.

This 6.5 percent (or higher) mortgage interest rate reflects all the relevant factors in the market for investable resources: the supply of savings from saver/lenders and the investable resources they represent, the desire of various borrower/spenders to borrow these savings in order to purchase or hire investable resources, and the judgments of all parties as to the riskiness of the various enterprises and mortgages. That 6.5 percent mortgage interest rate is a *market price* based on all the relevant knowledge of all the market participants. As such it has an important story to tell. It tells would-be homebuyers not to buy a house unless they are willing and able to pay 6.5 percent interest on whatever amount they borrow, because otherwise the resources would be more valuably used elsewhere (e.g. on a new hospital building, runway, or whatever).

Now let's change the thought experiment by substituting Fannie Mae for Bear Stearns, keeping everything else the same except that we allow for Fannie's government guarantee, and we assume that that guarantee means they can borrow for half a percentage point less than can their private-sector competitors for funds (funds representing investable resources). Now what would be the lowest mortgage interest rate the mortgage originators would offer?

\* \* \* \* \*

The same arithmetic would apply, but starting from Fannie's and Freddie's lower borrowing rate of 5.0 percent instead of 5.5 percent. Assuming the same 1 percent to cover expenses, Fannie could afford to buy mortgages paying only 6.0 percent instead of 6.5 percent, so mortgage originators could lower the rates they charge, thereby drawing more house buyers into the market, and still sell the mortgages. Mortgage interest rates could fall another 0.5 percentage points. House buyers who would have had to pay 6.5 percent in a free market must pay only 6.0 percent (in our example) when the government guarantees Fannie's and Freddie's obligations with taxpayers' money.

As the thought experiment shows, Fannie's and Freddie's artificially lower borrowing costs reduce mortgage interest rates *in general*. Indeed, this is a main purpose of Fannie Mae and Freddie Mac. The legislators and interest groups promoting housing, such as realtors and mortgage bankers, want interest rates lower than the free market rate so that more people will buy houses, and the houses will be bigger. Their aim is not really to help more people own houses, but to increase business and income for themselves by increasing the demand for housing and raising housing prices. It's another ugly instance of the negative side of the Incentive Principle: the intervention is used by special interests to benefit themselves at the expense of others.

And it all has been at others' expense. The Price Coordination Principle cannot be ignored this way without interfering with overall coordination in society and therefore overall well-being. A mortgage interest rate reduced by Fannie's and Freddie's government guarantee no longer reflects all the relevant realities in the market for investable resources; it no longer reflects the full risk of default. This distorted price of 6.0 percent interest (in our example) tells a misleading story. It says to homebuyers who can afford 6.0 percent but not 6.5 percent, "Come along and buy! There are enough investable resources to go around!" But there aren't. The demand from additional buyers for new homes draws resources into housing and out of tractors, pizzerias, new runways, or whatever project does not get built because a distorted mortgage interest rate has drawn resources into housing.

The hundreds of billions of dollars in debts to Fannie's and Freddie's creditors that the government has been covering with taxpayers' money since Fannie and Freddie went bankrupt represent hundreds of billions of dollars' worth of wasted resources. Fannie and Freddie directed those resources into housing that created no net value when those same resources could have been used instead for a huge variety of other projects—tractors, pizzerias, research centers, runways—that would have created value.

The careful reader will have noticed that nothing in this section about Fannie Mae and Freddie Mac can explain by itself the housing *boom* of 1997 to 2007 and the financial fiasco that followed. Fannie and Freddie, with their implicit guarantees, had been around for many years before the boom and bust. For the first decades of their existence they acted responsibly, dealing mostly in high-quality, low-risk mortgages, so that there was no need for the government to make good on its implicit guarantee. In normal years their special privileges surely channeled a lot of resources into housing that would have created more value in other sectors of the economy, but that means just unfortunate waste, not a full-on boom in housing. What was different in the boom? How did Fannie and Freddie's privileges lead not just to housing prices higher than otherwise, but to *rising* house prices? What happened so that not just too much investment was flowing into housing, but an *increasing wave* of investment?

The answer is that Fannie and Freddie's privileges interacted catastrophically with still another government intervention into housing, an effort supported widely in Congress by both the Clinton and Bush administrations. The effort promoted what was called, ironically now in hindsight, "affordable housing." To that we now turn.

## Intervention #3 - "Affordable Housing" Mandates

The popular justification for "affordable housing" mandates is to make it possible for more lower-income people to buy homes than would be able to in a free market, by helping them receive mortgages they would have been denied without government intervention.

The "affordable housing" mandates imposed on Fannie and Freddie, in combination with their government guarantees, cut Fannie and Freddie loose from regulation by market forces. Instead of responding to profit-and-loss guidance to buy and guarantee mortgages only while taking moderate risk, they responded to political incentives to buy and guarantee mortgages willy-nilly so as to please politicians. Their imprudent lending, allowed to go on and on without apparent limit by the government's guarantee to their lenders, fed the housing boom and increased the riskiness of the borrower pool.

The "affordable housing" mandates started gently and ramped up over time. In the years before and during the housing boom, the Department of Housing and Urban Development (HUD) required Fannie Mae and Freddie Mac to purchase increasing proportions of "affordable housing" mortgages. In the words of Russ Roberts,

> In 1993, 30 percent of Freddie's and 34 percent of Fannie's purchased loans were loans made to individuals with incomes below the median in their area. The new regulations required that number to be at least 40 percent in 1996. The requirement rose to 42 percent in 1999 and continued to rise through the 2000s, reaching 55 percent in 2007. Fannie and Freddie hit these rising goals every year between 1996 and 2007.

In order to meet these mandatory targets, Fannie and Freddie loosened their lending standards for loans they bought and guaranteed, and for the loans in the mortgage-backed securities they bought. Banks and other mortgage originators, knowing they could sell lower-quality loans to Fannie and Freddie, lowered the soundness standards they required of borrowers. Increasingly they made loans to borrowers with lower credit scores, with higher ratios of their mortgage payments to their monthly incomes, with less (or no) documentation of their incomes (this reduction in standards was an invitation to fraud), with higher ratios of other debt to their incomes, and with smaller down payments. These smaller down payments led to higher loan-to-value (LTV) ratios, which make default more likely, especially in the event of a decrease in the market value of the house (as discussed in Chapter 8).

This loosening of standards meant a flood of lower-quality loans to new homebuyers likely to have difficulty paying them back. The availability of those loans greatly increased the demand for housing, pushing up housing prices and feeding the boom. The higher prices reinforced the growing impression that "housing prices always go up," thereby spurring still more speculative buying and still higher prices in a self-fulfilling spiral. The rising prices misled many lenders about the riskiness of these mortgages. As more and more years went by in which subprime and otherwise below-traditional-standards mortgages stayed out of default, the illusion grew that these mortgages were actually sound, so standards eroded further. Mortgage loans that during the boom appeared to promise acceptable risk-adjusted returns turned out to have negative returns once house prices started to fall.

While housing was booming, all this loosening of standards seemed beneficial. After all, more people who previously would have been denied loans with which to buy a house now received them. The home-buyers were happy, the realtors were happy, the mortgage originators were happy, the advocates for under-privileged groups were happy, and the politicians were happy. Unhappily for everyone, though, it could not last. Once the boom turned to bust, it became clear that shockingly many recipients of these "affordable housing" loans could not afford them.

Not everyone was misled. On September 30, 1999, *New York Times* reporter Steven A. Holmes presciently wrote the following:

> In a move that could help increase home ownership rates among minorities and low income consumers, the Fannie Mae Corporation is easing the credit requirements on loans that it will purchase from banks and other lenders....

> Fannie Mae, the nation's biggest underwriter of home mortgages, has been under increasing pressure from the Clinton Administration to expand mortgage loans among low and moderate income people and felt pressure from stock holders to maintain its phenomenal growth in profits.

> In addition, banks, thrift institutions and mortgage companies have been pressing Fannie Mae to help them make more loans to so-called

subprime borrowers. These borrowers whose incomes, credit ratings and savings are not good enough to qualify for conventional loans, can only get loans from finance companies that charge much higher interest rates—anywhere from three to four percentage points higher than conventional loans....

In moving, even tentatively into this new area of lending, Fannie Mae is taking on significantly more risk, which may not pose any difficulties during flush economic times. But the government-subsidized corporation may run into trouble in an economic downturn, prompting a government rescue similar to that of the savings and loan industry in the 1980's.

Let's sum up this discussion of interventions in housing finance by noting how it illustrates the negative side of the Incentives Principle first introduced in Chapter 3 and brought home with many examples in Chapter 5, including the case of hairdresser licensing. Government intervention always runs the danger of getting captured by particular groups and used in their own special interest at others' expense. All the apparatus of government intervention into housing finance—the tax-advantaging of capital gains on housing, Fannie and Freddie's existence as agencies for funding housing, their government guarantees, and the regulatory mandates on Fannie and Freddie to buy large quantities of "affordable housing" loans—were an irresistible temptation to politicians, advocates of low-income housing, mortgage bankers, the National Association of Realtors, and the officers of Fannie and Freddie themselves. For politicians, funneling money into housing let them promote a politically popular goal without having to pay for it with taxes. For the advocates of low-income housing it was a way to get money for their cause without having to earn it or persuade donors to give it. For mortgage bankers, it meant lots of fees and profits, at least while the boom lasted. For the National Association of Realtors it meant a nationwide boom in their business. For the officers of Fannie and Freddie it meant huge salaries and bonuses while the boom lasted.

Each of these groups undoubtedly has a public interest explanation for its role in the fiasco. As late as September of 2003, Congressman Barney Frank was making the case for the good that Fannie and Freddie were doing for low-income people. He said, "I do think I do not want the same kind of focus on safety and soundness that we have in OCC [Office of the Comptroller of the Currency] and OTS [Office of Thrift Supervision]. I want to roll the dice a little bit more in this situation towards subsidized housing...." In February of 2004, Senator Chris Dodd said of the work Fannie and Freddie were doing, "this is one of the great success stories of all time." It is ironic that these are the two members of Congress whose names are on the financial regulation law that was passed in response to the financial mess, that loads a great many new restrictions on a wide variety of financial dealings but—and it would be astonishing if it weren't the work of politicians—has *nothing* to say about restricting the dealings of Fannie Mae and Freddie Mac.

We would all be much better off if the government simply had no authority to intervene in housing or mortgage lending, either to subsidize or to restrict.

## Chapter Eleven

# Why the Boom Got So Big

While Congress can and does privilege housing with various policies, as we saw in the last chapter, those policies are probably insufficient, by themselves, to have caused the housing *boom*. The exclusion from taxes of capital gains on housing, Fannie and Freddie, and the "affordable housing" policies all channeled investment dollars toward housing, but they don't explain the remarkable size of the torrent. Why did so many dollars flow to housing? Two main interventions go a long way toward answering this question: One of these is the government's monopolization of money through the Federal Reserve System ("the Fed"). The Fed misused this monopoly privilege to put too much new money in the hands of investors, many of whom invested it in the red hot housing market. The other damaging intervention is the government's habit of bailing out lenders with taxpayers' money; doing so took away the caution investors would otherwise have felt before lending so heavily into that market. Both culprits interfere with price coordination and profit-and-loss guidance, and set up perverse incentives for special interests.

## Intervention #4 – Too Much Money

The central bank of United States—the Federal Reserve System—created more new money than it should have, especially in 2001-2004. This was a fundamental cause of the boom itself, and therefore of the bust that had to follow. All this new money had to go somewhere—those who received it were eager to spend or invest it in something. Many chose to invest in housing. Some loaned it directly to new house buyers as mortgage loans; some loaned it to house buyers indirectly by buying mortgage-backed securities. This new money fueled the boom.

It is important to understand that the Fed intentionally manages the supply of money in the economy and does so largely through the banking system. The Fed does not have complete control over the money supply, because the actions of banks and the general public affect the money supply, too; but the Fed has by far the greatest influence. By manipulating the money supply the Fed also affects interest rates, though it cannot tightly control them. (See Appendix A for a more detailed description of how this works.)

To manage the money supply, the Fed generally buys or sells U.S. Treasury securities from banks or other institutional investors. When the Fed wants to increase the money supply, it buys some of these securities *with brand new money*. When the Fed wants to reduce the supply of money in the economy, it sells some of those securities. The money banks pay the Fed for those securities is thereby taken out of the economy.

By manipulating the money supply the Fed also indirectly influences interest rates, some more directly than others. (There are many different interest rates, of course, e.g. for car loans, student loans, mortgage loans, business loans, long-term loans, short-term loans, or loan sharks' loans.) The interest rate the Fed controls most directly is called *the fed funds rate*, the interest rate in the market where banks borrow reserves from one another for short periods. By buying and selling U.S. Treasury securities, the Fed intentionally changes the supply of reserves (cash on hand) available for banks to borrow and lend to each other. The supply of cash reserves that banks hold directly affects the fed funds rate. The Fed intentionally *targets* this fed funds rate—it chooses a level at which it means to keep this rate and it keeps it there (or close) by buying or selling U.S. Treasury securities as necessary to do so.

As shown in Figure 11.1, during the period when the housing boom was at its most intense, roughly 2001 to 2006, the fed funds rate was well below its historical range. Indeed, as shown by the dashed line in Figure 11.1, from 2002 through 2004 (shaded in gray) the Fed's target interest rate was 2 percent or lower. Adjusting for inflation, the fed funds rate was *near zero* from 2002 to 2005, as shown by the solid line in Figure 11.1. That is, when banks borrowed money at the fed funds rate in that period, what they repaid in principal and interest had no more buying power than what they had borrowed; it was like paying no interest at all. Think what having to pay almost no interest does to people's incentive to borrow money and invest it.

**Figure 11.1 The Federal Funds Rate, Nominal and Inflation-Adjusted**

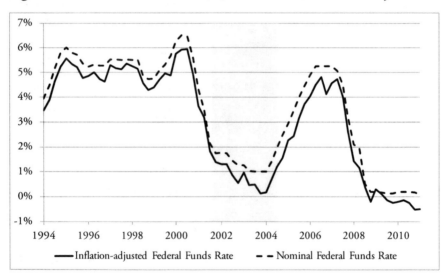

What was the consequence for mortgage interest rates of the Fed's creating so much new money that it kept the fed funds rate near zero? Mortgage interest rates fell below their historical range, as illustrated in Figure 11.2. The gray shading shows the period when the Fed's target for the fed funds rate was two percent or lower, as in Figure 11.1.

With new money flowing from the Fed into the economy, banks and other mortgage originators competed to lend the new money in the booming housing market by offering it at increasingly low mortgage rates.

**Figure 11.2 Mortgage Interest Rate**

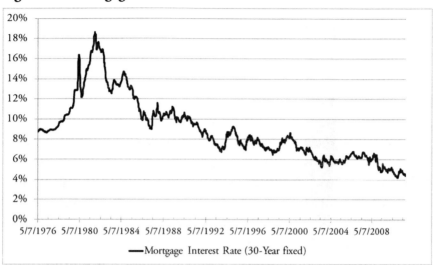

Attracted by these low rates (and the large profits being made in housing as prices rose), more and more people chose to enter the market for a new house, a bigger house, or another house. By doing so, they helped bid up the price of housing and reinforce the boom's illusion that "housing prices always go up."

Additionally, the very low short-term interest rates led lenders to offer a lot of adjustable-rate mortgages (ARMs). Lenders who believed that interest rates were unlikely to stay so low for thirty years wanted to be able to adjust upward the interest rate they were receiving if rates overall rose. These ARMs with very low initial rates attracted many borrowers who assumed that they would later be able to refinance their (then more valuable) houses, or to sell them at a profit, before the interest rate reset. As housing prices stopped rising and started falling, however, many people found themselves with *less* valuable houses when their interest rates reset to levels higher than they could afford. For this reason, adjustable rate mortgages make up a disproportionate share of mortgages in default.

The Fed's reckless creation of new money helped cause and worsen the housing boom. Without the fuel of new money, the fire could not have burned so brightly. On this point there is widespread consensus among scholars in economics: the Fed created too much money too fast in the early

2000s, especially from 2001 to 2004, when the Fed held the fed funds rate below 2 percent.

At this point I expect some readers to wonder, "Where is the intervention? All I see is a mistake: the Fed created too much money." The answer is that the Fed itself is an important—maybe the most important—government intervention in our economy.

The Fed is a government-created central bank. The fundamental interventions that it represents, and that underlie its over-issuance of money in the early 2000s, are 1) its legal monopoly on issuing paper money, and 2) the irredeemability of the Fed's money in any underlying commodity such as gold or silver. These two legislated privileges, starkly at odds with freedom of exchange, exempt the Fed from market discipline. Lacking market-based feedback, the Fed always faces a bad case of the knowledge problem: In a free economy, profit-and-loss would guide banks to discover pretty nearly the correct money supply—how this works is to me one of the most fascinating instances of spontaneous order; we'll discuss it shortly. With the right money supply (we'll discuss what the "right" levels are shortly also), the competitive interactions of saver/lenders and borrower/spenders would generate pretty nearly the right interest rates (those crucial "prices of time"). Free-market interest rates would give us the benefit of price coordination across time, *coordinating the actions of billions pursuing their myriad goals* that involve borrowing and lending.

Fed officials, however, lacking feedback from an unhampered market, *cannot know* the right quantity of money to supply or the right level of interest rates to try to achieve, no matter how conscientious they might be. Furthermore, the Fed's legal authority to control the lifeblood of the economy, money, gives special interest groups, including notably Congress and the President, a strong, unhealthy incentive to try to capture the money-creation process, pressuring the Fed to act in their particular interest at the expense of others. Almost always this pressure is to produce more money in order to keep interest rates artificially low.

In a truly free market there could be no over-issuance of money (for more than short periods), no artificially low interest rates, and hence no booms driven by artificially created credit. Let us see why.

In a free market, there would be no government-created central bank. Instead, entirely private banks would be free to issue their own distinctive currencies (hand-to-hand folding money) just as they issue their own distinctive checking-account money today. (Probably not all banks would choose to issue their own paper notes, and possibly the public would choose to accept and use only a few major brands.) All would be denominated in dollars, because dollars are familiar. Very important, all money would be *redeemable* in—"backed by"—the *base money*, some commodity, presumably gold or silver. Paper dollars, redeemable in something of independent value, is distinguished from *fiat money*, money by government decree, or "by *fiat*." (In our time, lamentably, all the world's monies are fiat currencies.)

In such a "free banking" system, as we'll describe below, the public's willingness to accept and hold onto money in their wallets and checking accounts would determine the amount of money in circulation. Banks would get prompt and clear profit-and-loss guidance from the market as to how much money they should issue. Their contractual obligation to redeem their notes and checks in gold or silver (or whatever other commodity might emerge as the base money) would prevent them from issuing more than the "right" amount.

The next two sections investigate how free market forces would tend to produce the right amount of money, and how central banking with fiat money tends to produce the wrong amount. The discussion is necessarily somewhat technical, but I hope, dear reader, that you will stick with me through it, because the way freedom works in banking is such a beautiful case of spontaneous order, and because getting the money supply right is so important to our standard of living.

## The Right Amount of Money

There is, in principle, a right amount of money. That is the amount the public wishes to hold at the going price level. When the amount of money in the system is exactly that amount, the system is in the ideal condition we call "monetary equilibrium."

A word on what is meant by the amount of money people wish to *hold*: Of course we all would like our incomes to be as large as possible, but we don't hold onto all of our income, nor keep all of our wealth in money. Most of our incomes we spend promptly on food, rent or the mortgage, electricity, transportation, communication, and other necessities. When we make these payments, the money becomes income for the grocery store, electric company, and other businesses; and these businesses in turn spend the money promptly on their employees' wages and salaries, inventory, supplies, equipment, maintenance, and other expenses.

Though each person or company spends the majority of her *income* pretty much as soon as she receives it, each of us also *holds* a certain amount of money in cash, checking, or savings accounts so that we have buying power immediately available when some need or opportunity arises. Different people and businesses choose to hold different amounts of money depending on their particular situations; but each has some approximate quantity that he or she would like to have on hand. (Of course the actual amount typically varies over payment cycles, from larger right after payday to smaller right before payday.)

When we find ourselves holding more money than we wish to—imagine a lovely fat balance in your checking account, perhaps due to unexpected income or lower-than-expected costs—we spend or invest the extra—we don't want that much on hand. When we find ourselves holding less money than we'd like, we build the amount back up by cutting back on our expenditures or cashing in an investment.

At any point, as myriad payments are made among all the different individuals and businesses in the economy, all the money in the system is held, at every moment, by someone. *The right quantity of money for the banking system to supply*, in cash and checkable deposits, is the total amount of money that all the different individuals and enterprises *wish* to hold at that time, prices being what they are. The reason prices matter is that ultimately people want to hold a certain amount of buying power, and at higher prices a given quantity of money has less buying power. Again, we call this match-up condition "monetary equilibrium."

It is important to the health of any economy that monetary equilibrium be maintained as closely as possible. The reason is that when the banking system chronically supplies more or less money than the public wants to hold (at prevailing prices), inflation or deflation respectively result. Either one, when it results from the wrong supply of money, causes a host of problems. Most important, inflation and deflation hamper the ability of prices to do their crucial job of coordination, in accordance with the Price Coordination Principle discussed in Chapter 1. When price changes are caused by decisions of entrepreneurs and consumers that reflect their changing local knowledge—as when, for example, computer makers lower computer prices to reflect extraordinary advances in building computers at lower costs—these price changes help coordinate the actions of all. When price changes are caused by artificial increases or decreases in the money supply, however, they send false signals and impede coordination.

To illustrate, suppose you are a business owner with rising profits: The price buyers are willing to pay for your product is rising while your labor costs and materials prices stay constant. What is that profit signal telling you? Does it mean the public's demand for your product has increased? If so, if these prices are "telling the truth," then you could profitably invest in new equipment, hire more people, and expand your operations. But if the higher price of your product is just the consequence of inflation spreading through the economy—inflation that will soon push up your workers' pay rates and materials prices and eliminate the profits you are temporarily enjoying—then expansion would be a waste of valuable resources. The increasing price of your product would have fooled you into making an investment that can't pay off; you'll just have to lay off the new hires and sell the new equipment, if you can, once prices start to "tell the truth" again.

Another bad consequence of having more money created than the public wishes to hold (we're coming up on the explanation of why this can be done for an appreciable time by a central bank but not by banks in a free market for banking) is that creation of excess money lowers artificially that all-important price: the interest rate. In a market free of government

---

### How Inflation or Deflation Result from
### Too Much, or Too Little, Money

The inflation process goes like this: When the banking system has provided more money than people want to hold in total, some people find themselves holding more money than they want, so they spend it away on goods, services, or investments. But each expenditure one person makes becomes another person's income; they can't all spend down their excess money holdings at the same time. The extra spending they are all doing pushes up prices, as their excess money holdings make each one willing to pay a little more.

The consequence is a general increase in prices, or, to put it another way, a general decrease in the purchasing power of money. The process will continue until the purchasing power of people's money holdings has decreased to the point where the amount of money they hold is no longer excessive to them—what used to be an excessive amount (when it could buy more) is now just enough to provide the purchasing power they want (because now it buys less).

For deflation, the process works in the other direction. People who find themselves with less cash on hand (less purchasing power) than they would like stop spending as much as they normally would, in order to rebuild their money holdings. They can't all do so at the same time, because one person's decision *not* to make a purchase reduces the income another person earns from selling. Sellers reduce prices in order to attract more purchasers, and the purchasing power of money thereby rises.

---

interventions in money, a falling interest rate results either from more provision of loanable funds (representing investable resources) by saver/lenders, or less desire for loanable funds (representing investable resources) on the part of borrower/spenders. Either way, a decreasing interest rate tells borrower/spenders that investable resources are relatively abundant, so they may borrow more freely and undertake projects that create a bit less value for customers or take longer to complete.

But when a central bank such as the Fed *creates* new money, that money does *not* represent any new savings (no additional investable resources have been made available), so the lower interest rate tells a lie about the amount of investable resources available. It misleads borrower/spenders into thinking that investable resources are more abundant than they actually are. Hence borrower/spenders over-invest, putting resources into time-consuming projects that cannot be completed with the resources available. That is what investors did with housing during the boom. That's what made it a boom.

To repeat the point of this discussion, maintaining monetary equilibrium is one of the most important things the banking system can do.

A main reason we need to free our market for money is that a free market would naturally tend to maintain monetary equilibrium—keep the quantity of money that banks supply equal to the quantity of money the public wishes to hold—as profit and loss guide banks' decisions in a spontaneous order. By contrast, in a system of government intervention via central banking, officials tasked with central planning of the money supply cannot possibly know the right amount of money to supply, as we shall see. In the absence of freedom and competition, they lack the profit-and-loss feedback that would help them discover what that amount is, in accordance with the Profit-and-Loss Guidance Principle discussed in Chapter 2.

## Free Market Forces
## Get the Money Supply (Just About) Right

Here we describe how, if we were to free our markets for money and banking, a truly free market would regulate the supply of money and dependably get it very nearly right (just as it gets the supply of pencils very nearly right). The general topic of "free banking" is rich and fascinating in its theory and history. We have space here only to lay out the main elements and processes (readers can pursue the topic by following the references in the chapter notes).

In a truly free market, what is used as money would emerge from the choices of people in the economy. (Of course. That's what freedom means.) Historically, as civilization deepened and commerce spread, precious metals emerged as the preferred monies, and for most of history most money was either the precious metals themselves, e.g. gold and silver coins, or paper *promises to pay* the bearer in gold and silver. That is, paper money was *redeemable* in the underlying commodity (called "base money"). This redeemability of paper money is an essential characteristic of a free market monetary system. Free to choose, the vast majority of people will always insist that their paper money be backed by—exchangeable for—*something* of independent value. Only within the last century, and only by governmental command, has unbacked paper money—"fiat money"—come to dominate the world economy.

In a truly free market, there would be neither a central bank nor any government role in banking beyond government's standard task of securing rights by preventing theft and fraud. Anyone would be free (to try) to establish a bank and issue paper money, redeemable in gold or silver, of course. To stay in business and grow its business, a bank would have to earn enough trust so that the public would accept its paper money.

Just as they do today, banks would offer money in the form of checking accounts using that bank's own checks, printed with its name and logo. In exactly the same way, banks would also offer paper money—their own particular banknotes printed with that bank's name and logo.

Just as all banks today denominate their checking account money in the unit of account familiar to the people of their own regions (e.g. dollars in the U.S., pounds in England, and yen in Japan), free banks would denominate their notes in the same familiar units of account. The key difference from today's fiat money system is that "dollar," "pound," and "yen" would each mean—*would be defined as*—some particular weight of gold or silver.

As strange as individual banks' issuing their own notes may sound, it has been common in other times and is still common in other places. When I went to study in Scotland in 1978, I was surprised to find four different kinds of notes circulating: those of the Bank of Scotland, the Royal Bank of Scotland, the Clydesdale Bank, and the Bank of England. All were denominated in pounds, and all businesses accepted them all. (Of course they weren't redeemable except in other notes also denominated in pounds; sad to say, it is now many years since a British pound note was redeemable in a pound of sterling silver.)

Scotland is also the country that had the longest episode of fairly free banking (to this point in history at least; let us hope for the future). From 1792 to 1847, banking in Scotland was largely free. While it had problems, it had far fewer problems than the neighboring English system, which had a whole variety of restrictions as to who could open banks, where, and so forth. Importantly, only Bank of England notes were allowed to be used in London, the country's financial center.

In a truly free market, governments would not restrict how much money any bank issues, whether as checking deposits or banknotes. This freedom from government restriction does not mean that banks could legally get away with issuing too much money, however. On the contrary, the banks' promises to redeem their notes and checks in gold (or silver or whatever other base money were to evolve)—and their court-enforceable legal obligation to keep that promise—would regulate the amount of money any bank dared to issue. That is, market forces would regulate the money supply.

In free banking, competition would (and historically did) force banks to accept routinely the notes and checks of other banks. The reason is that banks must offer their customers convenience. A businessperson who is paid for her goods or services in the notes and checks of various banks wants to be able to deposit all those notes and checks in one stop at her own bank. All banks simply have to provide such a service to attract depositors. Here again, market forces regulate bank behavior for public convenience.

Having accepted the notes and checks of other banks, all banks would wish promptly to return those other banks' notes and checks for redemption in gold or silver (or whatever is the base money). It would be time-consuming and wasteful for each bank to return notes and checks to every other bank individually. Instead, the banks in a region save expense by establishing a central clearinghouse to which they all send one another's notes and checks for consolidation and return to one another.

Furthermore, because so many of the payment obligations from bank to bank cancel one another, it makes sense to have the clearinghouse determine the *net* obligations among the different banks. For example, if in a given day Bank A receives from its customers $50,000 worth of the notes and checks of Bank B, and Bank B receives from its customers $50,000 worth of the notes and checks of Bank A, then the quantities cancel entirely—they clear with no adjustment needed—and no gold or silver need change hands to settle the obligations.

More normally there will be some net obligation to settle. For example, if Bank A receives $40,000 of Bank B's notes and checks while Bank B receives $50,000 of Bank A's notes and checks, then at the end of the day Bank A owes Bank B $10,000. When notified of this debt by the clearinghouse, Bank A could pay by taking $10,000 in gold out of the reserves it keeps in its vaults and truck it across town to Bank B, but banks found it much less costly instead to keep a quantity of reserves of gold (or silver) on deposit at the clearinghouse itself and let the clearinghouse make the transaction. It might literally move $10,000 in gold coins from Bank A's drawer to Bank B's drawer, but more likely it would keep all the different banks' gold coins together in its vault, and move the $10,000 from Bank A's account to Bank B's account on its books.

In this way, all the banks of a particular clearinghouse association would settle their varying daily claims on one another at the clearinghouse. On some days, a given bank would see its reserves of gold or silver coins increase as it receives and sends to the clearinghouse a greater dollar amount of other banks' notes and checks than they return to the clearinghouse of its own. This we call "positive net clearings." On other days, its net clearings would be negative and the bank would see its reserves decrease. Some days its net clearings would be large, other days small.

Notice that in the kind of mature free banking system we are describing here, gold or silver coins are hardly ever used day to day by the public; paper money and checkable deposits (and subsidiary coins for small transactions) are used instead. Precious metal coins come to be almost exclusively the reserves banks use to settle their mutual claims on one another at the clearinghouse.

With this quick overview of free banking as background, we can now describe the marvelous spontaneous order by which free banking regulates the quantity of money supplied by banks, keeping it very nearly the same as the quantity the public wishes to hold, and thereby staying close to the ideal of monetary equilibrium.

The key incentive that tends to keeps the money supply "right" is each bank's desire to maintain reserves large enough to cover its redemption obligations at the clearinghouse (or, rarely, at the teller window), but no larger. On the one hand, banks have a strong incentive to keep on deposit at the clearinghouse and in their vaults enough gold (or whatever is the base money) to cover any net obligations to other banks they may have at the end of any day. This coin (also called "specie") is the banks' "reserves." In free banking there would be no legislated reserve requirement; rather, banks would learn from experience how large their largest negative net clearings tend to be in usual periods and in extreme cases, and therefore how much they need to keep in reserve to cover days of unusually large drains on their reserves. Banks want to avoid the embarrassment and damaged reputation that would come from being unable to pay as they promise, and/or the expense of having to borrow reserves at short notice from a competitor.

Another incentive for banks to maintain adequate reserves is that the other banks that use the same clearinghouse—the banks' partners in that clearinghouse association—will be willing to accept any particular bank's notes and checks only as long as they are confident that that bank can meet its obligations to redeem those notes and checks as promised. A bank that lets its reserves at the clearinghouse fall too low would risk being suspended from the clearinghouse. *That* could be the road to ruin because it might shake its customers' confidence in the bank and motivate them to take their business elsewhere.

On the other hand, no bank wants its reserves to exceed the amount necessary to cover its normal redemption obligations, because that would mean missing the opportunity to earn income by lending out more notes and checking balances.

In short, any bank must discover through experience a safe but not excessive level of reserves to hold, and try to maintain that level. It is this effort by each bank, along with the public's actual behavior in spending or holding each bank's notes and checking balances, that keeps the money supply "right" in a free market.

To see how the feedback system works, consider what happens when a bank tries to expand too aggressively, lending more of its notes and checking balances into existence when the public is already holding all of that bank's money it wishes to hold. It might do this by attracting new borrowers with slightly lower interest rates on loans and then lending those new borrowers notes it has newly printed or checking account money it newly creates in the borrowers' accounts. When some bank does this (let's call it Bank A for "aggressive"), people to whom its borrowers pay the excess Bank A notes will spend them away (because by assumption they are already holding all they want to hold). As those notes are spent, they will eventually be deposited in various other banks and go from there to the clearinghouse. Similarly, people paid by checks drawn on the new checking accounts at Bank A will deposit those checks in their own banks, from where they will go to the clearinghouse.

Eventually (perhaps quickly) all the new notes and checking account money Bank A has issued in excess of what people wish to hold will come back to Bank A through the clearinghouse. Thereupon Bank A will have to redeem the notes and checks in base money (gold, silver, or whatever). The bank will thereby experience negative net clearings, "adverse clearings," *which reduce its reserves.* Low reserves will mean losses for Bank A on the next day it has unusually large negative net clearings at the clearinghouse and runs out of reserves. When that happens, the bank will have to borrow reserves from a sister bank or from the clearinghouse itself at a penalty rate of interest. That's costly. It reduces the bank's profits or causes a loss. That feedback gives the bank an incentive to stop over-issuing money and, indeed, to issue less than normal for a time, while it replenishes its reserves.

Of course, not all banks will necessarily learn the right amount of reserves to hold and money to issue. People (including bankers) make mistakes. From time to time, on account of their persistent over-issuing of money and the large expenses and diminished reputation that would result, some banks would go out of business or be taken over by a more capable rival. Driving bad banks out of business is one way in which the Profit-and-Loss Guidance Principle regulates the quality of banking.

If a bank (let's call it Bank T for "timid") is over-cautious and issues less in notes and checking balances than the public wishes to hold, the process works in reverse. The public will try to get their holdings of Bank T's notes and checking balances up to their desired levels by saving (not spending) them. Hence fewer will return to the clearinghouse. With less of its notes and checks to redeem at the clearinghouse, Bank T will experience positive net clearings—its reserves will increase. Observing that increase, Bank T will learn that it can safely lend out more.

Not all banks will avoid being over-cautious, of course, but market forces tend to weed out timid banks. Those banks make smaller profits than they could, or they make losses overall because their income is so low, and therefore they become attractive targets for takeover by better-managed, and hence more profitable, rivals. There's the Profit-and-Loss Guidance Principle again.

Each bank regulates the quantity of notes and checking balances it issues to the public based on the changing levels of its reserves. Profit and loss force each bank to do this pretty well or go out of business. With each bank regulating its own portion of the money supply more or less correctly based on its feedback from the clearinghouse, the system as a whole tends to provide the amount of money the public wishes to hold. As with pencil making, no mastermind is necessary to plan or comprehend the process as a whole. Free banking would regulate the money supply well in an entirely decentralized fashion.

## Why Central Banking
## Cannot Keep the Money Supply Right

Under a regime of central banking, in contrast to free banking, no feedback mechanism operates to tell the central bank how much money the public would like to hold at prevailing prices. When the central bank upsets monetary equilibrium by creating too much money, it has *no* competitors returning its notes and checking account money through the clearinghouse for redemption in the underlying reserve commodity. There *is* no underlying reserve commodity, so the notes and checks are not redeemable. The money a central bank creates does not come back to it from the clearinghouse; there *is* no independent clearinghouse (in most countries, the central bank clears commercial banks' checks). The new money stays out in the economy, unless and until the central bank intentionally removes it (see open market sales in Appendix A). A bank that receives the new central bank money holds it as reserves *instead of* gold, silver, or some other commodity. In a fiat system, central bank notes and checking account money *become* reserves for that bank as soon as the notes hit the teller's drawer and the checks clear. All banks are happy to acquire more reserves; accordingly, banks are willing to accumulate indefinite quantities of central bank money. Thus, in all central banking regimes in which the central bank has a legal monopoly on issuing notes, the central bank's fiat money serves as reserves in place of an underlying commodity.

Hence, when more fiat money is issued than the public wishes to hold, the central bank experiences no depletion of its reserves (the money it created *is* reserves!). The erring central bank faces no losses, embarrassment, or expulsion from its clearinghouse association (clearinghouses for notes no longer exist).

This difference in the nature of reserves is fundamentally important. In free banking, reserves consist of quantities of a physical commodity valuable in its own right; increased quantities can be obtained only by expensive mining operations. In central banking, reserves consist of printed paper and bookkeeping entries that can be created with the click of a mouse. With underlying ("base") money so easy to create, there is great danger, all too often realized in history, that the central bank will create too much of it.

When too much money is issued, spending rises. That is true under central banking or under free banking. The public spends away the excess on a variety of consumption and investment goods.  But because this new money stays in the economy in a central-banking regime (as it would not in free banking), this extra spending serves not to punish the over-issuing central bank (as it would a free bank) but to drive up prices. Prices tend to rise most in the sectors of the economy where the money is most freely spent. It might, for example, be spent most freely on housing and drive up housing prices. When prices rise, the buying power of money falls. Prices tend to rise until the buying power of money has fallen enough so that the new, larger quantity of money has only the buying power that people wish to hold.

So, in the absence of feedback from a clearinghouse, how does the central bank know how much money to create? It doesn't know. It can't know.

Because a central banking system lacks the natural, decentralized regulation provided by clearinghouses in free banking, there is no systemic limit to how much money the central bank can produce. In the face of political and social pressure on the central bank authorities, the public has little to rely on to restrain excess money issue other than the understanding, independent judgment, good intentions, and good luck of the bank authorities themselves.

Unfortunately for the public, even with the best of intentions to get the money supply right, central bankers lack the information and understanding necessary to do so. This is no slander of them: The world economy is too complex for anyone to understand well enough to intervene in it and reliably get good results. As I said above (and discussed in Chapter 2), this is another instance of the knowledge problem—a problem that free market processes solve, if they are allowed to. Unfortunately for the public, sometimes central bankers lack the best of intentions. After all, they are human beings. Like all of us they respond to the incentives at work on them. In a central banking system, impersonal profit-and-loss incentives (as well as, in the extreme, the unanswerable compulsion of bankruptcy) are replaced by a host of other incentives. Those incentives range from a magnanimous desire to do a good job and win the esteem of a grateful population (perhaps years in the future after the public comes at last to appreciate the wisdom of policies they once decried), to a selfish desire to pacify at once a clamorous public and legislature, to the desire to exercise yet again the intoxicating power to lower (short-term) interest rates and create new money and credit out of nothing at all.

I fear that, most often, political incentives prevail. This certainly seems to be what happened in 2001-2004, when the Fed created so much new money that it kept its target interest rate at historical lows, thereby enabling hundreds of billions of dollars of over-investment in housing.

## Intervention #5 - Rescuing Lenders

Another major government intervention into the economy that stoked the boom is the federal government's regular rescuing of the creditors of big institutions that have gotten into financial trouble. Such rescues obstruct the operation of the Profit-and-Loss Guidance Principle by shielding lenders from the losses they have earned, and which they need to suffer, if saver/lenders are to discover—and learn and remember—the kinds of investments they should avoid. The government has been rescuing lenders for decades. Its doing so has led creditors of big financial institutions to expect to be rescued in the event of trouble. This expectation in turn has led lenders both to lend more freely and to reduce (or quit entirely) their monitoring and curtailing of the risks their borrowers take.

Such carelessness and free lending allowed (even induced) major financial intermediaries—Fannie and Freddie, Bear Stearns, Merrill-Lynch, Citibank, Bank of America and others—to invest huge amounts of borrowed money in housing. These bad investments fed the housing boom.

The government's habit of rescuing lenders is harder to identify as an intervention than other culprits we've considered because it is implicit policy, nowhere explicitly written on the books and not consistently followed, as we shall see. The exemption of housing from capital gains tax, Fannie and Freddie's "affordable housing" goals, and the Basel capital adequacy rules (to be discussed in the next chapter) are all explicit policies "on the books." On the other hand, the government's strong tendency to rescue lenders over the last thirty years has shaped the expectations and decisions of lenders and borrowers.

I am indebted for my understanding of this problem to Russell Roberts. In discussing this intervention, I digest and quote extensively from his paper, "Gambling With Other People's Money, How Perverted Incentives Caused the Financial Crisis."

We already touched on the basic problem Roberts describes when we discussed the U.S. government's once-implicit, now-explicit guarantees to those who have loaned Fannie Mae and Freddie Mac money by buying their bonds or their mortgage-backed securities. In the next chapter we discuss guarantees in the form of government-provided deposit insurance for those who have loaned banks their deposits. The law promises to rescue these depositors from any losses on their deposits up to the amount specified by law (now $250,000).

Roberts discusses not only these guarantees—he discusses Fannie and Freddie at length—but also the government's record of rescuing lenders to institutions *not* "sponsored" by government and depositors whose deposits were *not* insured by the FDIC.

Roberts makes his point with a metaphor of a very good poker player who borrows most of his stake from a friend at an agreed rate of interest. His illustration merits quoting at length:

> Imagine a superb poker player who asks you for a loan to finance his nightly poker playing. For every $100 he gambles, he's willing to put up $3 of his own money. He wants you to lend him the rest. You will not get a stake in his winning. Instead, he'll give you a fixed rate of interest on your $97 loan.

The poker player likes this situation for two reasons. First, it minimizes his downside risk. He can only lose $3. Second, borrowing has a great effect on his investment—it gets leveraged. If his $100 bet ends up yielding $103, he has made a lot more than 3 percent—in fact, he has doubled his money. His $3 investment is now worth $6.

But why would you, the lender, play this game? It's a pretty risky game for you. Suppose your friend starts out with a stake of $10,000 for the night, putting up $300 himself and borrowing $9,700 from you. If he loses anything more than 3 percent on the night, he can't make good on your loan.

Not to worry—your friend is an extremely skilled and prudent poker player who knows when to hold 'em and when to fold 'em. He may lose a hand or two because poker is a game of chance, but by the end of the night, he's always ahead. He always makes good on his debts to you. He has never had a losing evening. As a creditor of the poker player, this is all you care about. As long as he can make good on his debt, you're fine. You care only about one thing—that he stays solvent so that he can repay his loan and you get your money back.

But the gambler cares about two things. Sure, he too wants to stay solvent. Insolvency wipes out his investment, which is always unpleasant—it's bad for his reputation and hurts his chances of being able to use leverage in the future. But the gambler doesn't just care about avoiding the downside. He also cares about the upside. As the lender, you don't share in the upside; no matter how much money the gambler makes on his bets, you just get your promised amount of interest.

If there is a chance to win a lot of money, the gambler is willing to a take a big risk. After all, *his* downside is small. He only has $3 at stake. To gain a really large pot of money, the gambler will take a chance on an inside straight.

As the lender of the bulk of his funds, you wouldn't want the gambler to take that chance. You know that when the leverage ratio—the ratio of borrowed funds to personal assets—is 32–1 ($9,700 divided by $300), the gambler will take a lot more risk than you'd like. So you keep an eye on the gambler to make sure that he continues to be successful in his play.

But suppose the gambler becomes increasingly reckless. He begins to draw to an inside straight from time to time and pursue other high-risk strategies that require making very large bets that threaten his ability to make good on his promises to you. After all, it's worth it to him. He's not playing with very much of his own money. He is playing mostly with your money. How will you respond?

You might stop lending altogether, concerned that you will lose both your interest and your principal. Or you might look for ways to protect yourself. You might demand a higher rate of interest. You might ask the player to put up his own assets as collateral in case he is wiped out. You might impose a covenant that legally restricts the gambler's behavior, barring him from drawing to an inside straight, for example.

These would be the natural responses of lenders and creditors when a borrower takes on increasing amounts of risk. But this poker game isn't proceeding in a natural state. There's another person in the room: Uncle Sam. Uncle Sam is off in the corner, keeping an eye on the game, making comments from time to time, and, every once in a while, intervening in the game. He sets many of the rules that govern the play of the game. And sometimes he makes good on the debt of the players who borrow and go bust, taking care of the lenders. After all, Uncle Sam is loaded. He has access to funds that no one else has. He also likes to earn the affection of people by giving them money. Everyone in the room knows Uncle Sam is loaded, and everyone in the room knows there is a chance, perhaps a very good chance, that wealthy Uncle Sam will cover the debts of players who go broke.

Nothing is certain. But the greater the chance that Uncle Sam will cover the debts of the poker player if he goes bust, the less likely you are to try to restrain your friend's behavior at the table. Uncle Sam's interference has changed your incentive to respond when your friend makes riskier and riskier bets.

If you think that Uncle Sam will cover your friend's debts . . .

> you will worry less and pay less attention to the risk-taking behavior of your gambler friend.

> you will not take steps to restrain reckless risk taking.

> you will keep making loans even as his bets get riskier.

> you will require a relatively low rate of interest for your loans.

> you will continue to lend even as your gambler friend becomes more leveraged.

> you will not require that your friend put in more of his own money and less of yours as he makes riskier and riskier bets.

What will your friend do when you behave this way? He'll take more risks than he would normally. Why wouldn't he? He doesn't have much skin in the game in the first place. You do, but your incentive to protect your money goes down when you have Uncle Sam as a potential backstop.

Capitalism is a profit *and loss* system. The profits encourage risk taking. The losses encourage prudence. Eliminate losses or even raise the chance that there will be no losses and you get less prudence. So when public decisions reduce losses, it isn't surprising that people are more reckless.

Roberts holds that the expectation of rescue induced creditors to lend too liberally and borrowers to make the very risky housing bets that went bad. The tremendous amount of borrowing induced by creditors' expectation of rescue if things went bad was another necessary condition of the financial fiasco:

> Without extreme leverage, the housing meltdown would have been like the meltdown in high-tech stocks in 2001—a bad set of events in one corner of a very large and diversified economy. Firms that invested in that corner would have had a bad quarter or a bad year. But because of the amount of leverage that was used, the firms that invested in housing—Fannie Mae and Freddie Mac, Bear Stearns, Lehman Brothers, Merrill Lynch, and others—destroyed themselves.

Is it reasonable to believe that creditors in general expected rescue in the event of big financial trouble? Roberts makes a strong case that the record of the last twenty-five years supported such an expectation:

- In 1984, the government rescued

> Continental Illinois, then one of the top ten banks in the United States before it could fail. ... In the government rescue, the government took on $4.5 billion of bad loans. ... Only 10 percent of the bank's deposits were insured, but *every depositor was covered in the rescue* [emphasis added].

That last is very significant; even the 90 percent of deposits in Continental Illinois *not* eligible for FDIC insurance were paid off with taxpayers' money.

- Irvine Sprague reported a rash of rescues in his 1986 book, *Bailout*, here quoted by Roberts:

Of the fifty largest bank failures in history, forty-six—including the top twenty—were handled either through a pure bailout or an FDIC assisted transaction where no depositor or creditor, insured or uninsured, lost a penny.

- Of the drawn-out collapse of the savings and loan industry through the 1980's, Roberts writes,

  [The] government repeatedly sent the same message: lenders and creditors would get all of their money back. Between 1979 and 1989, 1,100 commercial banks failed. Out of all of their deposits, 99.7 percent, insured or uninsured, were reimbursed by policy decisions.

- In 1990, the government actually let a big financial firm fail without rescuing its creditors. The firm was Drexel Burnham. "The failure to rescue Drexel put some threat of loss back into the system," says Roberts, "but maybe not very much— Drexel Burnham was a political pariah. The firm and its employees had numerous convictions for securities fraud and other violations."

- In 1995, there was another rescue, not of a financial institution, but of a country—Mexico. The United States orchestrated a $50 billion rescue of the Mexican government, but as in the case of Continental Illinois, it was really a rescue of the creditors, those who had bought Mexican bonds and who faced large losses if Mexico were to default.

- In 1998, "Long-Term Capital Management (LTCM), a highly leveraged private hedge fund," faced insolvency when billions of dollars' worth of its investment bets went bad. Although the government did not use any taxpayer money to rescue LTCM, it did call a "voluntary" meeting of LTCM's creditors, in which they agreed to take 90 percent ownership of LTCM in exchange for $3.625 billion of rescue funds. Roberts says,

Ultimately, LTCM died. While creditors were damaged, the losses were much smaller than they would have been in a bankruptcy. No government money was involved. Yet the rescue of LTCM did send a signal that the government would try to prevent bankruptcy and creditor losses.

In short, from the troubles of Continental Illinois to the beginnings of the current financial mess, the government let the creditors of only one major firm (Drexel Burnham) lose their loans to an insolvent major financial firm. Roberts reasons that "[g]iven the systematic rescue of creditors in recent decades, it is hard to believe that the strong possibility of rescue did not play a role in the increasing amounts of leverage and risk" that characterized the housing boom and made the financial mess so big.

If creditors of the big players financing the housing boom *did* expect to be rescued should those big players get into trouble, they got it right in every case but that of Lehman Brothers:

That brings us to the current mess that began in March 2008 ... The government played matchmaker and helped Bear Stearns get married to J. P. Morgan Chase. The government essentially nationalized Fannie and Freddie, placing them into conservatorship, honoring their debts, and funding their ongoing operations through the Federal Reserve. The government bought a large stake in AIG and honored all of its obligations at 100 cents on the dollar. The government funneled money to many commercial banks.

Each case seems different. But there is a pattern. Each time, the stockholders in these firms are either wiped out or see their investments reduced to a trivial fraction of what they were before. The bondholders and lenders are left untouched. In every case other than that of Lehman Brothers, bondholders and lenders received everything they were promised: 100 cents on the dollar. Many of the poker players—and almost all of those who financed the poker players—lived to fight another day. It's the same story as Continental Illinois, Mexico, and LTCM—a complete rescue of creditors and lenders.

The only exception to the rescue pattern was Lehman.

Even the case of Lehman, however, supports Roberts's thesis that creditors expected rescue. "The balance sheet at Lehman looked a lot like the balance sheet at Bear Stearns—lots of subprime securities and lots of leverage." Accordingly, after the collapse of Bear Stearns many expected Lehman to collapse as well. Nevertheless, Lehman was able to continue borrowing. Think what this means: lenders were willing to lend to a firm that was likely to collapse and be unable to pay them back! Roberts asks, "How did [Lehman] keep borrowing at all given the collapse of Bear Stearns?" The answer must be that lenders "expected a rescue in the worst-case scenario."

To sum up:

- Depositors at the many banks making shaky mortgage loans or buying subprime mortgage-backed securities knew they'd be rescued by the FDIC if their banks' investments failed, so they kept their deposits there anyway and took no actions to find out about, much less discipline, the banks' risky investing.

- Large institutions, banks, and foreign governments that bought the bonds that financed Fannie Mae's and Freddie Mac's purchases of shaky mortgages and subprime mortgage-backed securities were almost certain—and certainly correct—that they'd be rescued by the U.S. government if Fannie and Freddie could not pay them back, so they kept buying Fannie and Freddie's bonds and mortgage-backed securities.

- Lenders to Bear Stearns, Lehman Brothers, and other major private-label securitizers, who financed those firms' purchases of billions of dollars' worth of shaky mortgages that they bundled into mortgage-backed securities, had good reason to expect that they'd be rescued by the government if financial disaster occurred, so they kept lending to Bear Stearns, Lehman, and the others long after the risks became evident. (They lost confidence in Bear Stearns in March of 2008 and Lehman in September of 2008, but even so, the government made sure Bear Stearns's creditors received 100 cents on every dollar they were owed.)

As Chapter 2 stresses, profit is society's indispensable means of rewarding the goods and services—and investments—that create value for people; loss is society's indispensable means of eliminating those that destroy value. Over the years, the government has protected creditors from losses their loans have earned, and doing so has systematically obstructed the healthy process by which losses clear bad investments out of the economy. And it was certainly a major culprit in creating the boom, bust, and financial mess. In Roberts's words, "public policy over the last three decades has distorted the natural feedback loops of profit and loss." For Roberts, this rescuing of creditors is the *primary* cause of the financial fiasco of 2008 and afterwards:

> The most culpable policy has been the systematic encouragement of imprudent borrowing and lending. That encouragement came not from capitalism or markets, but from crony capitalism, the mutual aid society where Washington takes care of Wall Street and Wall Street returns the favor. Over the last three decades, public policy has systematically reduced the risk of making bad loans to risky investors Over the last three decades, when large financial institutions have gotten into trouble, the government has almost always rescued their bondholders and creditors. These policies have created incentives both to borrow and to lend recklessly.

What government interventions generated the housing boom of 1997 to 2007? The culprits include special tax treatment of capital gains on housing, Congress's requirement that Fannie and Freddie buy large quantities of shaky mortgages, the Fed's creation of great quantities of new loanable funds in the absence of new investable resources, and the crony-capitalist protection of lenders just discussed. The unsustainable boom these interventions combined to create had to end in a painful bust. But the story didn't end there, because after the *housing* bust came a *financial* crisis.

Why?

Chapter Twelve

# Why the Housing Bust Led to a Financial Crisis

The interventions in mortgage-making and in money that we have discussed so far help to explain the housing boom and bust. But the bursting of an asset bubble does not always, or even usually, lead to a financial crisis. The dot-com bust did not. The stock market crash of 1987 did not. Why did the *housing* bust lead to *financial* turmoil?

## Intervention #6 - The Basel Bank Capital Restrictions

It did so because so many banks and investment banks had invested heavily in mortgage-backed securities (MBSs). When the housing boom went bust, the banks holding all these MBSs were threatened with insolvency. But *why* were banks holding so many MBSs, including "toxic" subprime and low-down-payment mortgage-backed securities? After all, they were not holding a lot of technology stocks when the dot-com boom went bust. What made the difference this time around?

Mortgage-backed securities are not inherently problematical. In a healthy economy, they serve the useful function of allowing banks to pass off to others the risk of investment in housing. When banks *sell* a pool of their mortgages to a securitizer, who then sells the MBSs to lots of different institutional investors, banks become *less* exposed to the risks of housing, not more, and the risk is spread among many different investors. But as it transpired, many banks themselves *purchased* a lot of the MBSs that securitizers had created. Indeed, banks purchased *a disproportionate share* of them. U.S. commercial banks by 2008 owned about thirty percent of all AAA-rated MBSs held in the U.S. (apart from those held by Fannie, Freddie, and the Federal Home Loan Bank). As a proportion of their total assets, U.S. banks invested in AAA-rated MBSs at a rate three times higher than that of non-bank investors. Accordingly, when the housing boom went bust and the MBSs lost value, the banks holding them got in trouble. *That* is why the problems in the housing industry caused problems in the financial industry. Banks had loaded up on MBSs, many of which turned out to be "toxic."

Why did they do that?

They were pushed to do it by well-intended but misguided government intervention: restrictions on banks' freedom to decide the kinds and amounts of *capital* they hold. Bank capital functions essentially as a cushion against unexpectedly large losses. (For an explanation of what bank capital is, and why it matters, please see Appendix B.) The kinds and amounts of capital banks must hold are mandated by the *Basel capital adequacy rules*, named for the Swiss city where they were developed (and are even now being revised again) in an international accord. Those rules linked the housing and financial markets by giving banks strong incentives to buy mortgage-backed securities.

But let us step back a moment. Why does the U.S. government regulate American banks' capital in the first place, instead of leaving that to market forces? It does so because of still another, earlier intervention (Intervention #7, to be discussed later in this chapter), the government's insuring of deposits (up to $250,000) through the Federal Deposit Insurance Corporation (FDIC). Ultimately taxpayers' money stands behind the FDIC's insurance fund, so the government arguably has an obligation to those taxpayers to require insured banks to maintain a capital cushion adequate to absorb unexpected, large losses. That way the banks are less likely to fail, so the taxpayers are less likely to have to pay.

But how much capital—and what kinds—are adequate? When governments take over capital regulation from market forces, regulators—imperfect human beings—must specifically answer those questions and impose their answers on all the banks they regulate. That's a problem: if the regulators require a bad approach due to poor judgment or simple ignorance on their part, all banks must take that bad approach. That's what happened, as we'll see.

Bank capital requirements are another case of well-intentioned restrictions on freedom of exchange. In a free economy, banks would be free to exchange their services with willing customers while holding any amount and description of capital they choose—or, indeed, no capital at all—so long as they do so without fraud and they honor their contracts. Of course, in a market free of tax-backed deposit insurance, banks suspected to have insufficient capital would have a hard time attracting customers.

While government restrictions on the kinds and quantities of capital maintained by banks may be well intended, those restrictions block the operation of the Profit-and-Loss Guidance Principle: It makes it impossible for bankers and their insurers to *discover*, in an on-going process of entrepreneurial innovation and profit-and-loss selection, the different quantities, kinds and combinations of bank capital that sufficiently hold down the chances of insolvency. In place of that free-market discovery process, government regulation gives us a set of directives issued by a small number of legislators and agency officials, each of whom has only a limited view and understanding of the complex, dynamic system he is interfering with. Those directives are imposed on all banks and fixed until legislation or bureaucratic rule-making changes them.

A good system for regulating bank capital cannot be achieved by such top-down design any more than can a good system for regulating the safety and efficacy of hairdressing or pharmaceuticals, as we saw in Chapters 5 and 6. No group of financial system planners can possibly know enough to come up with a good design. There is too much to know—too many factors interact: there is too much change, too much accident, too many different ways in which regulations and innovations and outside factors may interact—for anyone to know for sure what to allow and what to forbid.

F.A. Hayek wrote, "The curious task of economics is to demonstrate to men how little they really know about what they imagine they can design." When a system of restrictions is designed centrally, as was the Basel Accord, and imposed on enterprisers trying to cope with an uncertain world, more harm than good usually results. Such is the case with the Basel rules: their intended positive consequences are swamped by their unintended negative consequences.

## The Basel Rules

The Basel rules, those known as Basel I, which were in place during the housing boom and bust and the onset of the financial mess, were implemented in the U.S. in 1991, and importantly amended ten years later in the United States by what is known as the "Recourse Rule." How the Basel rules induced banks to load up on mortgage-backed securities is crucial to understanding the financial fiasco, and it is also a great illustration of how well-intended regulation can do more harm than good through its unintended consequences.

A bank's "capital ratio," in general terms, is the ratio of a bank's capital to its assets (we'll tighten the definition below). Capital adequacy rules such as the Basel rules have the worthy intention of making sure banks have big enough capital cushions to keep them solvent even if a lot of their assets go bad. But how much capital is enough?

In the United States, the Federal Deposit Insurance Act gives the government's answer to this question by restricting banks' freedom of action more or less depending on their capital ratios.

Accordingly, this ratio is very important to banks.

Banking is one of the most highly regulated industries in the United States. Even when a bank is in good standing with its regulators because its capital ratio is high, coping with regulation is time-consuming and expensive, requiring bank employees to do paperwork for the government rather than create value for their customers. But when a bank gets into trouble as its capital ratio falls, its regulators, just doing their jobs, become increasingly intrusive and restrictive. The regulatory burden becomes suffocating.

To appreciate the importance of the capital ratio, imagine that you are the manager of a bank and consider what it would mean to the tranquility of your life, not to mention the health of your bank, to have your bank at the different capital levels specified in the Federal Deposit Insurance Act (we'll see how the percentages are calculated shortly).

- As long as your capital ratio is 10 percent or greater, your bank is considered "well capitalized;" accordingly your bank enjoys full privileges.

- When your capital ratio is between 8 and 10 percent, your bank is considered "adequately capitalized." It does not enjoy all the privileges of a "well capitalized" bank, but regulators let it be.

- If your capital ratio should fall below 8 percent, however, your bank is considered "undercapitalized," and the regulatory grip tightens significantly. Your regulators are now required to "closely monitor the condition" of your bank; you are required to submit a detailed "capital restoration plan;" you may not increase your assets, e.g. make new loans, without permission from your regulators; you must obtain permission from your regulators to make any acquisitions, open a new branch, or engage in any new line of business; and your regulator may, at its discretion, require or forbid various further actions.

- If your bank's capital ratio should fall below 6 percent, it is considered "significantly undercapitalized." Among various other provisions, your pay can be restricted; you can be fired; the board of directors can be replaced; your bank can be sold to or merged with another bank.

- If your bank's capital ratio falls below 2 percent, it is considered "critically undercapitalized" and your regulator must take control of your bank.

Clearly, the capital ratio matters.

But how is this ratio calculated? Some assets are risky, and others are safe. Shouldn't banks hold more capital against risky assets than against safe assets? How much more?

The Basel rules—still in effect as of this writing—address these questions by distinguishing categories of assets according to their presumed riskiness and giving each category a risk weight. The capital ratio *for regulatory purposes* is computed as the bank's capital divided by the bank's total *risk-weighted* assets:

*capital ratio = bank capital ÷ risk-weighted assets*

As of January 1, 2002, these were the categories and weights:

- Business loans, considered the most risky. Risk-weight: 100 percent.
- Mortgages, considered only half as risky as business loans. Risk-weight: 50 percent.
- State government bonds, considered not very risky. Risk-weight: 20 percent.
- Bonds and other securities, including mortgage-backed securities ("Agency" MBSs) of government-sponsored enterprises such as Fannie Mae and Freddie Mac, considered not very risky. Risk-weight: 20 percent.
- Asset-backed securities of private sector securitizers such as Bear Stearns or Lehman Brothers, including their mortgage-backed securities ("private-label" MBSs), *that had received an AA or AAA rating* from one of the three nationally recognized statistical rating organizations were considered, under the "Recourse Rule" adopted for the U.S. in 2001, to be no more risky than mortgage-backed securities of Fannie Mae and Freddie Mac. Risk-weight: 20 percent.
- U.S. government bonds and cash, considered not risky at all. Risk-weight: zero—no capital has to be held against them.

For illustration of the effect of the different risk weights, suppose again that you are the manager of a bank. Suppose your bank has $8 million in capital and total assets of $100 million. But now look at how wildly your regulatory capital adequacy varies depending on the *kind* of asset your $100 million is invested in:

*Suppose you hold all business loans.* Because business loans are risk-weighted 100 percent, your bank's risk-weighted capital is 100 percent of $100 million, which equals $100 million. Your bank's capital ratio under the Basel rules is therefore 8 percent:

*$8 million in capital ÷ $100 million in risk-adjusted assets = 8 percent*

With this 8 percent capital ratio, your bank is considered just barely "adequately capitalized." Your regulators are worried; you are anxious. If any of those loans should go bad, you'll face all the hassles—regulatory scrutiny of every decision, the necessity to submit a "capital restoration plan" and the like—that face an "undercapitalized" bank.

*Suppose you hold all mortgages.* Because mortgages are risk-weighted only 50 percent, your bank's risk-weighted capital is 50 percent of $100 million, or $50 million, so your capital ratio is 16 percent:

*$8 million in capital ÷ $50 million in risk-adjusted assets = 16 percent*

With this 16 percent capital ratio, your bank is considered better than "well-capitalized." Your regulators are happy; you are tranquil.

*Suppose you hold all mortgage-backed securities issued by Fannie Mae or Freddie Mac, or AA- or AAA-rated mortgage-backed securities issued by a private company such as Bear Stearns.* Because such mortgage-backed securities are risk-weighted at only 20 percent, your risk-weighted capital would be 20 percent of $100 million, or $20 million, so your capital ratio is 40 percent:

*$8 million in capital ÷ $20 million in risk-adjusted assets = 40 percent*

With a 40 percent capital ratio, your bank is considered far better than "well-capitalized." Your regulators are gratifyingly bored.

## How the Basel Capital Adequacy Regulations Induced Banks to Load Up on Mortgage-Backed Securities

These numbers begin to suggest how the Basel rules led many banks to invest heavily in the mortgage-backed securities that turned out to be bad investments when the housing boom went bust.

Let's do another thought experiment to understand how the Basel rules gave banks an incentive to switch out of other investments and into mortgage-backed securities. In this thought experiment, you, the reader, are again the president of an imaginary bank, call it Bank X. We assume that Bank X also has $8 million in capital. We further assume that:

- business loans pay 7 percent interest,
- mortgages pay 6 percent interest, and
- mortgage-backed securities pay 5 percent interest.

Initially, Bank X has interest-earning assets of $100 million in business loans. On those you stand to earn income of $7 million annually if none default. Suppose you wanted to increase the income you could earn (potentially, at least, if the investments all pay off). How could you do so and still stay within the Basel rules? If you took full advantage of the different risk weights of the different kinds of investments, what's the largest income you could (potentially) earn with only $8 million in capital?

Table 12.1 lays out the various options, which are also described in what follows. If you, the reader, would like to figure for yourself your largest potential income, pause here to do so before reading on.

* * * * *

Initially (holding $100 million in business loans), what is your capital ratio? As we saw above, because business loans carry a 100 percent risk weight, you have risk-weighted assets of the whole $100 million, so your regulatory capital ratio is your capital of $8 million divided by that $100 million in risk-weighted assets. That's 8 percent, so your bank is just barely "adequately capitalized." This original strategy is shown in Table 12.1 as Strategy A.1: Hold Business Loans (look ahead to see the table).

Suppose your stockholders (including yourself!) want a higher rate of return on their $8 million in capital, if you can earn it without too much risk. How might you increase your bank's income? The first alternate strategy you consider might simply be to take in more deposits and make more business loans with those deposits. (That's called "expanding your balance sheet." See Appendix B.) Will that work? If you were to take in $50 million more in deposits and make $50 million more business loans with them, you would increase your potential income from $7 million to $10.5 million, but look at Strategy A.2: Increase Business Loans in Table 12.1 to see what would happen to your capital ratio if you were to do so. Those new loans would all carry a 100 percent risk weight, so your risk-weighted assets would increase to $150 million. Your capital of $8 million divided by that $150 million in risk-weighted assets would yield a capital ratio of only 5.33 percent. That's "significantly undercapitalized," so your regulators would relieve you of your duties and install new management if you were to take this approach. It won't do.

What else might you do to increase the income your bank earns on its $8 million in capital? What if you make mortgage loans instead of business loans?

Following Strategy B.1: Replace Business Loans with Mortgage Loans, you could give up your business loans (sell them to another bank or let them mature without renewing them) and use the money to make mortgage loans instead. The Basel rules give you an incentive to do this because they treat mortgages as only half as risky as regular business loans. If you were to follow this strategy, your potential income would decrease to only $6 million per year, but look what happens to your capital ratio for regulatory purposes. Because mortgages carry only a 50 percent risk weight, your $100 million in mortgages amount to *risk-weighted* assets of only $50 million. Dividing your $8 million in capital by that $50 million in risk-weighted assets gives you a capital ratio of 16 percent, well into "well-capitalized" territory. That gives you some regulatory breathing space! How might you use that breathing space to increase your bank's potential income?

## Table 12.1 How the Basel Rules Led Banks to Buy Mortgage-Backed Securities

| Capital | Kind of Asset | Amount | Potential Income | Risk-weighted Assets | Regulatory Capital Ratio |
|---|---|---|---|---|---|
| **Strategy A.1: Hold Business Loans** <br> Consider a bank with $8 million in capital. If it makes only business loans, in order to stay "adequately capitalized," it can make only $100 million in such loans and therefore earn only $7 million in income. | | | | | |
| | Business Loans (paying 7%) | $100 | $7 | | |
| $8 | *risk weight = 100%* | | | *$100* | *8%* |
| **Strategy A.2: Increase Business Loans** <br> If the bank were to increase its business loans by $50 million, it could earn more income, but its capital ratio would go below "adequately capitalized," so this strategy won't do. | | | | | |
| | Business Loans (paying 7%) | $150 | $11 | | |
| $8 | *risk weight = 100%* | | | *$150* | **5.33%** |
| **Strategy B.1: Replace Business Loans with Mortgage Loans** <br> If the bank gives up its business loans and puts the $100 million into mortgage loans instead, its income decreases, but its capital ratio for regulatory purposes doubles, so it has capital to spare… | | | | | |
| | Mortgages (paying 6%) | $100 | $6 | | |
| $8 | **risk weight = 50%** | | | **$50** | *16%* |
| **Strategy B.2: Increase Mortgage Loans** <br> …and that in turn means it can borrow $100 million more (e.g. by taking more deposits), put that additional $100 million into mortgages, thereby double its (potential) income, and still be "adequately capitalized." | | | | | |
| | Mortgages (paying 6%) | **$200** | **$12** | | |
| $8 | *risk weight = 50%* | | | *$100* | *8%* |
| **Strategy C.1: Replace Mortgage Loans with Mortgage-backed Securities** <br> But the bank can increase much further the (regulatory) adequacy of their $8 million capital if they sell the mortgages to a securitizer and buy mortgage-backed securities (MBSs) with the proceeds… | | | | | |
| | MBSs* (paying 5%) | $200 | $10 | | |
| $8 | **risk weight – 20%** | | | **$40** | *20%* |

**Strategy C.2: Increase Holdings of Mortgage-backed Securities**
...and that in turn means the bank can expand its balance sheet further with still more deposits and more MBSs, make even more income (unless the MBSs go bad!), and still stay "adequately capitalized."

|  | MBSs* (paying 5%) | $500 | $25 |  |  |
|---|---|---|---|---|---|
| $8 | risk weight = 20% |  |  | $100 | 8% |

*\* (from Fannie or Freddie, or AAA- or AA-rated if "private label")*

You could take Strategy B.1 to the next step, B.2, by "increasing leverage"—borrowing more—to expand your balance sheet with more mortgage loans: Take in another $100 million in new deposits and use the whole amount to make more mortgage loans, doubling the quantity you hold to $200 million worth. That doubles your potential income to $12 million, while you remain "adequately capitalized" for regulatory purposes, because your $200 million in mortgages amount to risk-weighted assets of only $100 million.

This process of changing the composition of a bank's assets in order to escape the constraints of capital regulations is known as *regulatory capital arbitrage*. It allows a bank to accumulate more total assets with the same capital ("increasing leverage"—borrowing more—to pay for those assets) while staying within the regulatory rules.

The most significant and ultimately dangerous kind of regulatory capital arbitrage caused by the Basel rules, as amended by the Recourse Rule, involved buying mortgage-backed securities (MBSs). To increase their regulatory capital ratios, many banks did buy many MBSs, and many of the MBSs they bought were backed by subprime mortgages. Let's continue the example to see why banks bought MBSs.

Consider Strategy C.1: Replace Mortgage Loans with Mortgage-backed Securities: You could sell your $200 million worth of mortgages (from Strategy B.2), to a private-label securitizer such as Bear Stearns or Bank of America, or to Fannie Mae or Freddie Mac. That securitizer could turn those mortgages into a mortgage-backed security that either receives an AAA rating from one of the big ratings agencies (Moody's, Standard and Poor's, or Fitch), or has the government's (implied) guarantee if the securitizer is Fannie or Freddie. You could then use your $200 million to buy that MBS—*which is based on the very mortgage loans you sold.* (This is slightly oversimplified, because banks bought only the AAA-rated portions, called "tranches," of the securities backed by the mortgages. This means they were not buying back rights to *all* the potential income from the mortgages, just most of it. The simplification does not affect the point being made here. See the end notes for an explanation of tranching, and how a MBS based on subprime mortgages can get a AAA rating.)

Strategy C.1 in Table 12.1 shows what would happen to your capital ratio if you made this switch from whole mortgages to MBSs. Because AAA-rated MBSs have a risk weight of only 20 percent, your $200 million in MBSs would amount to *risk-weighted* assets of only $40 million (20 percent of $200 million). Your capital ratio, accordingly, would jump from 8 percent to 20 percent, giving you still *more* regulatory breathing room. While your actions have decreased your *total* capital ratio from 8 percent ($8 million in capital ÷ $100 million in business loans) to 4 percent ($8 million in capital ÷ $200 million in MBSs), you have increased your *regulatory* capital ratio from 8 percent to 20 percent. That's regulatory capital arbitrage.

The move to MBSs would reduce your (potential) income to $10 million, but that reduction can be temporary if you then use Strategy C.2: Increase Holdings of Mortgage-backed Securities. Your comfortably high regulatory capital ratio would allow you to increase your holdings of mortgage-backed securities again, by more than double if you are willing to take the risk of letting your *total* capital ratio to fall to a new low. You can increase your holdings by another $300 million. Going to this extreme would increase your annual income (until and unless just a few of the mortgages go bad!) to $25 million, even while you remain "adequately capitalized" according to the regulators, as shown in Table 12.1, Strategy C.2.

The progression of Strategies A, B, and C (shown in Table 12.1) illustrates how regulatory capital arbitrage allows banks to increase their leverage and decrease their overall capital ratios even as they reduce their capital ratios for regulatory purposes. In the example, by taking advantage of the low risk weight assigned to MBSs as in Strategy C.2, you could accumulate millions of dollars' worth of MBSs as you increase the leverage of Bank X from 11.25 to 1 ($92 million in deposits to $8 million in capital while holding $100 million in business loans) to 61.5 to 1 ($492 million in deposits to $8 million in capital while holding $500 million in MBSs) *and yet maintain constant the bank's capital ratio for regulatory purposes.* Doing so would increase the bank's potential income (remember, this is before expenses and assuming all those mortgages pay off!) from $7 million to $24 million per year.

The upside of regulatory capital arbitrage for less-prudent banks—those willing to increase their leverage to expand their balance sheets—is obvious. It gives them a chance for high returns on investment within the constraints of the Basel rules. Accordingly, during the boom, banks willing to let their *actual* capital ratios decrease sought out AAA-rated mortgage-backed securities to buy. Note that until quite late in the housing boom, almost everyone trusted the AAA rating to mean that these mortgage-backed securities were very safe.

The downside of this kind of regulatory capital arbitrage for banks is greater vulnerability to losses on their mortgage-backed securities if the housing market should get into bad trouble (a development almost no one considered likely until late in the boom). In our example, it would take losses on 8.0 percent of Bank X's business loans to wipe out its capital at the outset, but after loading up on mortgage-backed securities, it would take losses on only 1.67 percent of those MBSs to wipe out its capital.

Again, this is a made-up example with simple numbers, and it is intentionally as extreme as I can make it in order to make the underlying arithmetic clear. But it illustrates how the Basel capital adequacy rules gave banks an incentive to borrow more deeply and to use the borrowings to load up on mortgage-backed securities.

The point of the example is *not* that all bankers expanded their balance sheets in a reckless grasping for more and more income, regardless of risk, as in Strategy C.2 of the example, just because the Basel rules made it possible for them to do so. Of course, some did expand their balance sheets imprudently; but not most. The point is rather that the Basel rules gave all bankers, cautious or incautious alike, an incentive to *over*invest in MBSs, to buy more of them than they would have if not for the Basel rules.

The distinction is very important, because in fact commercial bankers (as distinguished from investment bankers) on average did *not* take on more leverage so as to expand their balance sheets during the housing boom, and most were demonstrably not disregarding risk. A strong case can be made, in fact, that, on average, commercial bankers stayed quite cautious.

Commercial banks in general maintained about the same moderate overall capital levels in the run up to the financial crisis. According to Jeffrey Friedman and Wladimir Krauss, "[i]n the aggregate, the regulatory (risk-weighted) capital level of U.S. commercial banks as of mid-2007 [near the peak of the boom] was 12.85 percent …, nearly 30 percent higher than the 10 percent level mandated for well-capitalized banks, and 60 percent higher than the 8 percent level mandated for 'adequately capitalized' banks."

Even banks that did leverage up and expand their balance sheets to buy mortgage-backed securities were still being cautious in other ways: like almost everyone, the banks believed the AAA-rated securities were very safe, and they invested almost exclusively in these safest ones even though riskier, lower-rated (AA-rated) MBSs would have paid them a higher return (because they are slightly riskier) while receiving the same low, 20 percent risk weight as the AAA-rated ones. If bankers had been willing to take more risk for higher return, they would have bought AA-rated MBSs. They didn't. They bought the safest, AAA-rated MBSs despite their lower return.

Even banks which maintained conservative overall capital ratios *did*, on average, engage in regulatory capital arbitrage, however. Like the more risk-tolerant banks, many of them also loaded up on mortgage-backed securities because the Basel rules and the Recourse Rule gave *all* banks an incentive to buy far more MBSs—both from Fannie and Freddie and from "private-label" issuers—than they otherwise would have. As pointed out above, U.S. banks overall invested *three times* as heavily in AAA-rated, privately-issued securities as did non-bank investors. (Recall that these "private label" securities lack the government guarantee given securities issued by Fannie and Freddie, so these are the ones everyone worried about when the housing boom turned to bust and mortgages started to default.)

Why would risk-averse banks engage in regulatory capital arbitrage and load up on mortgage-backed securities even if they did not intend to use the capital relief to leverage up? They did so to give themselves a bigger cushion above the 8 percent regulatory capital ratio below which their banks would be considered "undercapitalized." For banks, this is their *usable* capital cushion as opposed to their *regulatory* capital cushion. The distinction is important. The eight percent (for "adequately capitalized") regulatory capital floor is a cushion for the FDIC, which has to make good on insured deposits when a bank fails, and for taxpayers, who have to make up the difference when the FDIC's Deposit Insurance Fund runs short. But that floor is not a cushion for a *bank*. A bank gets in expensive trouble with its regulators if it falls out of the "adequately capitalized" category. If it stays "undercapitalized" for ninety days, it can be seized by the FDIC and have its management replaced. For the banks, therefore, the regulatory floors are much more (hard marble) floors than cushions.

Accordingly, banks wish to hold some capital in addition to the amounts required by regulation. That additional capital is a cushion they can use to avoid the legal penalties of falling below the *regulatory* floors. Regulatory capital arbitrage based on the Basel rules and the Recourse Rule gave them a way to plump this cushion at low cost.

To see how, let's continue our example from above. Suppose to begin with, as before, that your Bank X has $8 million in capital and $100 million in assets, all business loans. This is Strategy A.1 from Table 12.1, repeated for comparison purposes in Table 12.2. Because the Basel rules assign a 100 percent risk weight to business loans, your risk-weighted capital ratio is 8 percent ($8 million ÷ $100 million).

That *regulatory* capital ratio is perilously low: you have no *usable* capital to protect yourself from consequences with your regulators if you should make even small losses on your loans. So suppose your executive committee decides it must raise that ratio. Suppose (to pick a number that will be useful for comparison purposes shortly) your executive committee decides you must raise your capital ratio by a tenth, from its current 8.0 percent to 8.8 percent.

What would you have to do to achieve that goal if you engage in no regulatory capital arbitrage, but stay invested entirely in business loans? You would have to reduce the dollar amount of the loans you make to $91 million, as shown in Table 12.2 Strategy D: Increase Capital Ratio by Reducing Assets. That change would have the unpleasant consequence of reducing your expected income from $7 million to $6.37 million. So you explore another option.

Doing some regulatory capital arbitrage (Strategy E) will let you raise your capital ratio the same amount—to 8.8 percent—while reducing your potential income less and letting you maintain the dollar amount of your interest-earning assets. You can switch out of *some* of your business loans and into mortgage-backed securities, and thereby take advantage of the lower risk weight the Basel rules and the Recourse Rule assign them. Table 12.2 shows Strategy E: Increase Capital Ratio by Regulatory Capital Arbitrage. Shifting the composition of Bank X's assets from all business loans to a mixed portfolio, as shown, does not expand your balance sheet but does increase your bank's capital ratio as desired, while reducing your expected income from $7 million, not to $6.37 million, but only to $6.78 million.

This regulatory arbitrage lets you achieve the same increase in your usable capital cushion while investing in (what were generally considered) very safe assets, and give up less than half the income you would have had to give up if you had stayed entirely in business loans. The example illustrates why *even many banks that did not increase their leverage* to expand their balance sheets nevertheless altered their balance sheets to include mortgage-backed securities.

I have chosen the proportions of MBSs in the mixed portfolio of Strategy E to match the proportions of these different kinds of securities that U.S. commercial banks actually did hold in 2008. In aggregate, they held 7.7 percent of their assets in MBSs issued by Fannie Mae and Freddie Mac (and Ginnie Mae, a smaller player whose securities were always explicitly guaranteed by the government) and 3.5 percent in MBSs issued by private-sector securitizers.

**Table 12.2 Increasing Usable Capital with Regulatory Capital Arbitrage**

| Capital | Kind of Asset | Amount | Potential Income | Risk-weighted Assets | Regulatory Capital Ratio |
|---|---|---|---|---|---|
| **Strategy A.1: Hold Business Loans** | | | | | |
| $8 | Business Loans (paying 7%) risk weight = 100% | $100 | $7 | $100 | 8% |
| **Strategy D: Increase Capital Ratio by Reducing Assets** | | | | | |
| In order to raise its capital ratio up to 8.8% while holding all business loans, it would have to reduce its total assets and expected income. | | | | | |
| $8 | Business Loans (paying 7%) risk weight = 100% | $91 | **$6.37** | $91 | 8.8% |
| **Strategy E: Increase Capital Ratio by Regulatory Capital Arbitrage** | | | | | |
| If the bank trades some business loans for MBSs, it can raise its capital ratio to the desired 8.8% while maintaining its total assets and reducing its expected income less. | | | | | |
| | Business Loans (paying 7%) risk weight = 100% | $88.8 | $6.22 | $88.80 | |
| | "Agency" MBSs (paying 5%) risk weight = 20% | $7.7 | $0.39 | $1.54 | |
| | "Private-label" MBSs* (paying 5%) risk weight = 20% | $3.5 | $0.18 | $0.70 | |
| | | $100 | **$6.78** | | |
| $8 | | | | $91 | 8.8% |

*rated AAA

That 3.5 percent of assets may not seem large, but remember, it is an aggregate figure, an average. For every bank that held no private-label MBSs there was one that held 7 percent of its assets in them. When the housing boom went bust, the solvency of banks that held a lot of MBSs immediately came into question, because no one could readily tell which MBSs were based on a lot of shaky mortgages, or which banks owned those that did. Banks themselves could not tell for sure the value of the MBSs they owned without laboriously examining all the different mortgages in the securitized pool. In that tense time of sudden uncertainty, banks hoarded cash just in case, lending fell off, and the wheels of commerce slowed.

I call the reader's attention here, in passing, to two other government interventions that interacted with the Basel rules in important and damaging ways. We won't discuss these at length lest this long account run longer still.

One of these two other interventions is the legal oligopoly granted to the "Nationally Recognized Statistical Ratings Organizations": Standard and Poor's, Moody's, and Fitch. The law privileges these three agencies *alone* to qualify a mortgage-backed security with a AAA or AA rating for the favorable 20 percent risk weight under the Recourse Rule. The other intervention is "mark-to-market" accounting, which requires banks to assign values to their assets (e.g. mortgage-backed securities) in a particular manner when they do their capital ratio computations.

In a free market there would be no legal oligopoly for Standard and Poor's, Moody's, and Fitch, but free competition in the rating of securities; and banks would be free to do their accounting in any non-fraudulent manner they chose and to discover the most useful ways to do so. The completely unforeseen, damaging interaction of these two interventions with the Basel rules is fascinating. I recommend that those interested read Chapter 3 of *Engineering the Financial Crisis*, by Jeffrey Friedman and Wladimir Kraus.

## From Housing Bust to Financial Crisis

In the absence of governmental restrictions, banks would seek the best balance they could achieve between the risks and rewards of various asset classes—residential and commercial mortgages, business loans, credit card loans, auto loans, mortgage-backed securities, other asset-backed securities, student loans, and so on—and decide for themselves how to diversify their portfolios and how much capital to maintain. Under the Basel rules, however, whether motivated to increase their leverage aggressively (as some did) or to broaden their usable capital cushions conservatively (as most did), *banks had an incentive to load up on mortgage-backed securities.* In consequence of this government intervention in banking, banks invested in these at three times the rate of non-bank investors. The securities included the "private-label" MBSs which had no guarantee, as well as the "agency" MBSs which did.

Banks' overinvestment in MBSs helped cause the financial mess in two ways.

First, banks' eagerness for mortgage-based assets fueled the housing boom: With such a lively market for their product, banks and mortgage originators sought out house buyers, offering attractive rates and conditions. With mortgages easy to obtain, lots of buyers entered the housing market, bid up prices, and fueled the boom.

Second, when housing prices started downward, increasing numbers of mortgages began to go into default, and the value of MBSs became questionable, the solvency of American commercial banks holding these MBSs became questionable also.

That is why, when mortgages started to default in record numbers, the problems in the housing sector spilled over into the financial sector: Wrong-headed government regulation had induced too many banks to invest in too many securities backed by shaky mortgages. The losses on those mortgage-backed securities reduced banks' capital; banks' solvency came into question; lenders everywhere got cautious, not knowing which banks were sound and which were shaky; lending dried up; and the financial crisis began.

There is a painful irony here: capital adequacy regulations imposed to keep banks sound made them unsound instead.

## The Knowledge Problem of Centralized Bank Regulation

The lesson to draw from this is not that we need better bank capital regulation by government. Regulators probably are and have been doing the best they can. The lesson to draw is that we need regulation by market forces instead. Why? Because top-down regulators in the Basel Committee on Banking Supervision, the Federal Reserve, the Federal Deposit Insurance Corporation, the Office of Thrift Supervision and the Office of the Comptroller of the Currency—these are the U.S. bureaucracies that apply the Basel rules to American banks and issued the Recourse Rule—face the knowledge problem of central planning. These individuals, no matter how well-meaning and well-educated, cannot know all they would need to know to regulate well. The banks did not get into trouble with mortgage-backed securities because they were hiding from regulators or because the regulators were not paying attention. The regulators *supported* regulatory capital arbitrage. But they, like most bankers and economists, did not foresee where it would lead. Government regulation of bank capital is a classic case of the knowledge problem and the corresponding need to allow the Profit-and-Loss Guidance Principle to regulate bank activity.

In his illuminating paper on the policies that produced the crisis, economist Arnold Kling writes, "The phenomenon of regulatory capital arbitrage was well understood by the Federal Reserve Board." Kling quotes a paper by a Fed researcher from the year 2000 whose "tone ... was generally sympathetic to the phenomenon." Here are some illustrative passages, quoted in Kling's paper:

> In recent years, securitization and other financial innovations have provided unprecedented opportunities for banks to reduce substantially their regulatory measures of risk, with little or no corresponding reduction in the overall economic risks—a process termed "regulatory capital arbitrage" (RCA).
>
> ... Ultimately, RCA is driven by large divergences that frequently arise between underlying economic risks and the notions and measures of risk embodied in regulatory capital ratios.... Efforts to stem RCA ... for example, by limiting banks' use of securitization ... would be counterproductive.... In some circumstances, RCA is an important safety-valve that permits banks to compete effectively (with nonbanks) in low-risk businesses they would otherwise be forced to exit owing to unreasonably high regulatory capital requirements.

That is from a Fed researcher. Kling shows that the International Monetary Fund held similar views (note that 2006 was the year in which more subprime and otherwise shaky loans were made and securitized than in any other year):

> [T]he annual report of the International Monetary Fund in 2006 stated that financial innovation "has helped to make the banking and overall financial system more resilient."

Federal Reserve Chairman Ben Bernanke agreed also. Here are some remarks of his from June, 2006, again quoted in Kling's paper (my emphasis):

> The evolution of risk management as a discipline has thus been driven by market forces on the one hand and developments in banking supervision on the other, each side operating with the other in complementary and mutually reinforcing ways. Banks and other market participants have made many of the key innovations in risk measurement and risk management, but *supervisors have often helped to adapt and disseminate best practices* to a broader array of financial institutions.
>
> … The interaction between the private and public sectors in the development of risk-management techniques has been particularly extensive in the field of *bank capital regulation*, especially for the banking organizations that are the largest, most complex, and most internationally active.
>
> … To an important degree, banks can be more active in their management of credit risks and other portfolio risks because of the increased availability of financial instruments and activities such as loan syndications, loan trading, credit derivatives, and *securitization*.

Kling concludes,

> Thus, regulators were well aware of the innovations in credit risk management. However, they viewed these developments with sympathy and approval.

The regulators were overseeing a system that was broken and headed for big trouble, and *they didn't know*. They did not comprehend the damaging ways in which financial innovations were interacting with the vast web of financial regulations. They thought everything was in pretty good shape. They were wrong. They didn't know enough. The regulators were not asleep at the switch; they did not lack sufficient authority; they just were not supermen; they were not able to foresee all the ramifications and interactions of all the many regulations. They were fallible. They are human.

The Basel bank capital regulations were but a minor cause of the *housing* boom and bust. In their absence, there might still have been a housing boom and bust, but it would have been smaller and less destructive: without banks' hungry demand for AAA-rated mortgage-backed securities, banks and other mortgage originators would have had less money with which to originate mortgages, and the pressure in the boom would have been lower.

But the Basel regulations were a major cause of the *financial* mess that followed the bust, because in the absence of the Basel rules, banks and other financial institutions would not have held so many toxic mortgage-backed assets when borrowers started to default. Accordingly, banks would not have gotten into so much trouble when mortgages started to go bad. There might still have been a (milder) housing boom and bust, but there would have been no financial crisis to follow it.

## Intervention #7 – Deposit Insurance with Taxpayers' Money

Why have the Basel rules at all? Why shouldn't banks be free to try out various combinations and amounts of capital as they see fit as long as they are honest with their depositors about what they are doing? Why not let profit and loss shape what bankers do?

That's the way it should be, and would be in a truly free market.

In our present mixed economy, however, bank capital restrictions and other government regulations on banking are considered to be necessary to reduce the bad effects of a *prior* government intervention: insurance of bank deposits. Because it is the reason for bank capital regulation, government-provided deposit insurance is itself, indirectly, a major cause of the financial mess. In this case, as in many others, the ill effects of one intervention lead politicians to intervene further, the ill effects of the second intervention lead them to intervene in still a third way, and so on. One of the goals of this book is to show that the more sensible response to most problems is not to intervene further but to identify and repeal the interventions that cause the problems in the first place.

The Federal Deposit Insurance Corporation (FDIC) was instituted by the Banking Act of 1933 (the Glass-Steagall Act). At the outset, the maximum deposit insured by the FDIC was quite small, only $2,500: the government promised that if a bank became unable to pay back its depositors in full, the government would make up the shortfall up to $2,500. By 2008, the limit was up to $100,000 per depositor. In the financial crisis of 2008, Congress raised the limit "temporarily" through 2013—up to $250,000 per depositor.

Nearly all banks are required to pay annual fees to support the insurance fund, and when, as in 2009, these normal fees are insufficient to cover the deposits in failed banks, healthy banks are assessed additional fees. Of course, all that fee money comes ultimately from the general public in their role as bank customers, and any additional shortfall would come from the general public in their role as taxpayers.

Government-provided deposit insurance shifts the risks on bank deposits from depositors to the general public. In a free market, risk and responsibility would both lie with the depositors, people such as you and me. In accordance with the Profit-and-Loss Guidance Principle, each depositor would enjoy the profits or suffer the losses that result from her decision to deposit—to invest—her money in a particular bank. Each depositor would be responsible for judging the soundness of her bank. She would have a strong incentive to do that carefully, either by herself, or in other ways we will discuss below. If she were to come to doubt her bank's soundness, it would be up to her to withdraw her money and deposit it—invest it—elsewhere. The general public would not be at risk from her decision.

Under government-provided deposit insurance, by contrast, risk, reward, and responsibility are all separate. Each depositor still enjoys the benefits of his or her bank accounts, but the government imposes on the general public any losses that may occur. The government, accordingly, bears responsibility to the general public for making sure the banks don't lose a lot of money. Because the government has put the general public at risk, the government has an obligation to monitor and restrict banks' activities so as to protect the public from losses.

Government-provided deposit insurance creates yet another hazard: increases in risky investments by banks. This is so because deposit insurance reduces or eliminates the incentive of *depositors* to monitor their banks' activities. How might depositors behave if there were no compulsory, government-provided "insurance"? Any time a depositor worried about the soundness of his bank's investments, he could withdraw his deposits. If many depositors became worried at the same time and made withdrawals, those withdrawals would constitute a bank run. The threat of a run is a very healthy restraint for banks tempted to make too many risky investments, and actual runs on banks that *do* make too many risky investments serve society well by weeding out banks that waste investable resources.

Under government deposit insurance, by contrast, lost is the market check on bankers' behavior that comes from depositors' actions to protect their money. After all, depositors won't bear any losses from the unwise, reckless, or just unlucky investments a bank might make—the general public will. Hence there is a real danger that some banks will—and plenty of evidence shows that some do—make more risky investments than they would if market forces were regulating bank activity. The government, having increased the risk of bad investments, must protect the general public from that risk as best it can, by such measures as the Basel rules and the Recourse Rule.

To sum up: government-provided deposit insurance necessitates capital adequacy requirements, and the Basel capital adequacy requirements were primary causes of the financial mess. That's regrettable, but isn't government-provided deposit insurance *necessary*?

## Why We Have Deposit Insurance

It is widely believed that market forces failed to regulate bank safety and soundness effectively before 1933 when the FDIC was created. In particular, banking regulated only by market forces is believed to be very unstable, subject to bank runs and panics, such as those that occurred in 1873, 1893, and 1907, and in the Great Depression, when thousands of banks failed.

Government-provided deposit insurance is seen as necessary to protect the economy from (unjustified) bank runs and bank panics. A bank run is unjustified when the bank being run on is solvent—when its assets exceed its liabilities, so that it has more than enough to pay off all its depositors—but depositors nevertheless come to fear that the bank is *in*solvent. Believing that not everyone will be able to get his money out, depositors "run" to the bank to get their own out while they can.

A bank *panic*, as opposed to a run, is a rash of bank runs caused by a kind of contagion: A run on one bank, whether justified or not, makes depositors at *other* banks fear that perhaps their banks are at risk, too. If depositors at other banks don't have reliable information that their banks are sound, they run on their banks, too, in a panic that can bring down sound banks along with the unsound ones. Deposit insurance does prevent bank panics by assuring depositors that they will be able to get their money back even if their bank fails. The FDIC has been very successful in preventing bank panics in the U.S.

This discussion raises two further questions, however: *Were* market forces failing to regulate banks' safety and soundness properly? And was government-provided deposit insurance itself safe and effective?

If the first question means "Were *free*-market forces failing to regulate banks' safety and soundness properly?" the answer must be "no," because there was no free market in banking before 1933. Banking in the U.S. has been hampered by legal restrictions from early on. Instability in banking was caused not by the freedoms the banks retained but by these legal restrictions.

One important government intervention was a restriction on the freedom of banks to issue banknotes (the standard paper money we are accustomed to, but issued by individual banks—remember this was before the Federal Reserve). Between the Civil War and 1913, virtually all banknotes were issued by individual banks, but banks were allowed to issue notes only if they followed the government's rules. By those rules, a bank in effect had to loan the federal government an amount of money roughly equal to the quantity of bank notes they issued. A bank did this by purchasing certain U.S. government bonds. A consequence of this restriction was that from time to time, typically during harvest season, banks were unable to find and buy those bonds in sufficient quantity to produce as much paper money as their customers needed to pay their bills. A shortage of money at harvest season was the trigger for the bank panics of 1893 and 1907.

Another important intervention was the prohibition on branch banking that lasted in the U.S. until the 1980s. In a free market, businesses are free to expand to wherever customers are willing to do business with them. But in the United States, banks based in one state were not allowed to open branches in other states. In some states, in fact, "unit banking" rules allowed banks no branches at all, not even in their own regions: they were allowed to have one location only!

This legal restriction greatly weakened banks by preventing them from diversifying the kinds of loans they made. A bank in farm country, for example, would lend almost exclusively to farmers, and so was as vulnerable as its farmer clients to bad weather and drops in crop prices. If banks had been allowed to branch widely around the nation, they could have made loans to a wide variety of businesses in different places, so that when one region of the country or one sector of the economy fell on hard times, the bank's branches in healthier regions or sectors could support branches in the troubled areas. Also banks with many branches can quickly move cash to branches that are running short of reserves from branches that have plenty. George Selgin addresses the importance of freedom to branch in this way:

> No episode illustrates more dramatically the weakening effect of anti-branching laws than the Great Depression. Between 1931 and 1933 several thousand US banks—mostly unit banks—failed. In contrast

Canada's branch-banking network did not suffer a single bank failure even though in other respects Canada was just as hard hit by the depression.

And Canada did not have government-provided deposit insurance until 1967.

Government-provided deposit insurance thus does *not* seem to be necessary: the problem of bank runs and panics it supposedly addresses would be better addressed by repealing the legal restrictions which lead to runs and panics.

In fact, government-provided deposit insurance in the United States has historically been not only unnecessary but damaging. When it was instituted in 1933, it was known to cause problems. Though he signed the Federal Deposit Insurance Act, Franklin Roosevelt himself opposed the idea in the 1930s, as did many others, because already evidence was clear that government-provided deposit insurance at the state level was harmful. According to Clifford Thies and Daniel Gerlowski, "[f]rom 1908 to 1917 eight states passed deposit guaranty legislation.... Of the eight, all but the Texas guaranty fund [had] left depositors with uninsured losses." The general pattern was that the deposit insurance allowed a few unscrupulous and/or incompetent bankers to attract a lot of deposits which they then loaned out unwisely. The troubles of imprudent banks put the insurance fund in jeopardy; prudent banks then pulled out of the system, leaving only the worst banks participating. Thies and Gerlowski's account of events in Kansas is representative:

> In Kansas, the 1923 failure of the American State Bank of Wichita, the third largest bank in the system, embarrassed a guaranty fund already deep in debt. Interest on the fund's outstanding debt plus interest on the debt expected to be incurred to make good on losses at the American State Bank approximated revenue from assessments, meaning no money would be available to cover future losses. This situation led to a massive exodus of banks from the system and left a remaining

risk pool of banks that were uninsurable. When the guaranty law was repealed in 1929, depositors of 88 failed banks were left with nothing.

Given its well-understood bad record at the state level, how did deposit insurance get passed at the national level in 1933? Take a moment to anticipate the answer: recall the Incentive Principle about how government intervention tempts people to benefit themselves at others' expense and what we said in Chapter 7 about the special interest effect. What special interest group might benefit from government-provided deposit insurance?

Federal deposit insurance, as originally passed, was supposed to be a temporary, emergency measure. It was promoted by Senator Henry Steagall of Alabama, a state whose many small banks were politically powerful. Recall that, at the outset, the maximum amount insured by FDIC was quite small, only $2,500; this is a significant clue. What interest group would benefit from insurance on such comparatively small amounts? It would be less important to larger banks whose clients typically had much larger sums on deposit. But to smaller banks with many smaller depositors, this insurance was particularly useful, because it *shielded small banks from having to compete* with larger banks on the basis of safety. No bigger bank, say, from Birmingham or Montgomery, could take customers away from a small Alabama bank by claiming, "Your money is safer with us," because your money—up to the $2,500 insured by the federal government—*was* just as safe in the small, local bank.

Federal deposit insurance in the U.S. began, as so much intervention does, as special interest legislation. It aimed at benefiting small banks by eliminating some of the competition they would otherwise have had to face. As frequently happens, the "temporary" intervention became permanent and the amounts insured rose steadily. To protect taxpayers, bank regulations such as the Basel rules were imposed, and these interventions triggered their own ill consequences as we have seen.

The Federal Savings and Loan Insurance Corporation (FSLIC), FDIC's sister organization which insured depositors in savings and loan associations, collapsed dramatically in the 1980s. FSLIC not only failed to protect depositors but also had the effect of encouraging risky business. Covering the deposits it insured required over $25 billion of taxpayer money on top of special assessments on healthy insured banks. The luridly colorful tale includes accounts of politicians obtaining "regulatory forbearance" for banks that supported them politically, and "zombie" S&L's—banks already deeply insolvent but not yet closed by the understaffed FSLIC—losing hundreds of millions of additional dollars on go-for-broke investment gambles. They were gambling with depositors' money, of course, but the depositors were insured, so they paid little attention. In consequence, resources were misallocated badly and taxpayers paid dearly.

How much simpler, cleaner, more effective and adaptive would the regulation of banking be were market forces the regulator? We can't be certain, of course, but there is much reason to believe it would be far better.

## The Need for Regulation by Market Forces

Government regulatory agencies face no market competition; they cannot be driven out of existence by failure to attract repeat business when they do a bad job. The rules they propose for regulating business behavior cannot be refused by enterprises that prefer to do business according to other rules. The revenue stream of government regulators is captive: It originates not in satisfied clients in repeated dealings day after day, but in taxpayers' surrender of their property to the IRS every April 15th. Government regulatory agencies can botch their jobs—as the Basel Committee surely has done—they can implement restrictions that hamper enterprises' ability to create value for customers, and yet stay in business year after year. There is no process in government regulation for getting rid of a bad regulator, or for rejecting bad regulations.

What governmental regulatory agencies are attempting to do is central economic planning. It differs from Soviet central planning only in its extent, not in its nature. Whereas Soviet attempts to plan the entire economy prevented improvement in the standard of living of the Soviet people, the U.S. government's partial planning of sectors of the economy merely slows down improvement of Americans' standard of living. The damage to economic well-being is proportional to the extent of the top-down planning attempted.

And that brings us back to the fundamental reason for relying on regulation by market forces that we discussed in Chapter 6: In a world of pervasive uncertainty and frequent human error, society has no better way of discovering what standards and practices best protect the public health and safety—in this case financial safety—than entrepreneurial innovation and profit-and-loss selection *of those standards and practices*. We need a market process through which a variety of different regulatory approaches is tried out, with those that perform better being increasingly used, and those that perform worse being abandoned.

The decisive advantage of regulation by market forces over regulation by legislative restriction is that regulation by market forces fosters continuous experimentation and adaptation, *informed by success and failure in accomplishing its purposes*. Banks that manage their capital poorly in a free market will tend to make losses; banks that manage it well will tend to make profits. Through profit-and-loss selection, beneficial regulation spreads and useless or counter-productive regulation dies out.

The best we can do is to let banks and associations of banks regulate themselves on a contractual, consensual basis, aiming not at the high social goal of good systemic performance, but at the humble individual goal of creating value for their customers and thereby profiting as much as possible. Good systemic performance will emerge spontaneously from the choices free banks and free customers make under such general rules. The system and its results will not be perfect because human beings are so imperfect, but they will be the best achievable.

It is easy for me to assert that, but how might it work in practice?

## How Regulation of Bank Capital by Free Market Forces Might Work

In the absence of taxpayer-funded deposit insurance and one-size-fits-all bank capital regulation, we would have ... who knows what, but lots of innovation through which banking would evolve. We could expect the emergence of robust methods of making sure depositors don't lose their money. It's impossible to say what would evolve—one of the beauties of innovation is how often it surprises us with goods and services far better than we could have imagined—but let's speculate.

One possibility is private deposit insurance. Depositors and/or their banks would have to pay for it themselves rather than pass the expense on to others through the FDIC. George Selgin writes:

> Such insurance, provided on a competitive basis, would have a distinct advantage over present government-administered insurance. Government insurance assesses individual banks using a flat-rate schedule, charging them only according to their total deposits. This procedure subsidizes high-risk banks at the expense of low-risk ones.... In contrast, profit-maximizing, competing private insurers would attempt to charge every bank a premium reflecting the riskiness of its particular assets.

Some banks might contract with individual insurance companies; others might work with several at once, offering their depositors a choice of plans. Banks might also offer their depositors the option of going with no deposit insurance in exchange for slightly lower fees or higher interest rates on their deposits. Banks would probably advertise the benefits of their insurance options.

Unlike today, this would be real insurance: it would be a contract between insurer and insured, with freedom to exit on both sides. That freedom assures that each side is creating value for the other. By contrast, banks today are not permitted to decline the "insurance" by the FDIC, which assesses banks' "premiums" based not on the quantity of deposits insured, but on the bank's total assets. By this means virtually all bank customers are forced to pay for FDIC, including those with no deposits and those with deposits over the insurable maximum. The fees charged by FDIC are better understood not as premiums but as a tax.

There are various other ways of providing depositors with assurance that their deposits are safe, some of them probably better than deposit insurance as such. One such way is extended liability. In various times and places, bank shareholders have accepted double, triple, or even unlimited liability for the bank's obligations. That means that a shareholder who had invested, say, $1000 in a bank would agree to be personally liable for $2000 or $3000 worth of bank obligations, or any amount the bank owed. Similarly, some banks' by-laws have obliged shareholders to respond to calls for additional capital, if necessary. In these cases the wealthy individuals who own the banks in effect insure deposits out of their own property.

In other cases, notably in the bank panics of the late 19th and early 20th centuries in the U.S., sound banks have assured the public of the safety of their deposits and thereby headed off possible runs by publishing their balance sheets in the newspapers. This disclosure of the details of their assets and liabilities gave depositors the confidence they needed.

A promising kind of private deposit insurance is a system of cross-guarantees among a large number of banks. The group of banks would collectively insure the obligations of each member, so that, in effect, each bank's obligations are backed by the capital of all. Such a policy would provide strong motivation for all the banks in the insurance pool to monitor one another's solvency and banking practices. The group would almost certainly set rigorous capital requirements and require regular inspection of member banks to identify any problems before they grow large. Any bank that should fail inspection would run the risk of suspension or expulsion from the group; *that* would give it a strong incentive to behave prudently.

In a free banking system, clearinghouse associations would be natural groups for cross-guaranteeing deposits. According to George Selgin, the discipline on bank soundness exerted through clearinghouses historically was so strong that other ways of assuring the safety of deposits, such as extended liability, were neither necessary nor even particularly significant as a check on banks' risk-taking.

Undoubtedly banks would fail on occasion. Failures would not usually mean losses for depositors, however, either because a rival bank takes over the failed bank's assets and liabilities or because of the kinds of insurance we have been discussing. Surviving banks and their insurance companies or clearinghouse association partners would study the causes of those failures and make changes to their business practices accordingly. Then those new practices would be put to the market test. Unlike in today's one-size-fits-all regulation by a centralized bureaucracy, we would see various competing systems of regulation generated and tested by actions of many market participants as the industry evolves.

In such a setting, whoever is on the hook for deposits—the insurance companies, the depositors themselves if they choose to go uninsured, the shareholders with extended liability, or the sister banks in a cross-guarantee pool—would have a strong incentive to monitor the capital adequacy and risk levels of the banks that hold the deposits ... or pay someone else to monitor them.

I would not expect depositors to do much monitoring; I certainly wouldn't monitor my bank. Like most people, I don't have the time or knowledge required. But most of us also don't have the time and knowledge to evaluate the fire resistance of the insulation in our homes or the competence of our auto mechanics. We pay Underwriters Laboratories (UL) and The National Institute for Automotive Service Excellence (ASE) to certify them for us. Or rather, we pay manufacturers and service stations a bit more for the certifications they provide us, and they pay UL and ASE to do the certifying.

Similar kinds of certification (or something better not imagined yet) would evolve in a free market for banking and financial services. Many depositors would be willing to pay a bit more, or give more business, to banks that offered trusted third-party certification of their safety and soundness. Insurance companies would offer better rates to certified banks, so banks would pay for that certification. Cross-guarantee pools and clearinghouse associations might hire bank-examination specialists to conduct regular examinations in order to assure the public, and themselves, of their members' soundness. One way or the other, unlike today, banks would have to compete on safety and soundness.

We can imagine the emergence of enterprises analogous to Underwriters Laboratories that would specialize in monitoring, inspecting, and certifying banks. We can imagine an evolution of best practices and standards that insurance companies or bank associations would routinely impose on their clients or members as a condition of receiving insurance or association membership.

We can imagine most depositors being unwilling to deal with banks that do not meet the standards that gain acceptance over time. In short, we can imagine a dynamic system of private, contractual, market-based regulation of bank capital and risk.

# Part III

# Conclusion

The housing boom and bust and financial turmoil could not have been a consequence of free markets because we don't have free markets. The U.S. government has been intervening long and heavily in mortgage markets, money, and banking. These interventions caused the problems.

In order to protect ourselves from future booms, busts, and financial turmoil, we need to repeal those interventions and free those markets. We need to let our economy order itself spontaneously, with free market prices coordinating everyone's different actions, profit and loss guiding entrepreneurial innovation, and free market incentives motivating everyone to try to benefit others.

What should housing-finance policy be in a free society? It should be to let markets work. Leave housing finance to the free choices of individuals interacting voluntarily with one another.

The special treatment of housing in the Taxpayer Relief Act should be eliminated; all capital gains should be taxed at the same rate: zero percent.

Fannie Mae and Freddie Mac should be wound down and eliminated. Their very existence creates a dangerous incentive for politicians to seek votes by funneling into housing resources that would be better used elsewhere. As for Congress's guarantees of loans to Fannie and Freddie, legislative bodies should have no authority to guarantee some people's investments with other people's money. The actual performance of investments in creating value should determine how well they pay off, if at all.

But what about helping low-income people find more affordable housing? This admirable goal is best pursued through private enterprises and voluntary associations, not through the coercive powers of government.

What should money policy be in a free society? It should be free banking—non-intervention in money. The Fed should be retired, shut down. The kinds and quantities of money used should be determined by entrepreneurial innovation and profit-and-loss feedback in an unhampered market. Interest rates, like other prices, should be determined by the free play of market forces.

How might we make the transition from central banking with fiat money to free banking and free-market money? That's a fascinating, challenging question; others have offered pathways to get there (see the end notes for references). For our purposes, what is essential is that excessive money creation helped fuel the feverish overinvestment in housing, and excessive money creation is possible only when governments control the supply of money. Had the money supply been regulated by market forces, one major cause of the housing boom and financial mess would have been eliminated. Free banking and market-determined money is the ideal toward which we should shape our course.

What about lenders who make bad investments? Governments should have nothing whatever to do with them apart from enforcing contracts and punishing fraud. What I said above with respect to lenders to Fannie Mae and Freddie Mac goes just the same for lenders to big investment banks: legislative bodies should have no authority to guarantee some people's investments with other people's money. Such authority distorts the price of risk and blocks the profit-and-loss feedback on which improvements in well-being depend. Expectations of rescue distort incentives. And allowing government the power to give taxpayers' money to particular investors is a pernicious temptation to politicians to advance their careers by doing favors with other people's property.

Likewise, the government should never bail out bank depositors. The FDIC should be retired, and deposit insurance should be taken over by private insurance companies and/or by other arrangements banks might make to persuade depositors that their deposits are safe.

Of course any private individuals, institutions, or companies that want to rescue creditors or depositors should be free to do so with their own funds.

How should bank capital and banking and financial services be regulated? Efforts in Washington and Basel to *design* new and better systems of financial and capital regulation are futile. The would-be architects of a system that *this time* will get it right literally do not know what they are doing. They do not understand "how little they really know about what they imagine they can design."

The well-meaning bureaucrats in the alphabet soup of financial regulatory bodies cannot know for sure, before the fact, what principles of deposit insurance and bank capital management will create value any better than H.M. Warner knew that nobody wanted to hear actors talk, or Michael Dell knew that Apple Computer should be shut down, or the leadership at Motorola knew that the future of telecommunications was satellite phones. They were all mistaken; they were ignorant. We all are. That's why it's dangerous to give anybody the power to coerce.

The best we can do is to let the relentless discipline of consumers' decisions, transmitted via profit and loss, regulate banks and other financial institutions. Good systemic performance will come about not top-down by intentional design, but bottom-up as the unintended consequence of individual banks seeking to profit by creating value for customers. This dynamic market process cannot be perfect because those engaged in it are so ignorant and prone to mistakes. But the *process* tends to overcome that ignorance, punish the mistakes, and reward those who do create value.

Free-market discipline is the best regulator of financial services. It is an imperfect regulator, to be sure, but it is the least imperfect regulator available.

The lessons we learn from this one case study of one slice of our economy over one period in time can be generalized. The three principles of spontaneous economic order provide a lens for looking into all sectors of our economy to find the truth about how to advance well-being for all. In the concluding chapter we apply the three principles to a sector of economy that is near and dear to my heart: the education of the young.

# Chapter Thirteen

# Hope for the Future

I learned first-hand the importance *to the poor* of freeing our schooling markets over the ten years I served as chairman of the board of Children's Scholarship Fund Baltimore. CSF Baltimore is one of about thirty partner organizations across the country offering privately funded, partial scholarships to low-income children for kindergarten through eighth grade, to help them pay tuition at non-government schools. Since its founding in 1998, Children's Scholarship Fund partners have provided scholarships of nearly $500 million to some 125,000 students. In my home town, CSF Baltimore has provided almost $10,000,000 in scholarships to 6,166 students over that time.

CSF Baltimore grants only partial scholarships, covering 25, 50, or 75 percent of a child's tuition up to a maximum scholarship of $2,000, depending on the family's income. Parents must pay the remaining tuition, a minimum of $500 per child. When families apply for the program, they are put on a waiting list that consistently holds about two thousand families.

Then, as funding becomes available, families are selected at random. Parents choose the schools, apply, and make sure their children meet any admission requirements. Admission is by families: if one sibling wins a scholarship, all do, including younger siblings just reaching school age. Children may attend any legally operating school anywhere, but the great majority of our families choose relatively inexpensive private and/or parochial schools in and around their home neighborhoods.

There are around two hundred such schools in the Baltimore area—Bethlehem Christian Day School, Calvary Lutheran School, Community Initiatives Academy, St. Agnes School, School of Original Thought, St. Joseph School, Bais Yaakov School for Girls, Kingdom Academy, The Unselds' School, and scores of others. CSF Baltimore has been awarding on average around $1 million in scholarships each year. In the 2012-2013 academic year, CSF Baltimore supported two hundred thirty students at forty-seven schools. The average scholarship was $1,823; the median tuition per child was $6,400. The average family contribution per child was $3,360, out of an average family income of $32,918.

My strongest memory of my work with CSF Baltimore is of one night in the auditorium of Immanuel Lutheran School, at a meeting of families who had just won the selection lottery for the following year's new scholarships. They had come to learn about their responsibilities in the program. These included documenting their income, selecting a non-government school for their child, applying and getting their child accepted, and keeping up with payments of their portion of the child's tuition.

About two hundred parents and grandparents were there that night. My job was to explain the various aspects of the program. While I was explaining how the dollar amount of the scholarships is determined, I emphasized that in all cases families are required to pay a minimum of $500 per year per child to be eligible for a scholarship. (They are not allowed, in other words, to combine CSF Baltimore's scholarship with other scholarship support to bring the total they have to pay below $500.) I had felt some concern about making this point, fearing that some people might think us stingy. But when I told them that the founders of the program believed it was important for each family to have meaningful financial responsibility for their children's education, all around that large room heads slowly nodded; all those serious, carefully listening faces showed no trace of resentment, but agreement and support.

At that moment, and every time I have thought of it since, anger flares in me at the broken system these parents were trying to escape. The Baltimore city and Maryland state governments tax residents and businesses enough to spend more than $14,000 per child in the Baltimore City Public Schools—far more than the tuition charged by nearly all the schools CSF Baltimore students attend, and more than double the tuition of most. Yet the schooling the city system offers is generally so poor that these parents are eager to pay again out of their modest incomes to put their children into better, safer schools. The excitement and profound gratitude the parents often express is moving. The waste of taxpayers' money in the Baltimore City Public Schools is infuriating.

I learned two clear lessons from my work with Children's Scholarship Fund Baltimore. One is that I dislike raising money. The other is that the poor have far more to gain from free market schooling than do well-off people like me.

But it's not just low-income families who are getting a lousy deal. Many government schools in upper-income areas are mediocre at best. Every term I'm shocked once again at the proportion of my students at Towson University, from supposedly good government schools, who don't write correctly. They write sentence fragments, use inappropriate words, punctuate confusingly, shift tenses, misplace modifiers, and often just don't write down what they mean. They have not been instructed well.

And taxpayers are paying more and more for this mediocrity. Nationwide, over the past three decades, as inflation-adjusted per pupil spending has doubled, student performance by most measures hasn't improved at all.

What is wrong with American schooling?

American schooling is poor because it is centrally planned by government rather than spontaneously ordered in free markets. It lacks the necessary foundations of healthy economic order: free-market prices, profit-and-loss selection, and the incentives of private ownership and free exchange. Schools attended by most American children are government owned, so we don't have profit-and-loss feedback to guide discovery of better methods. Schools that create value are not rewarded; those that destroy value are not punished. Without that feedback to guide innovation, schooling stagnates.

There is little freedom of exchange between American parents and schools; most parents surrender their taxes and send their kids where they are assigned. If a parent would prefer to have her child in a school run by one of the charter school companies beginning to operate across the country, she can't just switch; she and other parents must go through the slow, political process of persuading the school board to authorize the charter school company to open another school. Thus school performance and school funding are almost totally disconnected. Regulation of schools is by legislation and bureaucracy. That regulation has been largely captured by the teachers' unions and administrative bureaucracies who use government schools as a jobs program. (I do not blame the teachers themselves, many of whom are excellent, heroic, and very poorly served by the system.)

Reformers in various regions are trying to improve education *within the system of state control* by means of charter schools. Charter schools are tax-funded schools that are in various degrees independent of the school system, including, importantly, being free to hire (and fire) non-union teachers. Progress via charter schools is slow and uncertain, however, because the teachers' unions and school system bureaucracies oppose them politically and make it difficult for new charter schools to open.

Let us close *Free Our Markets* with one last thought experiment about education based on the principles of spontaneous economic order we have been considering: creative destruction in a totally free market. Suppose all schools were privately owned, and thus subject to profit-and-loss selection. Suppose parents and schools were free to exchange tuition money for schooling on terms they see fit. Suppose educational entrepreneurs stood to make significant profits when they find better, cheaper ways to help children succeed. What then?

What might spontaneously ordered schooling look like? Who might own schools? What entrepreneurial innovations might we see in organization, in teaching methods, and in curriculum? Who would decide on the curriculum? How might market forces regulate school quality? Would it be affordable? Even to poor families?

We can't know, of course, but let's speculate.

We concede at the outset that free market education would not be perfect—nothing human is perfect. But we'll find good reasons to believe that the principles of spontaneous economic order apply to education, and that education ordered from the bottom up would far outperform the top-down government schooling of today.

## What Needs to Happen: Parents Decide Where the Money Gets Spent

The essential reform is to let parents, not bureaucrats, decide where tuition dollars get spent. Here's a simple way to think about how this could happen. It's not what I recommend—that's coming in a moment—it's just a simple way to start to think about it: Take all the tax money that now goes to the country's government schools. Instead of giving it to school boards to allot to all the district schools, good or bad, give it to the parents. Divide the money up into equal shares for the children in each grade, and *let the parents spend it on any school they choose*, anywhere in the area, or the world, for that matter. THEN the schools would have to perform. If they didn't, parents would take their children and their money elsewhere. Just like other businesses—and churches and charities and clubs—schools would have to perform well or close. Again: parents, not bureaucrats, must decide where the tuition dollars get spent.

Now one step further—and this *is* what I recommend: Cut out the government middleman. Repeal all the taxes now raised for schooling, and leave it to parents to pay for their children's schooling themselves, as they pay for their children's food and clothing. Parents are paying for schooling now through their taxes; take the tax collectors and school bureaucracies out of the loop. Let parents deal directly with schools. Separate school and state, in the same manner—and for many of the same reasons—we separate church and state. Religion is too important to be in the hands of politicians. We don't let government provide churches, synagogues, or mosques; we don't let it pay the salaries of clerics, or decide the nature of worship. We leave religion entirely to the private sector, and religion thrives, in poor areas as well as rich. We should treat schooling the same.

I want to acknowledge the concerns of my readers who are anxious for families too poor to pay for adequate schooling with their own resources, or even with help from others in the private sector. I don't believe there would be any such families because there are so many voluntary ways in which schooling for the poor might be paid for, some of which we'll explore later in this chapter. But for those worried that the poor would not get schooling in a free market, I suggest thinking in terms of a part-way measure: complete free markets in schooling, except using tax money to provide "school stamps" for those who otherwise would not be able to go to school. Like food stamps, which can be spent at any business that sells groceries, "school stamps" (the common term for which is "school vouchers") could be spent at any legally operating school, on school supplies, on courses online, and the like.

Providing food to poor people at government-run food dispensaries would be absurd. Government food-supply bureaucracies would be inefficient and expensive. The public would constantly protest about the poor quality of the food, and taxpayers would complain about its high cost.

It makes much more sense, if the government is to concern itself at all with getting poor people fed, to give them food stamps and let them spend those at ShopRite, Safeway, Kroger's and Walmart—stores that have to compete with one another on price, quality, variety of foods offered, location, etc. The government helps the poor *pay* for their food, but it leaves food *provision* to private enterprise.

Providing schooling to poor people—and everyone else—at government-run schools is equally foolish. The government school bureaucracies are inefficient and expensive, and they offer schooling that is mostly mediocre to lousy. If the poor had "school stamps" to spend, schools would have to compete with one another on price, quality, variety of instruction offered, location, and you name it.

## How to Make the Change

How might we make the change from our current system, in which some eighty-eight percent of American children go to education dispensaries owned and run by government, to a free market in schooling, in which every family chooses its entrepreneurial education providers?

Freeing our schooling markets would be as simple on the government end as it would be wild and unpredictable on the entrepreneurial end. All a government would need to do—and state or district level governments could take the initiative—is to repeal the taxes that pay for schooling and to auction off government school property: buildings, land, books, desks, computers, chalk, maps—the works. The state or locality might announce that:

1. effective immediately, the state or locality will begin to take bids on the school system's land, buildings, and other property;

2. effective at the end of the next complete school year, the land, the buildings, and other school property will be sold to the highest bidders; and

3. effective at the end of the next complete school year, all the taxes that pay for schooling will be repealed.

A full school year's lead time would probably be necessary to allow the private sector to make plans, arrange financing, etc. At the end of that school year, on the effective date of the tax repeal, payment for all school property would be due from the high bidders, and that state or locality would be out of the schooling business. From then on it would be up to parents to make sure their children's education is paid for.

What gales of creative destruction would blow across that region's educational landscape! What innovations we'd see in organization, curriculum, and teaching techniques! What new kinds of schools would emerge! What cost savings would be discovered!

What would schooling—what would education—come to look like? We can't possibly know until real entrepreneurs are set free to innovate, and parents are set free to reward some with profit and punish others with loss, but let's speculate.

## Then What? Who Might Own and Operate Schools?

Who might want to buy government school buildings and land? Who might want to run schools? Please consider the questions for a while before reading on.

I foresee property management companies and real estate investment trusts buying many of the government schools' land and buildings. I would expect them immediately to turn around and rent back most of the space to education providers of various kinds.

In particular, I imagine groups of the really good teachers in today's really bad government schools gathering in joyful relief and hope and excitement, thinking, "NOW, we'll be able to teach the way we've always wanted to!" I imagine teachers joining together, laying plans to lease a wing of their current building, and organizing a school of their own, free of union rules, burnt-out colleagues, impertinent bureaucracy, endless testing, and the like. I imagine them eagerly contacting the parents of their current students, urging them to sign up to come back to the same building and even the same classrooms in the fall, to a much better, new school there.

I have already mentioned that in and around my home town of Baltimore there are some two hundred small independent schools, many of them connected with local churches and synagogues. Once they and others like them were free from competition from tax-funded schools, they would have the incentive to expand. Money that interested parents once had to pay in taxes could go to pay private school tuitions. Many of these independent schools might expand right into the buildings that used to house the government schools they would replace.

No longer needing the permission of a regional board of education to open a new school, many organizations now running charter schools, such as Green Dot, KIPP (Knowledge Is Power Program), and Aspira, would likely set up new schools of their own brands. All they would need is the willingness of enough parents to give them a try.

Parent groups might take the initiative in organizing schools, much as they now organize charter schools: hiring teachers and a principal they know and trust, leasing space (again, probably in a formerly government-school building), laying out a curriculum, and eagerly taking control of their children's education.

In a true free market for schooling, a wide variety of new schools might just happen. A young woman providing day care for small children, for instance, might discover the joy of teaching them, and do it well enough that the children's parents ask her to keep the children for a kindergarten year. She does so and teaches the children to read and do basic arithmetic; other parents learn of her good results and ask her to teach their children, too, so she hires a colleague to help her, looks for some larger space, and a new elementary school is born.

Similarly, groups of home-schooling parents, who even in the present day organize themselves into cooperatives, might actually evolve into schools, perhaps just focused on subjects that are learned best in groups, and meeting maybe only two or three times a week.

Ethnic or immigrant groups might establish schools to smooth the adjustment of immigrants to their new homes, or to preserve their home country's culture and language.

Universities might set up schools, in part as a service to their communities, and in part as teaching labs to give university students the experience and satisfaction of teaching the subjects they are studying.

Museums might set up schools designed to make intensive use of the museums' educational resources.

More schools for children with special needs would probably arise, and possibly companies dedicated to creating and running schools for special-needs children.

Large education corporations, such as Sylvan Learning, might invest in running schools. To make the transition as smooth as possible, they might contract with selected teachers and principals in the year or so before privatization in order to be staffed when the schools go private.

Large companies with a lot of employees might sponsor schools or even provide schools on site so that parents could be near their kids and not have to worry about leaving work to pick them up. Of course we wouldn't expect companies making, say, fuel injectors or smoke alarms to set up their own schools—they don't have the skills or expertise to do so. No, they would probably contract with schooling companies that specialize in setting up little schools on corporation grounds. Done well, it would be a valued fringe benefit, attracting employees with children.

Other companies might set up and financially support trade schools that teach not only basic subjects and skills, but also the specialized skills they need in their industry.

Entirely new ventures would likely arise, including companies running chains of for-profit schools. One such company, Kunskapsskolan, was started in Sweden after that country went to a universal voucher system. (All taxes raised for schooling in Sweden now go not to schools but to parents in the form of a voucher, what I have called school stamps. Parents in Sweden now choose their children's schools; schools in Sweden now compete for students.) The company has been very successful, growing to thirty-four schools in Sweden and licensing its program to three schools in the United Kingdom and now one charter school in Manhattan. Its first school in India is scheduled to open next year.

Maybe education companies would evolve that specialize in delivering particular subjects at many different schools. A school might contract out, say, its science or art instruction to an education company that specializes in science and art. Perhaps language immersion schools might arise in which all (or most) subjects are taught in the foreign language.

If this kind of arrangement should prove efficient, children would in effect attend more than one school at the same site, learning different subjects from different education companies. For example, a child might get her reading and writing from a traditional teacher in a traditional classroom, her music instruction from a special arts school located in her same building, and science instruction from an online academy with which her local school has a contract.

What about the huge number of *good* government schools? The residents of the region might buy and own the school system, reconstituted as a non-profit corporation, much as those residents had "owned" it before in their role as taxpayers. We would expect them to continue on very much as at present, at least initially, with the same teachers, buildings, and administration. As long as those schools could attract funding through tuition and donations they could continue to operate.

Indeed, to an extent that is impossible now while they are subject to the political process, really outstanding school systems might expand as private-sector, non-profit entities. But if too many parents preferred the new educational offerings that emerge from competition, like any other enterprise, these schools would have to adjust, improve, or go out of business. We would expect them to adjust pretty quickly in a lot of small ways and a few big ones as they discovered their relative strengths and weaknesses and sought out ways to teach children more effectively and at lower cost, responding to their new competition and the need to earn student enrollments.

Again, it's impossible to know what forms of school ownership and management would emerge and last (for a while, at least) in a free market. It would be fascinating to watch the evolution.

## Unleashing Innovation in Teaching and Learning

What about curriculum and teaching techniques? An on-going tragedy of our current, government-owned, centrally planned schools is their of lack of innovation in teaching. Surely there must be much to discover about better teaching and learning, especially making use of the fantastic information technologies that have emerged in recent years.

For example, we might expect some schooling company to arise that offers much more individualized education than the standard classroom approach where all the kids work on math at the same time, then they all work on science, then history, with every student in every class studying the same material in the same place at the same time. Different children learn differently; they have different strengths and weaknesses, different aptitudes and rates of development, different interests at different times in their lives. Couldn't schooling be customized to each child's own aptitudes and interests, allowing her to proceed at her own pace and to some degree in her own way, using the latest information and communications technologies?

We can imagine a kind of school in which each child has personal goals and a learning plan, worked out in advance with the help of skilled instructors. Teachers at such a school might serve not just as instructors in a subject, but also as learning coaches with responsibility for overseeing the progress of particular students toward their individual goals. In weekly meetings with a personal teacher-coach, each student would be guided to make steady progress toward achieving her goals. She would proceed at her own pace, going on when she had mastered a subject but not before. She might lay out her weekly timetable in her individual logbook with her teacher coach each week, after reviewing her accomplishments of the previous week.

At such a school, with today's information technology, a lot of the work that students can do individually might be kept on a web-based "learning portal" where "students [could] find most of the learning material...: the courses, the content, objectives and criteria for every step, assignments, texts, pictures, links and tests." If a school were to use a web-based system such as this, the line between homework and schoolwork would be blurred or erased. A student would "have work to do, and [she could] get it done in school, at home or anywhere there is an internet connection."

Would such an individualized approach to schooling work well? Could it be provided cost-effectively? If so, would parents choose it for the children? Actually we don't need to speculate because such an approach is working well in practice right now. The Swedish company Kunskapsskolan mentioned above has been developing this individualized approach since 2000. The quotations in the last few paragraphs are taken from their website.

An intriguing characteristic of Kunskapsskolan's approach is the way it combines personalized schooling for each student with standardized, best-practice lessons. Their website explains that their (trademarked) "Learning Portal" "contains all the best material, developed by all the best teachers" in their network. The Learning Portal, accessible on the web to all schools in the network—from Manhattan to India—"assures students, families, and society that what is learned is not solely a function of an individual teacher." Making their best practices available throughout their network of schools also keeps costs down and increases the individual attention that teachers can give their students. As their website explains,

> [E]very minute saved for a teacher who doesn't have to prepare a lesson that has already been developed by colleagues is a minute that could be spent on personal coaching instead of preparation. That is one of the reasons why it is possible for [Kunskapsskolan] schools to provide more personal coaching time with the same staff resources as a conventional school.

Like for-profit businesses in other fields, Kunskapsskolan invests in on-going research and development aimed at continuously improving its product and lowering its costs. Their Learning Portal "is under continuous development and review as teachers contribute with new material and experiences."

Even the architecture of Kunskapsskolan schools is consciously aimed at facilitating learning: the layout is open and airy; there are spaces of different sizes for different purposes; glass walls provide both privacy and supervision; computer workstations here and there around the building give students many places to get their work done.

Kunskapsskolan is compelling evidence of the kind of ingenuity that would be applied to schooling—no, let us say *will* be applied to schooling—as we increasingly free our markets in education. Impressive as it is, Kunskapsskolan is just one relatively small enterprise, started by one entrepreneur in only the first major country to let its parents decide where their children's education money will be spent. (Sweden instituted vouchers for all in 1992; Kunskapsskolan opened its first school eight years later.)

Imagine how much more ingenuity would pour into education, how many other innovations in curriculum and educational technology would be tried if a large country such as the U.S. were to free its schooling markets, so that every square inch of American schooling were open to entrepreneurial innovation. It would be magnificent.

Consider one other curriculum innovation, also based on our remarkable advances in technology, this one based in the US. In 2009, Salman Khan, an MIT graduate with degrees in math and computer science and an MBA from Harvard, offered to help his niece with her math homework over the internet, using software with which he could talk to her and let her see on her computer the graphs and calculations he drew up on his own. When they were unable to find the time to work together simultaneously, he recorded instruction for her in a file that showed her his equations and graphs as he drew them, with his voice explaining what he was doing. It was not long before his niece told him she preferred the recorded lessons because she could replay portions at will when she didn't fully understand the first time through.

Khan had a flash of entrepreneurial insight. He could make such lessons available not just to his niece, but to anyone with an internet connection. Khan Academy was born.

Khan Academy's virtuosic use of information technology makes it possible for teachers to "flip" class work and homework. This means letting children watch "lectures" and other presentations of content at home instead of in class, and then, in class, apply and develop what they have learned, working problems and practicing where the teacher can help them. Students are set free to work at their own pace and receive more individualized attention from their teachers.

If this is the first you have heard of Khan Academy, look at its website; it is astonishing. Founded in 2009 as a web-based, non-profit enterprise, Khan Academy aims "[to change] education for the better by providing a free world-class education to anyone anywhere."

All of the site's resources are available to anyone. It doesn't matter if you are a student, teacher, home-schooler, principal, adult returning to the classroom after 20 years, or a friendly alien just trying to get a leg up in earthly biology. The Khan Academy's materials and resources are available to you completely free of charge.

They declare that their mission is "to help you learn what you want, when you want, at your own pace." The rapidly growing company invites us to:

Watch. Practice.
Learn almost anything for free.

Khan Academy makes this approach to learning possible by offering literally thousands of short (eight to fourteen minute) video lessons available on its website, initially in math, but now in science, finance and economics, and history also. The site's software also generates practice questions and problems on which students can practice hundreds of skills. As of this writing, new content is going up constantly.

With this technology, teachers don't have the problem (painfully familiar in my own teaching) of deciding how to pitch a presentation to a class with a wide range of ability and current understanding. If it is not so fast as to leave behind the slowest learners, a presentation is likely to be so slow as to bore the fast learners; generally we have to pitch it at the middle, losing both the fast and slow learners to some degree. But with the kinds of individualized learning tools offered by Khan Academy and Kunskapsskolan's Learning Portal, students can race ahead on what they find easy or take extra time to master a difficult concept, with the teacher free to answer questions and explain concepts for each student wherever she is in her learning.

Suppose "flipping" class work and homework is a great idea, at least for certain subjects. We can't know for sure that it is until it has been tried out in enough schools for enough years, but suppose it should turn out to be a terrific approach for most children in certain subjects. If so, how long will it take to spread in our current government-run school system? I fear that it would spread only to the most innovative teachers and schools, then tail off and stop spreading. It would never reach schools where it would be most valuable. Why? Because government schools don't have market forces regulating them; they don't have creative destruction driving them to innovate or close down. Would an average American school district support having, say, some of their fourth graders learning "fourth grade math" while others race ahead to math traditionally taught in fifth, sixth, or ninth grades? Or would that kind of disruption to established practice be blocked? I fear that no matter how good the idea turns out to be, most government schools will continue to keep class work as class work and homework as homework in the same old, familiar way.

If "flipping" homework and class work should turn out in fact to be a great idea, we need the discipline of unhampered market forces to drive its adoption throughout our schools. In a free market for schooling, as the innovation shows itself to work well, more and more schools will embrace it or lose students to those that do.

It has taken Kunskapsskolan only twelve years to offer its personalized approach in thirty-three schools in Sweden. Why so fast? Because parents are free to take their tuition money wherever they choose. No bureaucracy needs to be persuaded to adopt the personalized approach. Schools determined to teach in the old way are free do to so; they just start to lose students if the old way is not as good. And Kunskapsskolan's and Khan Academy's approaches are surely not the last word in educational innovation. Indeed, they are just early applications of modern information technology in education. What other splendid innovations might be developed by free educational entrepreneurs? We can't possibly know. We must free our education markets to find out. The results are likely to be far more impressive than we can foresee.

## Who Would Determine What is Taught?

Should sex education be taught or not? If so, should the children be instructed in birth control techniques or taught to abstain from sex until marriage? Or both? Should creationism and the theory of evolution be taught as equally valid theories? Or is creationism not science? How about reading instruction? Should children learning to read be taught intensive phonics, learning to sound out words? Or should they be taught by the whole word, look-and-say method? And in mathematics, should schools use the "new math" or the old math? Or something else?

Who should answer such questions? How should we decide what goes into our schools' curricula, what topics should be emphasized, and how they should be taught?

A common argument for government schooling is that, in common schools, we all learn a body of knowledge and a set of values common to all Americans; it is believed that this shared education holds us together. Without a common curriculum shared by all, it is feared, we would splinter into separate, isolated groups, each teaching its own ideas and values. Free-market schooling, it is believed, would divide us, while government schools unify us.

The argument is false on a number of counts. First, as the questions above make clear, we do *not* all share a body of knowledge and set of values. Second, the necessity for government schools to decide what to teach *to all*, regardless of parents' values and beliefs, itself divides us. When, for example, the schools that we all pay for must decide whether to teach creationism or not, those with strongly held beliefs on different sides of the question battle with one another in the school board meetings to get their beliefs taught.

One of the great strengths of free market education would be to depoliticize these questions. What is taught and how would be decided jointly by many different schools and parents who would choose one another, in part according to shared beliefs and values. We would expect that those who establish schools in different areas, whether educational entrepreneurs, groups of parents, or religious institutions, would be sensitive to the beliefs and values of the parents in that area. Instead of having tough questions of what is to be taught decided centrally for all, they would be decided in different ways for different groups. No group would have to worry about having others' values imposed on them. Hebrew schools and evangelical Christian schools and totally non-religious schools could coexist harmoniously in the same neighborhoods, the different parents mingling amicably in the afternoons as their children play together on the same recreational-league teams.

As for questions of instructional technique, such as the relative merits of intensive phonics *versus* the look-and-say method in reading instruction, or "new math" *versus* old math, and the many other such questions that will arise, our best approach is not to let experts dictate to an entire state school system. The market-based solution is to let the different techniques compete for parents' favor on the basis of their actual results. Experts disagree, and they make mistakes. When experts who turn out to be mistaken win the political battle over how some subject shall be taught in some state school system, every child in the state suffers. In a free market lots of mistakes will be made, but profit or loss feedback from satisfied or dissatisfied parents will tend to correct those mistakes.

A free market's continual testing of instructional techniques is a strength. Let's find out by experience which ones work best; that's the most effective way to discover better methods and means.

## How Would Quality be Assured?

What about accountability? What would assure decent quality of teachers and schools in a free market for education? The key is this: Accountability should be to parents, not politicians.

Let's approach this question with a thought experiment: Picture a school. Picture the children, perhaps in uniform, the buildings, the grounds. Now suppose that that school has begun to deteriorate, that teacher quality and motivation have eroded, that the children are not learning to read and write very well, that discipline has become lax, that there is bullying in the hallways and even a certain amount of drug-dealing in the schoolyard.

What would happen to the funding of that school?

It depends, doesn't it? If that school is a non-government school, perhaps one affiliated with a church or other religious institution, its funding would drop, fast. Parents would not tolerate it. They would pull their children out and send them to school somewhere else.

But what if the school is a government school? What *has* happened to the funding of such government schools over the last twenty or thirty years? According to the National Center for Education Statistics, it has nearly doubled, in inflation-adjusted terms. Some wag has said that in American government schooling "nothing succeeds like failure." With each new public outcry against the poor condition of our schools, the teachers' unions and school bureaucracies cry to their state legislatures, "How can you expect us to perform with so little money!?" But it is not a matter of money. It is a matter of incentives.

In government schools, supported by taxes, performance and funding are largely disconnected; hence the personnel in public schools have a weaker incentive to do a good job than they would if their incomes depended on satisfying parents, as tuition payments do at private schools. This is not to say that all private schools perform better than all public schools, nor to deny that there are many dedicated, superb—even heroic—teachers and administrators in government schools. There are. And I certainly don't mean to suggest that teachers are motivated mainly, or even primarily, by money. I'm a teacher myself, and I could earn more doing something else; like many teachers, I teach because I love it and believe it is important.

The point is the much simpler one: People do respond to financial incentives, as well as the non-financial incentives of pride in one's work and concern for the students' learning. Teachers who stand to lose their jobs if their teaching is poor are more likely to work hard and teach well than if their jobs are effectively guaranteed. School principals whose budget dollars are paid over to them by state boards of education, almost regardless of how well their children learn, are less likely to strive to improve their schools than principals whose children's parents can leave and take their tuition dollars with them. When performance and funding are connected, performance tends to be better than when they are disconnected.

This thought experiment captures why the regulation of school quality is fundamentally stronger in private than in government schools. The current system is bad because quality regulation is top-down, by legislation and bureaucracy. Such regulation can't work well, because of the problem of who will regulate the regulators, and because every layer of regulators is farther away from the children and less interested in and informed about them. If teachers do a poor job, they are supposed to be regulated by their principals. If the principals do a bad job, they are supposed to be regulated by the school boards. If the school boards do a bad job, they are supposed to be regulated by their state legislatures. If the state legislatures do a bad job, they are supposed to be regulated at the ballot box, once every two years, by the voters—that is, the parents. Why have the parents four steps removed from the original problem, able to act only once every two years, and then only by majority vote? It's nuts.

Make the accountability bottom-up. Let every different parent regulate schools directly by his freedom to say, "I'm not satisfied, and if the problem does not get fixed by next month, my child and her tuition dollars are going elsewhere."

Here is a story about the ineffectiveness of top-down regulation, in this case all the way down from Congress in far-away Washington, through the No Child Left Behind Act. In the spring of 2009, Alex McCoy, twenty-two, just graduated from Haverford College, was teaching 9th grade math at William Penn High School in Philadelphia in the Teach for America program. She was told by her principal not to give any of her students a failing grade. The message was not framed in those terms, but that was the message. Under the No Child Left Behind Act (NCLB), her school administration would get in trouble if too many of William Penn's children got left behind—failed—so the principal instituted the no-failures policy. The dictate operated by making it too time-consuming and difficult for teachers to give a failing grade. In Alex's words,

You [the teacher] had to prove that you had gone above and beyond to try to save the kid. You had to hold a number of conferences with parents. You had to prove that you had spoken to parents and gotten them involved. That was extremely difficult because you could only get parents' phone numbers through the school, and usually the phone numbers were out of date. You spent hours just to make contact. And that was only the beginning of the process. There was lots of paperwork needed to prove that you had done a lot of intervention. It was almost impossible because it all required so much time. All of those things together seem to have been put in place to keep teachers from failing anybody. There were so many hoops to jump through that we [the teachers in the school] were not failing anyone.

Alex gave all her ninth graders passing grades, even though some were doing math at fifth, third, or even first grade level. She considered only a fifth of them actually prepared for the tenth grade.

Alex also describes a perverse response to the emphasis on testing in the government's top-down approach to assuring quality. For purposes of NCLB, the students were categorized as "below basic," "basic," "proficient," or "advanced" according to their test scores. The school needed to show "adequate yearly progress" in moving students up from "below basic" toward "advanced" in order to stay out of trouble.

All the focus was on the 11th graders, because that's when they were tested. In the last month before testing we would pull kids thought to be on the edge of basic and proficient from their expressive arts classes to give them extra tutoring [in reading and math]. Because if they scored *proficient*, they satisfied NCLB.

Thus the well-roundedness of the children's education was sacrificed to the desires of the school administration to meet the letter of the No Child Left Behind law.

To see how market forces would regulate the quality of schooling better, if only market forces were allowed to work, consider the case of Kelley

Williams-Bolar, an Ohio mother of two who recently spent nine days in jail and was convicted on two felony counts of grand theft. Her crime? "Educational theft." She had "used her father's address to enroll her two daughters in a better public school outside of their neighborhood." The *Wall Street Journal* reported on the case:

> [P]arents in Connecticut, Kentucky and Missouri have all been arrested … for enrolling their children in better public schools outside of their districts. …
> From California to Massachusetts, districts are hiring special investigators to follow children from school to their homes to determine their true residences and decide if they "belong" at high-achieving public schools.

Here are American parents acting so as to reward better-performing schools with more business and to penalize worse-performing schools with less business. This is the kind of natural behavior that in a free market underlies profit-and-loss selection of high-quality goods and services. In our government schooling system, however, the bureaucracies spend additional taxpayer money to keep new customers out. Something is wrong.

The only kind of quality regulation schooling needs is to have Kelley Williams-Bolar and other parents in charge of their children's tuition dollars. Let them spend those dollars at any school that chooses to accept the child. The millions of Kelley Williams-Bolars in the country, all choosing educational options for their children based on their particular knowledge of their children's needs and the options available, would provide much stronger and more immediate accountability than Congress and the president can devise in dozens of tries at managing education top-down. No matter what schemes they devise for measuring children's progress or evaluating teachers and schools, they will never regulate as precisely and promptly as will parents with the freedom to say, "We're not satisfied; we're leaving." That, coupled with freedom for educational entrepreneurs to say, "Try our school! Look at what we offer!" would be the best possible regulator of quality. Again, it would not be perfect—nothing we fallible humans create can be perfect—but it would be the best possible.

But what about the children of parents who don't pay attention to school quality, whether because they must struggle so hard to put food on the table that they don't have time, or because they are just not good parents? They might just send their children to the closest school, even if it were a poor one. Wouldn't some children get sent to poor schools for this reason?

I don't think so; not in a free market for schooling. Many parents also can't take time to research the merits of different grocery store chains or kinds of shoes they might buy, or the different churches they might attend. Nevertheless, they have only pretty good grocery, shoe, and church options to choose from. Why? Because in a free and competitive system enough other people *do* do such research and *do* make such informed choices that only reasonably decent grocery stores and shoe brands and churches can stay in business. So it would be for schools. If only, say, half of all parents made careful school selections in a free system, no poor schools could survive.

## Would Free-Market Schools be Affordable?

What about expense? Aren't private schools too expensive? Would they be affordable?

Yes, they would be affordable. Remember that the essential schooling children need in order to get to that take-off point where they can learn on their own is the three R's: reading, writing, and 'rithmetic. That can be provided very inexpensively, so the lowest-budget schools might teach just those skills. Entrepreneurs earn an acceptable return selling clothes and shoes and groceries to low-income people and renting them places to live; why shouldn't entrepreneurs make an acceptable return selling low-income people affordable instruction in reading well, writing clear paragraphs with correct sentences, and doing basic math?

If that sounds like far too little schooling to offer, remember that government schools in low-income areas today systematically fail to give children even that. Free-market schooling just needs to be better to be preferable.

Slightly more expensive schools might offer history or science, too. The next most expensive might add art, music, and foreign language instruction. Some schools would offer athletic programs; some would not. Increasingly expensive schools might offer additional options and increasing depth of instruction. Competition would tend to assure variety and good value at each level.

Also on affordability, remember that we citizens bear the cost of government schooling now; we just do so indirectly through the taxes we pay. If those taxes were repealed, we would have all that money in hand to pay for schooling directly, rather than through the tax man and school bureaucracy.

And we'd get far more for our money. Government school systems are government bureaucracies, with guaranteed funding and guaranteed customers. Like all such bureaucracies, they are grossly inefficient. Think of the Post Office, Amtrak, the Department of Motor Vehicles, or Medicare. If schools had to compete for their students and their funding, and if they had to compete not just on quality but also on price, competition would force them to find cost savings.

Peje Emilsson, the founder of Kunskapsskolan, is often asked how his schools in Sweden can earn a profit, when the voucher they receive for each student is no more than the amount spent per student at government schools. He responds, "Anything the government does, you can of course get a better result at twenty percent lower cost. Seriously."

Emilsson's "twenty percent" may be way off. What do you suppose is the median tuition charged by the private sector schools in Baltimore attended by Children's Scholarship Fund Baltimore students? How do you suppose that compares to the spending per child in the Baltimore City Public Schools? I have looked up the figures for the 2010-2011 academic year. How large do you suppose the difference is? Please take a moment to make some estimates.

Median annual tuition charged by private, Baltimore schools
attended by Children's Scholarship Fund Baltimore students,
2010-2011: _____?
Annual spending per child in the Baltimore City Public Schools,
2010-2011: _____?

The actual figures are $5,050 and $15,464. These aren't directly com-
parable because many of the CSF schools include only grades K-8 while
the Baltimore City schools include high schools, which are more expensive;
nevertheless, the numbers suggest that in Baltimore we could get better
schooling for our children for less than half of what's spent in the government schools. These numbers square with those found in a Cato Institute
study that contrasts total spending per child in government and private
schools in six major American cities. The authors "find that, in the areas
studied, public schools are spending [per pupil] 93 percent more than the
estimated median private school."

In short, we could get better schooling for about half what we spend
today. And those numbers are from today, when most kids go to government schools, so private schools lack the vigorous competition that would
bring prices down. If all schools had to compete for students, tuitions
would come down still more.

## How Might the Needy Get Schooling Without Taxes to Pay for It?

Now let us address a main concern many good people have with getting the
government out of education. That is the all-important question of how
very low-income families would afford schooling for their children without
money from taxpayers. There are many ways. Let me ask you to brainstorm
on this for a minute: How many different ways can you come up with in
which the schooling of the very poor could be paid for?

\* \* \* \* \*

One way some of it might be paid for is by the investments Bill Gates and Google and many others are making in Khan Academy, so that high-quality instruction in a growing list of subjects is now *free* to anyone with a computer and Internet connection. We can't tell yet how many different subjects and skills might be taught with that kind of technology, and how much learning requires face-to-face interaction with a knowledgeable teacher, but technology certainly is dropping the cost of education.

Next, what about having children who are old enough—high school kids—pay for their own schooling, by working part of the time for their tuition? Would that work? In fact it does work. In the network of Cristo Rey schools, founded by Father John Foley and the Jesuit order, students earn nearly seventy percent of the cost of their schooling by working five days a month in entry-level jobs at a major company in their city. They initially tried out the idea simply as a way to pay the bills, but they discovered that the experience of working in the business world is itself a valuable and empowering part of the children's education. The concept has worked so well that there are now Cristo Rey schools in twenty-four cities.

What other innovative, entrepreneurial approaches to paying for schooling might emerge if governments bowed out of schooling and left all that tax money in the private sector? I surely hope we get a chance to find out.

The second most important reason why even the poorest would get schooling—even if no tax money were available—is that most people really care that all children get a decent education. And most of those who care will donate money and time for the purpose. If the government just got out of the way, generous individuals, religious institutions, charitable foundations and corporations would do the job in any or all of the following ways:

- They would donate funds for scholarships at particular schools.
- They would support organizations like Children's Scholarship Fund, which makes scholarships usable wherever a child is admitted.

- They would donate to schools that charge little or no tuition. In this respect I think of Mother Seton Academy in Baltimore, a tuition-free Catholic school I admire and support, whose explicit goal is to "break the cycle of poverty through education." The Bill and Melinda Gates Foundation has given millions for the founding of new Cristo Rey schools.

- Individuals would donate their time teaching, tutoring, fundraising for, and doing upkeep on their children's schools. The popularity of Teach for America shows the willingness of young people to work for less than they'd be paid elsewhere. Teaching is rewarding. (It would be more rewarding still in functional schools.)

If the government withdrew from education, we would expect all of these options to increase dramatically in amount and number from what they are today, both because generous people see the need and because the repeal of school taxes would leave them with more money to donate.

Now I can't prove that this voluntary giving would be enough to get all kids decent schooling; nothing truly innovative can be proven in advance, but I'm confident that it would. A main reason why I'm confident is that for decades, as I have lectured to various audiences and advocated for free markets for schooling, the number one concern people respond with is how poor children would be educated. If so many people are so concerned, I reason, we have nothing to worry about: Enough of them would put their money or their time where their mouths are to make sure poor children get educated.

There is one other main source of funding for schooling for low-income families we must not forget, and this is the main reason for confidence that even the poorest would get schooling, even if no tax money were available to them: Low-income families themselves work hard and save to send their children to good schools. The poor are not helpless; they are resourceful and intelligent. They want their children educated. Most would sacrifice to pay for their children's education, as poor families have struggled and managed to do for generations. Here is a relevant quotation from the *Edinburgh Review* in 1813:

> Even around London, in a circle of fifty miles, which is far from the most instructed and virtuous part of the kingdom, there is hardly a village that has not something of a school; and not many children of either sex who are not taught, more or less, reading and writing. We have met with families in which, for weeks together, not an article of sustenance but potatoes had been used; yet for every child the hard-earned sum was provided to send them to school.

My experience has shown me this is true today, too. I recall again that evening I mentioned at the beginning of the chapter. Parents gathered to learn about CSF scholarships all nodded their willingness to pay at least $500 per child. Poor people in America will find a way—even if help from others like CSF Baltimore should disappear, which it won't—to pay for their children's schooling, as long as they are offered schooling worth paying for.

And remember, they will find it much easier when they do not have to pay property taxes to support schools that are failing them. And when free market competition among schools drives down tuitions.

As I imagine the schooling options that would emerge for the poor in a free market, I have great confidence in the ability of entrepreneurs to offer affordable schooling for profit. While I cannot forecast the variety of options that would emerge, I believe that in the mix of offerings there would be some free schools in the lowest-income areas, and increasing numbers of both non-profit and for-profit schools charging tuition, but offering free or reduced-tuition enrollments to those who had trouble paying the whole tuition.

What about adequacy? Would it be enough? If there were no taxes to support education, would low-income people really have enough decent schools? Well, do they have enough decent churches? There are no taxes supporting religion, and the poor seem to cover that for themselves pretty well. Would schooling be different in any decisive way? I don't see why it would.

## Evidence and Inspiration

I have argued that we should free our schooling markets for all of the reasons I have presented throughout this book:

We need free market prices to coordinate our various activities, including schooling. We need profit and loss to guide innovation in education. We need private ownership and free exchange to connect the performance of schools and teachers to the funding they receive, and thereby give them strong incentives to pay attention to the children's needs. We need regulation by market forces so that every parent is a regulator and so that the teachers' unions and school bureaucracies don't capture the regulation and turn it to their benefit at the expense of the children. I have claimed that free markets in education would produce schooling that is much better and much more affordable.

Let's close this discussion with some supportive evidence for this claim from an unexpected locale, the slums of poor countries.

Professor James Tooley of Newcastle University has done remarkable research on private schooling in some of the poorest areas in the world, in India, China, Nigeria, Ghana, and Kenya. His team of researchers mapped populated areas and then walked through them, street by street, counting schools in three categories: government schools, private schools that are "recognized" by the education authorities, and private schools that are "unrecognized," operating illegally, completely off the radar screen of the education authorities. The government schools are free of charge; the private schools charge fees. Tooley's team made unannounced visits to the schools, noted the facilities and student-teacher ratios, interviewed parents and teachers, and tested a large sample of both private and government schools students in English and math.

What do you suppose Tooley found? How numerous are the private schools in these very poor areas, and what percentage of children in them go to private schools? What do you suppose they charge per month (or per day)? How well do the private school children do when tested in math and English (parents around the world are evidently eager for their children to learn English), as compared with the government school children? Think about it a moment before I summarize for you the results.

\* \* \* \* \*

Tooley found that in the poorest areas, the slums of India, Nigeria, Ghana, and Kenya:

- Between sixty and seventy percent of all schools are fee-charging private schools, and between sixty and seventy percent of all children living there attend them.
- The schools are for-profit, commercial operations. Nevertheless, nearly all the proprietors, who also care about their communities, offer free places for the poorest children.
- In tests of academic achievement administered to large numbers of randomly selected children in both government and private schools, the private school children performed much better across the board.
- Facilities such as drinking water were more commonly available in private schools than in government schools.
- The private schools cost far less, with their teachers being paid a third to a quarter the salaries of teachers in the government schools.

In short, just as in America, the private sector provides better quality schooling for lower cost. These results, along with the whole remarkable story of how Tooley stumbled on these schools, whose very existence is widely denied by many Third World development "experts" and decried by many others, are written up in Tooley's charming, illuminating book on the subject, *The Beautiful Tree*. I recommend it highly.

To conclude, then, schooling in America, and everywhere else, needs liberty. Let governments just get out of the way. Schools should be privately-owned and run; payment should be by free exchange between parents and schools, not by taxation. Schooling should be improved steadily through entrepreneurial innovation with profit and loss guiding discovery. School quality should be regulated by market forces. Freedom works. Let's free our schooling markets.

While we are at it, let's free all our markets, as far and as fast as we can. Pencils get made without anyone in charge because ever-adjusting market prices let us coordinate our myriad activities, with no help from government except protection of our rights. Let us leave other activities free to be ordered the same way. Let the Sharissas of the world dress the hair of willing customers at low prices without a license. Let local villagers and ranchers manage the elephants on their land. Let the US Postal Service operate without subsidies and face competition as Iridium faced it. Let doctors and their patients decide whether or not to use new medicines, based on testing from competing third-party certifiers such as Underwriters Laboratories. Let the dairy and housing industries operate without subsidies, so that market prices can tell farmers and builders how much milk and housing to supply, given the need for scarce resources in other areas, too. Let us end the Fed, so that profit and loss signals can tell free banks how much money to supply. Let us stop bailing out banks, insuring their depositors with other people's money, and centrally planning their capital ratios. Banks' depositors, competitors, and clearinghouse association partners will regulate them better from the bottom up than the Basel Committee on Banking Supervision can regulate them from the top down.

Let us have done with government intervention in the peaceful exchanges among individuals that are a free economy. Let organized force, in Jefferson's words, "restrain [us] from injuring one another," but "leave [us] otherwise free to regulate [our] own pursuits of industry and improvement .... This is the sum of good government."

Hayek wrote, "The curious task of economics is to demonstrate to men how little they really know about what they imagine they can design." With humility to recognize our inability to design top-down even pencil-making, much less a country's health care or financial or education systems, let us embrace the marvelous spontaneous order that arises from individual liberty. Let us establish what Adam Smith called "the obvious and simple system of natural liberty." In Einstein's words, "God does not play dice with the universe." To institute in practice the moral principle that decent people allow one another to do "anything that's peaceful," would improve standards of living for people of every condition. We should free our markets because to do so frees human creativity, the most powerful force of all, and disciplines that creativity to serve others.

How should we go about freeing our markets, we who believe in doing so? Each in his or her own way. Each using his or her own special knowledge and talents. Some may write books or letters to the editor; some may teach and some preach. In our time there seems no limit to the scope of persuasive communication by blogs and video on the Internet. Some even may accomplish some good in politics, though I am skeptical of that route because power tends to corrupt.

All of us can make our principles known, respectfully and appropriately, to friends and family members who are willing to listen. One way or another, however best suits our individual aptitudes and opportunities, we must make the case for economic liberty. The outcome is uncertain, of course, but the effort is a joy.

# Appendix A

# How the Fed Alters the Money Supply and Thereby Interest Rates

The primary means by which the Fed seeks to manage the money supply and thereby affect interest rates is buying U.S. Treasury securities from, or selling them to, individuals and institutions in the public at large.

U. S. Treasury securities—bills, notes, and bonds depending on the length of the payback period—are essentially interest-paying IOUs from the U.S. Treasury to the holder of the security. The U.S. Treasury uses them to borrow money: it borrows $10,000 from your bank, for example, by selling your bank a $10,000 bond. Once sold to the general public, these securities are freely bought and sold in the huge secondary market for them, called "the bond market." Treasury securities are popular investments for banks and investment funds of all kinds, because they are relatively low in risk and "liquid"—easy to sell.

Days, weeks, or years after the Treasury has initially sold them to the general public, the Fed may buy some of these T-bills, T-notes, and T-bonds from individuals, banks, and other institutions that hold them as investments. Such purchases are called "open market purchases." Alternatively, having already bought lots (and lots!) of Treasury securities, the Fed may sell back some of those it owns to the general public (called "open market sales").

To see how an open market purchase works, suppose your bank has bought a $10,000 Treasury note, thereby loaning $10,000 to the federal government; it receives interest on the note from the U.S. Treasury every six months, and it is entitled to repayment of its $10,000 at the note's maturity (in one to ten years). When the Fed wants to create new money, it can buy that Treasury note from your bank at the market price. (The day's market price will usually be a bit more or less than $10,000 depending on whether market interest rates have fallen or risen since the T-note was first created by the Treasury and sold to its first purchaser.) Let's suppose, for example, the day's price is $10,400, so the Fed pays your bank $10,400. Now the Fed owns the T-note, so now the Fed is entitled to the interest on the note and the principle when it matures. What's key for the money supply is that *the Fed buys the T-note from your bank with $10,400 of brand new money. This is how new money is created.* It is perhaps easiest to think of this as money newly printed, and that would be the case if your bank asked for $10,400 cash in payment. More usually, the new money is created by "the magic of the bookkeeper's pen": the Fed simply writes a brand new credit of $10,400 to your bank's account on its books.

This new money immediately affects *the fed funds rate*, the interest rate in the market where banks borrow reserves (cash on hand) from one another for very short periods. (I don't know why this market is called "the *federal* funds market" as it appears to have nothing to do with the Fed.) The Fed is the 500 pound gorilla in the fed funds market because through open market operations it intentionally changes the amount of reserves available to be borrowed and loaned. In our example, that $10,400 of new money becomes part of your bank's reserves as soon as the computers that keep track of the exchanges credit your bank's account. Because it is brand new reserves, if your bank wants to lend it out in the fed funds market, if other things remain equal, your bank will have to offer it at an interest rate slightly lower than the going rate in order to induce another bank to borrow it. Hence the creation of new money via open market purchases tends to lower the fed funds rate. For those familiar with supply and demand analysis, the increase in the supply of reserves leads to a lower price—a lower interest rate—for reserves.

Conversely, when the Fed wants to reduce the money supply—it does so much less frequently than it increases the money supply—it conducts an "open market sale" in which it sells some of its own large holdings of Treasury securities. Perhaps your bank buys from the Fed one of those Treasury notes to increase its holdings of relatively safe investments for, say, $10,500. (The price would rise a little higher if market interest rates had fallen a little lower.) The $10,500 your bank pays essentially vanishes from the money supply—it is extinguished, annihilated—when it returns to the Federal Reserve. (Think of a $10,000 bill and a $500 bill being thrown into the furnace in the Fed's basement, or the bookkeeper highlighting the entry for $10,500 in your bank's account and hitting "Delete.") In this manner the money supply is reduced. Your bank still has the Treasury note, with its promised interest and principal payments, but there is $10,500 less money in the economy.

By removing money from circulation in this way, open market sales increase the fed funds rate. The $10,500 your bank pays for the Treasury security comes out of its reserves. Having fewer reserves on hand now, your bank would naturally require a slightly higher interest rate, other things remaining equal, of another bank seeking to borrow some of its now-reduced reserves. In supply and demand terms, the decrease in the supply of reserves leads to a higher price—interest rate—for reserves.

What is described here is the Fed's primary means of altering the money supply and thereby affecting interest rates. In recent years (as of 2013), the Fed has used other means of expanding the money supply and keeping interest rates lower than they would otherwise be, including rounds of "quantitative easing." The term means that it has "eased"—increased—the quantity of money in circulation. Among other means, it has done so by purchasing huge quantities of mortgage-backed securities. (See Chapter 12 for a discussion of these.) The process is essentially the same as what is described here; the only meaningful difference is in the kind of securities the Fed purchases with the new money it creates.

# Appendix B

# Bank Capital and "Leverage"

Bank capital can be understood as the net value of the bank or how much stockholders own after all obligations are paid off. It's the difference between the bank's assets (what the bank owns, mostly loans it has made) and its liabilities (what it owes). It functions as a cushion against loans that might go bad. To see the importance of having a good capital cushion, imagine that you, the reader, are a simplified bank that you have established with $20 million of stockholders' money. That's your capital as you begin to do business. Your balance sheet (which always balances, by the nature of the reckoning) looks like this:

| Assets | | Liabilities + Capital | |
|---|---|---|---|
| Cash in reserve | $20 million | Capital | $20 million |

At this point, your capital ratio—your ratio of capital to assets—is 100% ($20 million in capital/$20 million in assets); but because cash is essentially riskless, your ratio of capital to risky assets is infinite ($20 million in capital/$0 in risky assets). Cash also earns no interest, so you are really not in business as a banker yet. You could earn some interest by lending out some of this cash you have from stockholders. If you were to lend, say, a quarter of it, your balance sheet would look like this:

| Assets | | Liabilities + Capital | |
| --- | --- | --- | --- |
| Cash in reserve | $15 million | Capital | $20 million |
| Loans | $5 million | | |
| TOTAL | $20 million | TOTAL | $20 million |

Still you would not be operating like a real bank because you are not yet taking deposits and lending out some or all of them. Doing so involves "expanding your balance sheet"—increasing its length, so to speak, by taking on additional liabilities in the form of checking or savings deposits, and using those to increase your interest-earning assets. For example, instead of lending out your capital, you might take in $100 million worth of deposits. Those deposits are liabilities because you have effectively borrowed that money from your depositors, and you are responsible for ("liable" for) paying it back when depositors want it. Now your balance sheet has expanded from $20 million to $120 million:

| Assets | | Liabilities + Capital | |
| --- | --- | --- | --- |
| Cash in reserve | $120 million | Capital | $20 million |
| | | Deposits | $100 million |
| TOTAL | $120 million | TOTAL | $120 million |

Your capital ratio (capital/assets) is now technically $20 million/$120 million = 16.66%, but your ratio of capital to risky assets is still infinite because your cash is riskless.

You want to make money, however, and in order to do that you have to take some risks, so you might hold, say, 10 percent of your deposits ($10 million) in reserve and lend out your remaining cash. Your balance sheet then looks like this:

| Assets | | Liabilities + Capital | |
| --- | --- | --- | --- |
| Cash in reserve | $10 million | Capital | $20 million |
| Loans | $110 million | Deposits | $100 million |
| TOTAL | $120 million | TOTAL | $120 million |

Your ratio of capital to risky assets (your loans) is now $20 million/$110 million = 18.18%.

If all your loans pay off at, say, 7 percent interest on average, then you earn $7.7 million on your loans in a year, and that amount, less all your expenses, gets added to capital. You will be happy, having earned a return on capital of $7.7 million/$20 million = 38.5% before expenses. That's a decent return that can earn you a nice profit, depending on how well you keep expenses down.

Your capital meanwhile serves as a reserve against possible loan losses. Suppose instead of a good year you have a bad one in which ten percent of your loans go bad. (For simplicity's sake, let's suppose the other loans earn just enough to cover your expenses). Will your $20 million in capital keep you out of bankruptcy? Ten percent losses on $110 million in loans is $11 million lost, leaving you with loans worth only $99 million. The deposits for which you are liable have not changed; so on the right-hand side of your balance sheet, that $11 million loss reduces your capital by an equal amount. (Too bad!) Your balance sheet has shrunk by the amount of the loss as follows:

| Assets | | Liabilities + Capital | |
|---|---|---|---|
| Cash in reserve | $10 million | Capital | $9 million |
| Loans | $99 million | Deposits | $100 million |
| TOTAL | $109 million | TOTAL | $109 million |

You have taken a grievous loss, but you are still solvent: your assets ($109 million) are greater than your liabilities ($100 million of deposits), so you are able to pay what you owe. Your losses have wiped out more than half of your capital; therefore your ratio of capital to risky assets is now down to $9 million/$99 million = 9.09%, but you had enough capital to weather the storm.

By contrast, consider what would have happened to you, the bank, if you had been a lot more aggressive, expanding your balance sheet ten times more—to $1 billion—on the basis of that same $20 million in capital. Here is the sequence:

| Assets | | Liabilities + Capital | |
|---|---|---|---|
| Cash in reserve | $20 million | Capital | $20 million |

You begin as before, but this time, in order to make more money from loans, you take in not a million, but a billion dollars' worth ($1000 million) of deposits. That is, you borrow a billion from depositors, whom you must pay back. Before you make any loans, your balance sheet looks like this:

| Assets | | Liabilities + Capital | |
|---|---|---|---|
| Cash in reserve | $1020 million | Capital | $20 million |
| | | Deposits | $1000 million |
| TOTAL | $1020 million | TOTAL | $1020 million |

This kind of increased borrowing as a proportion of one's capital is called "leveraging" or "increasing leverage." In the first example above, your leverage was only $100 million in deposits to $20 million in capital or 5:1. In the present example, your leverage would be $1 billion in deposits to $20 million in capital, or 50:1; you are borrowing from depositors fifty dollars for every one dollar you have in capital. The point of doing so is to earn more income by lending out the borrowed money, although doing so is risky, as we'll see.

Suppose that, willing to take a lot of risk in hope you'll make a lot of money, again you hold back 10% of your deposits in reserve (that's $100 million now) and lend out the rest. Your greatly expanded balance sheet now looks like this:

| Assets | | Liabilities + Capital | |
|---|---|---|---|
| Cash in reserve | $100 million | Capital | $20 million |
| Loans | $920 million | Deposits | $1000 million |
| TOTAL | $1020 million | TOTAL | $1020 million |

Now your ratio of capital to risky assets (your loans) is $20 million/$920 million = 2.17%. If all goes well, that frighteningly low ratio will mean high profits (known as return on equity or ROE) for you and the bank's other shareholders; but if things go badly, it will mean disaster. Let's do the arithmetic:

If, as before, all your loans pay off at 7 percent interest on average, then you will earn 7 percent of $920 million on your loans in a year (less all your expenses). That is $64.4 million. You would have hit the jackpot, having earned a return on equity capital of $64.4 million/$20 million = 322% (!) before expenses. That's the payoff from expanding your balance sheet with such tremendous leverage when things go well.

But what if things go badly? Your $20 million in capital is all you have as a reserve against possible losses on $920 million worth of loans. Suppose you have a mildly bad year in which, say, three percent of your loans go bad. Three percent of $920 million is $27.6 million, so your remaining loans would now be worth only $920-$27.6 = $892.4 million. You still owe your depositors $1000 million, so you are in bad trouble. On the right-hand side of your balance sheet that $27.6 million loss completely wipes out your capital and leaves you $7.6 million deep in insolvency and shame, as shown here:

| Assets | | Liabilities + Capital | |
|---|---|---|---|
| Cash in reserve | $100.0 million | Capital | (-$7.6 million) |
| Loans | $892.4 million | Deposits | $1000.0 million |
| TOTAL | $992.4 million | TOTAL | $992.4 million |

The increased likelihood of insolvency is the downside of shooting for high returns by using high leverage (maintaining a small ratio of capital to risky assets): a small decrease in the value of its assets can pitch a bank that does so into insolvency.

This is the problem the Basel capital adequacy rules were supposed to prevent. They didn't.

# Notes

## Notes to the Introduction

Frederic Bastiat's *The Law*, first published in France in 1850, is widely available in English translation. The Dean Russell translation which the Foundation for Economic Education (FEE) gave me at my first seminar is available online at the Library of Economics and Liberty at http://econlib. org/library/Bastiat/basLaw.html. The quoted passage is in paragraphs 64 and 65. FEE provides a PDF file for download at http://www.fee.org/ library/books/the-law-by-frederic-bastiat-free-download/.

Jennifer Roback's illuminating article on racial segregation in the South describes the way many streetcar owners resisted segregation because it would be costly to do so. They would not segregate their streetcars voluntarily, so others who favored segregation had to force segregation on them with governmental force. See "The Political Economy of Segregation: The Case of Segregated Streetcars," published in December, 1986, in the *Journal of Economic History*, Vol. XLVI, No. 4. It is available on JSTOR, a digital library of academic journals, books, and primary resources, at http://www. jstor.org/discover/10.2307/2121814?uid=3739704&uid=2129&uid=2&u id=70&uid=4&uid=3739256&sid=21101128768711.

The quotation from Adam Smith's *The Wealth of Nations* comes from Book IV, Chapter IX, paragraph 51, available from the Library of Economics and Liberty at http://www.econlib.org/library/Smith/smWN19.html#B.IV. The whole sentence and the next bear quoting:

> All systems either of preference or of restraint, therefore, being thus completely taken away, the obvious and simple system of natural liberty establishes itself of its own accord. Every man, as long as he does not violate the laws of justice, is left perfectly free to pursue his own interest his own way, and to bring both his industry and capital into competition with those of any other man, or order of men.

The full text of Thomas Jefferson's first inaugural address is available on the web at http://jeffersonpapers.princeton.edu/selected-documents/first-inaugural-address-0.

# Part I: Principles of Spontaneous Economic Order

## Notes to Chapter 1
## "Prices Communicate Knowledge"

Leonard Read was the founder of the Foundation for Economic Education (FEE). His classic essay "I, Pencil" is available in an attractive pamphlet from FEE at http://feestore.myshopify.com/products/i-pencil, and online at the Library of Economics and Liberty at http://www.econlib.org/library/Essays/rdPncl1.html. Read put this footnote after the very first sentence of "I, Pencil": "My official name is 'Mongol 482.' My many ingredients are assembled, fabricated, and finished by Eberhard Faber Pencil Company, Wilkes-Barre, Pennsylvania."

*The Price of Everything*, a short novel by Russell Roberts available from Princeton University Press (2009), provides an engaging exploration of this chapter's point about prices.

Ludwig von Mises' statement that socialists without prices would be "groping in the dark" comes from "Economic Calculation in the Socialist Commonwealth," in *Collectivist Economic Planning*, F.A. Hayek, ed., George Routledge & Sons, 1938, p. 110.

The term "the knowledge problem," as applied to central economic planning was probably coined by Don Lavoie, or possibly his teacher at New York University, Israel Kirzner. Don was my beloved instructor, dissertation advisor, colleague and friend at George Mason University. He used this term to identify the main problem the scholars of the Austrian School of economics found with central planning in the famous Socialist Calculation Debate. Don's book on the subject is *Rivalry and Central Planning, The Socialist Calculation Debate Reconsidered*, Cambridge University Press, 1985.

Hayek's essay, "The Use of Knowledge in Society," was originally published in the *American Economic Review* XXXV, No. 4 (September, 1945), pp. 519-30. It was reprinted in *Individualism and Economic Order*, University of Chicago Press, 1948. It is available online at http://www.econlib.org/library/Essays/hykKnw1.html. The famous quotation about "knowledge of the particular circumstances of time and place" is in paragraph H.9 of this online version. The quoted passage giving the example of the market for tin is from paragraph H.21, and the quotation about "the economy of knowledge with which [the price system] operates" is from paragraph H.22.

Hayek's discussion of the tacitness of knowledge is in "Socialist Calculation II: The State of the Debate," in *Individualism and Economic Order*, University of Chicago Press, 1948, p. 155.

Details on the punishment for violating the price controls in Charleston after Hurricane Hugo come from the microeconomics textbook I use, Gwartney, Stroup, Sobel, and Macpherson's, *Microeconomics: Private and Public Choice*, Thomson-Southwestern, 2005, p. 87.

Tyler Cowen and Alex Tabarrok's wonderful statement that "a price is a signal wrapped up in an incentive" comes from their textbook, *Modern Principles: Microeconomics*, 2nd Edition, Worth Publishers, 2013, p. 113.

Professor Russ Sobel's story about using scarce generators to power a blow-dryer and an electric shaver is from an email he sent me on July 30, 2008.

## Notes to Chapter 2
## "Profit and Loss Guide Innovation"

The work to which I am most indebted for my understanding of the ideas in this chapter is Ludwig von Mises' "Profit and Loss," available online at http://library.mises.org/books/Ludwig%20von%20Mises/Profit%20 and%20Loss.pdf. The book containing my copy is *Planning for Freedom, and Sixteen other Essays and Addresses,* published in 1980 by Libertarian Press. The first quotation from Mises in this chapter is from page 23 of the online version and page 123 of the printed version. The second quotation is from page 13 of the online version and page 113 of the printed version.

For my understanding of the role of the entrepreneur and the entrepreneur's "propensity for alertness toward fresh goals and the discovery of hitherto unknown resources," I am most indebted to the work of Israel Kirzner, especially his *Competition and Entrepreneurship,* The University of Chicago Press, 1973. The quotation in the previous sentence is from page 34.

A short, clear story that illustrates the source of profit is Fred I. Kent's "Letter to his Grandson," available in *Free Market Economics, A Reader,* edited by Bettina Bien Greaves and available at https://mises.org/store/ Product2.aspx?ProductId=393.

The complete interdependency between market prices and profit (or loss) deserves note. Entrepreneurs base their actions on profit-and-loss projections, which are themselves based on expected market prices. Entrepreneurs' actions then determine actual market prices, and actual market prices determine actual profits and losses. Both the projected and the realized profits and losses help entrepreneurs discover what to do with scarce resources to create the most profit for themselves by creating the most new value for others.

The quotation from Adam Smith's *Wealth of Nations* comes from Book I, Chapter V, paragraph 17, available from the Library of Economics and Liberty at http://www.econlib.org/library/Smith/smWN2.html#B.I,_Ch.5,_ Of the Real and Nominal Price of Commodities.

Early in the 1870s, three economists working independently, Carl Menger of Austria, Leon Walras of France, and William Stanley Jevons of Britain all established the subjective theory of value, and showed that valuation occurs "at the margin." That is, the value we put on one more unit of a good (the *marginal* unit) depends on how much of that good we already possess. The major change in economic understanding these three economists initiated is called "the marginal revolution."

The claim that "both buyer and seller gain" from a voluntary exchange should perhaps be clarified: At least they *expect* to gain at the moment of decision. Of course we all make mistakes. In the example in which you and your friend buy and eat a pizza, you might feel uncomfortably stuffed after eating your half, and wish you had bought something smaller. Nevertheless, you bought the pizza because you *expected* to be better off as a result.

The question asked by Jesus, "For what is a man profited, if he shall gain the whole world, and lose his own soul?" is from Matthew 16:26.

The original Iridium company was called Iridium LLC. Its assets were bought out of bankruptcy in December, 2000, by a new company called Iridium Satellite LLC, which was immediately awarded a two-year, $72 million contract with the Department of Defense for unlimited use of the low-Earth orbit network. Note that that $72 million is approximately 1.15 percent of the low-end estimate of $5 billion spent building the system. The Department of Defense is still the company's main customer. More information is available at http://www.iridium.com/About/IndustryLeadership/fastfacts.aspx and http://www.defense.gov/releases/release.aspx?releaseid=2769.

Michael Rothschild's insightful and readable *Bionomics, Economy as Ecosystem*, originally published in 1990, is available in a reissued edition from Owl Books (1995). Russell Roberts's *The Price of Everything* is available from Princeton University Press (2009).

*Scarcity* in economics means the insufficiency of the amount of some good to satisfy all possible wants for it. It means there is not enough of it to do everything we might like to do with it. Scarcity does not rule out unemployment: human talent and other resources are scarce even when unemployed, in that there are many ways we would like to use them. Unemployment is a consequence of discoordination in the economy; it does not mean that we all have everything we would like to have.

To those who have studied economics, the first kind of discovery discussed in this chapter will be familiar as the standard textbook version of the economic problem: How do we use our limited resources to satisfy unlimited wants? F.A. Hayek is persuasive that this is *not* a good way to conceive of the economic problem, however, because it assumes that "we" know what resources are available and what people want. Hayek, in his indispensable "The Use of Knowledge in Society" (Paragraph H.3, available at http://www.econlib.org/library/Essays/hykKnw1.html) writes:

> The economic problem of society is thus not merely a problem of how to allocate "given" resources—if "given" is taken to mean given to a single mind which deliberately solves the problem set by these "data." It is rather a problem of how to secure the best use of resources known to any of the members of society, for ends whose relative importance only these individuals know. Or, to put it briefly, it is a problem of the utilization of knowledge which is not given to anyone in its totality.

The quotations from Joseph Schumpeter are from page 83 of his *Capitalism, Socialism and Democracy*, published by Harper & Brothers Publishers, New York, 1950.

I thank my friend and colleague Antony Davies for crystallizing for me this idea and for its wording: "We want entrepreneurs to take risks because, when the risks pay off, we all benefit from the new products and lower costs. But we don't want entrepreneurs to waste society's resources on foolish risks." I thank Russell Roberts for this way of putting the same idea at various times on *EconTalk* (http://www.econtalk.org/): "The lure of profit encourages entrepreneurs to take risks, while the fear of loss discourages them from taking imprudent risks."

Franz Oppenheimer's distinction of the economic means and the political means is in *The State: Its History and Development viewed Sociologically*, first published in German in 1908. The authorized translation by John M. Gitterman (New York: B.W. Huebsch, 1922), is available from the Online Library of Liberty at http://oll.libertyfund.org/title/1662.

Antony Davies points out that oil companies' profits are not out of line with those of other industries. In 2007, for example, "oil companies' return on assets were less than Pizza Hut's." He has a useful short presentation on this point at http://www.antolin-davies.com/conventionalwisdom/oil.pdf.

## Notes to Chapter 3
## "Free Market Incentives Foster Service to Others"

Walter Williams's statement comes from the ABC news special "Greed," with John Stossel, available from ABC News and at various place on You-Tube.

The *Anchorage Daily News* story, "Tongass forest river damaged by logging declared restored," available at http://www.adn.com/2011/08/25/2031770/tongass-national-forest-river.html, briefly describes some of the environmentally destructive logging practices and recent restoration of the watershed. The quotation from John Baden and various figures from this section are from Baden's *Destroying the Environment: Government Mismanagement of Our Natural Resources*, National Center for Policy Analysis, Policy Report No. 124 (October, 1986) pp. 12-13.

The Forest Service's website about the Tongass used to contain a FAQ page which was the source of much of the data in this section. It was located on the web at http://www.fs.fed.us/r10/tongass/forest_facts/faqs/forestmgmt.shtml. That page has been taken down. Any reader wishing to see it may email the author for a copy.

Information on another interesting restoration project in the Tongass can be found here: http://alaskaconservation.org/conservation-issues/tongass-rainforest/updates-field/sitka-conservationists-pursue-unconventional-path/.

My original source of information on the Rainey Wildlife Sanctuary is also John Baden's *Destroying the Environment: Government Mismanage-*

*ment of Our Natural Resources*; the quotations are from page 34. For a fascinating story of Audubon Society's handling of the political incorrectness of allowing oil and gas production inside a bird sanctuary, see "PC Oil Drilling in a Wildlife Refuge," a September 7, 1995, article in the *Wall Street Journal* (available at http://www.perc.org/articles/article167.php). A January 23, 2010, article entitled "Audubon Society considers allowing oil and gas drilling at sanctuary in Vermilion Parish" (available at http://www. nola.com/business/index.ssf/2010/01/audubon_society_considers_allo. html) discusses the Audubon Society's renewed interest in leasing oil and gas production rights.

The short quotations from James Buchanan come from his "Public Choice: Politics Without Romance," *Policy*, Vol. 19, No. 3, The Centre for Independent Studies (Spring, 2003), p. 3, available at http://www.cis. org.au/publications/policy-magazine/article/2379-feature-public-choice-politics-without-romance. This essay is a good introduction to public choice economics from its leading exponent. Another helpful essay on public choice is William F. Shughart II's "Public Choice," in *The Concise Encyclopedia of Economics*, 2008, Library of Economics and Liberty, available at http://www.econlib.org/library/Enc/PublicChoice.html.

Ludwig von Mises' noble statement "If honour cannot be eaten, eating can at least be foregone for honour" is from his book *Socialism*, Part II, Chapter 5, paragraph 15. In my version, published by Liberty Classics in 1981, the quotation is found on page 100. A full-text, searchable edition is available online from the online Library of Economics and Liberty at http://www.econlib.org/library/Mises/msS.html.

Thomas Sowell's immensely instructive *A Conflict of Visions* (Basic Books, 2007, first published in 1987) provides an illuminating discussion of the vision of mankind as inescapably self-interested, and the opposing vision of mankind as to a large degree perfectible.

# Part II: Regulation by Market Forces Outperforms Government Regulation

## Notes to Chapter 4
## "Ownership Matters"

The story of the elephants in Kenya and Zimbabwe began for me when I read "Herd Mentality: Banning Ivory Sales is No Way to Save the Elephant," by Randy T. Simmons and Urs P. Kreuter, in the Heritage Foundation's *Policy Review*, Vol. 50 (Fall, 1989), pp. 46-49. This article is my source for much of the information in the first part of this chapter, including information on poaching and smuggling in Kenya. The article is not available online. Additional information about wildlife management in Kenya and Zimbabwe and the problem of overpopulation in some regions in recent years comes from personal communications with Urs Kreuter.

Information about CAMPFIRE and quotations from Brian Child come primarily from Child's article, "Building The CAMPFIRE Paradigm, Helping Villagers Protect African Wildlife," PERC Reports: Volume 22, No.2 (Summer, 2004). This can be accessed at http://www.perc.org/articles/article138.php. The Property and Environment Research Center (PERC), located in Bozeman, Montana, is a world leader in "free-market environmentalism."

Urs Kreuter's statement that "In some areas villagers began to actively inform on illegal poaching in their areas (unheard of in the preceding colonial area)," the quotation about overpopulation on the Botswana-Zimbabwe border, and the statement that elephant populations "have led to the eradication of most trees in game reserves such as Amboseli" are from a personal communication.

Information on Community-Based Natural Resource Management in Namibia is from Karol Boudreaux, both from a personal communication and from her "Community-Based Natural Resource Management in Namibia: A Case Study," *Mercatus Policy Series*, Feb. 20, 2007. This article is available online at http://mercatus.org/publication/community-based-natural-resource-management-namibia-case-study. The phrase, "CAMPFIRE continues to limp along," is Karol's.

For an up-to-date (2011) account of conservation through private ownership in Africa, see "An African Success: In Namibia, The People and Wildlife Coexist," by Fred Pearce, available from PERC, the Property and Environment Research Center, at http://perc.org/articles/african-success-namibia-people-and-wildlife-coexist. Their website, www.perc.org, is a wonderful resource for those interested in the crucial role that private property rights play in effective stewardship of natural resources.

For a 1996 update on the failure of the ivory ban in Kenya (and early discussion of instituting community ownership rights there), see "Why the Ivory Ban is Failing," by Urs Kreuter and Linda Platts, at http://www.perc.org/articles/article171.php.

Information on African wildlife thriving on ranches in Texas comes from Terry L. Anderson's, "In Praise of 'Enviropreneurs'," in the *Wall Street Journal*, February 13, 2012, available at http://online.wsj.com/article/SB10001424052970204369404577209062592063958.html.

For a CBS News *60 Minutes* report on the conservation of African animals on Texas hunting ranches, see http://www.cbsnews.com/8301-18560_162-57366738/hunting-animals-to-save-them/.

The United States Postal Service states in its *2011 Report on Form 10-K* (p. 15) that its "[n]et losses were $5,067 million, $8,505 million, and $3,794 million for the years ended 2011, 2010, and 2009, respectively." The report is available at http://about.usps.com/who-we-are/financials/10k-reports/fy2011.pdf.

The Express Statutes grant a legal monopoly on first class mail to the U.S. Postal Service. No other companies are allowed to offer such service; those that have tried have been shut down. The example that follows is reported by James Bovard in *Cato Institute Policy Analysis* No. 47: "The Last Dinosaur: The U.S. Postal Service" (available at http://www.scribd.com/doc/57683405/Last-Dinosaur-the-U-S-Postal-Service-Cato-Policy-Analysis-Some-Hard-Facts-About-the-Incompetence-of-the-USPO):

In 1978, the P.H. Brennan Hand Delivery Service offered same-day delivery of mail in Rochester, New York, for 10¢ apiece; the Postal Service could not guarantee overnight delivery even for 15¢. The Brennan Service operated during snowstorms (when the Postal Service did not even try to deliver), never lost a letter, and never had a complaint. When U.S.P.S. attorneys closed in on the Brennans, Rochester lawyers provided them with a free legal defense. But the Postal Service persuaded a judge to issue a "cease and desist" order on account of the "threat to postal revenues."

About "the dole" in Britain, I was surprised to learn from fellow students that many of them collected unemployment compensation during summer and Christmas vacations. When I questioned this, a student explained that of course they should receive unemployment compensation during vacations, because their taxpayer-funded college grants covered only time actually spent in school.

CSF Baltimore supported 230 children at 47 different schools in and around Baltimore for the school year 2012-2013. Median tuition at these schools in that school year was $6,400.

## Notes to Chapter 5
### "Government Regulation Gets Captured by Special Interests"

The figure for the total price of beauty school tuition, fees, books and supplies was given on the webpage of the Maryland Beauty Academy, July 29, 2012, http://www.stateuniversity.com/universities/MD/Maryland_Beauty_Academy.html.

The classic article on regulatory capture is George Stigler's "The Theory of Economic Regulation," published in *The Bell Journal of Economics and Management Science*, Vol. 2, No. 1 (Spring, 1971).

Descriptions of the Institute for Justice cases on occupational licensing come from the Institute's website. They are available as follows (as of July 29, 2012):

- Clemens v. Maryland State Board of Veterinary Medical Examiners, et. al.: http://www.ij.org/victory-for-maryland-entrepreneur-in-animal-massage-dispute-2;
- Brown v. Hovatter: http://www.ij.org/brown-v-hovatter-2;
- Susan Roberts v. Jerry Farrell: http://www.ij.org/susan-roberts-v-jerry-farrell;
- Clayton v. Steinagel: http://www.ij.org/utah-hairbraiding-2.

Sidney Carroll and Robert Gaston's article on the effects of licensing electricians is "Occupational Restrictions and the Quality of Service Received: Some Evidence," in the *Southern Economic Journal*, Vol. 47, No. 4 (April, 1981) pp. 959-976.

The quotation from the Institute for Justice on the number of occupations requiring a license is from Chip Mellor's "IJ's Campaign to Restore the Constitution & Protect Economic Liberty" available at: http://www.ij.org/index.php?option=com content&task=view&id=2668&Itemid=194.

Of general interest on the subject of occupational licensing is *License to Work, A National Study of Burdens from Occupational Licensing*, published by the Institute for Justice in 2012. They provide a link to the study itself and to an interesting, five-minute video on its findings at http://www.ij.org/licensetowork.

For information on airline regulation and deregulation I am indebted to my friend Jerry Ellig, a regulation expert who, with Robert Crandall, has summarized the academic literature on airline deregulation in "Economic Deregulation and Customer Choice: Lessons for the Electric Industry," Center for Market Processes, 1997. This is available from the Mercatus Center at http://mercatus.org/publication/economic-deregulation-and-customer-choice-lessons-electric-industry.

Ellig wrote me in an email that, interestingly, his "impression from reading the literature" is that even though the Civil Aeronautics Board excluded competition, the "[a]irlines did not end up earning monopoly profits because they dissipated the profits in spending on meals, piano bars in airplanes, and scheduling excess flights (intending to appeal to passengers' desire for convenience, which also meant flights were less full)." Those interested in studying the subject "will find the whole story told very well in *Prophets of Regulation*," by Thomas K. McCraw (Harvard University Press, 1986) "in the chapter on Alfred Kahn."

The seminal works, recommended by Ellig, on the effects of deregulation are: Steven A. Morrison and Clifford Winston, "The Remaining Role for Government Policy in the Deregulated Airline Industry," in Sam Peltzman and Clifford Winston (eds.), *Deregulation of Network Industries: What's Next?* (AEI-Brookings Joint Center for Regulatory Studies, 2000); Morrison and Winston, *The Evolution of the Airline Industry* (Brookings, 1995); and James C. Miller III and George Douglas, *Economic Regulation of Domestic Air Transport: Theory and Policy* (Brookings, 1974).

Information on Mexican trucking is taken from Dan Griswold's "Attempt to Limit Mexican Trucking in U.S. Masks Union Agenda," *Los Angeles Daily Journal*, December 20, 2007, available at http://www.freetrade.org/node/818, and his "House Bans 'Driving While Mexican'," Cato@ Liberty, March 4, 2009, available at http://www.cato.org/publications/commentary/attempt-limit-mexican-trucking-us-masks-union-agenda.

Economists broadly agree that minimum wage laws have negative economic consequences overall, for reasons we discussed in Chapter 1. Like all price controls, they hinder the operation of the Price Coordination Principle. Whether or not minimum wage laws benefit or harm low-income workers on balance in the short run depends on what is called the elasticity of demand for labor. The reader can pursue this with any good microeconomics text. For our present purposes, the key point is another on which almost all economists agree: minimum wages set above market levels will cause at least some unemployment.

The quotation from Adam Smith is from *The Wealth of Nations* Book I, Chapter X (Part II), paragraph 67, available from the Library of Economics and Liberty at http://www.econlib.org/library/Smith/smWN4.html#B.I, Ch.10, Of Wages and Profit in the Different Employments of Labour and Stock.

For more on how the unionized coal interests influenced the 1977 Amendments to the Clean Air Act, see Bruce Yandle's classic article, "Bootleggers and Baptists: The Education of a Regulatory Economist," in *Regulation*, Vol. 7(3) (1983); and Bruce Ackerman and William Hassler's, *Clean Coal/Dirty Air: or How the Clean Air Act Became a Multibillion-Dollar Bail-Out for High-Sulfur Coal Producers* (Yale University Press, 1981).

The passage from George Stigler is as recounted to Russell Roberts by Bruce Yandle in the *EconTalk* podcast of January 15, 2007, (http://www.econtalk.org/archives/2007/01/bruce_yandle_on.html). Roberts quotes Yandle in his weblog *Café Hayek*, at http://cafehayek.com/2006/12/who_benefits_fr.html.

## Notes to Chapter 6
## "Market Forces Regulate"

The quoted passage about Automotive Service Excellence (ASE) comes from "Auto Service Goes High-Tech," accessed July 31, 2012 at http://www.ase.com/News-Events/Publications/Car-Care-Articles/Auto-Service-Goes-High-Tech.aspx.

The article about food industry self-regulation is Andrew Martin's "To Fill Food Safety Gap, Processors Pay Inspectors," *New York Times*, April 16, 2009. Accessed June 26, 2009, at http://www.nytimes.com/2009/04/17/business/17leafy.html?_r=3&hp.

Data on Underwriters Laboratories comes from "About UL" at Underwriters Laboratories' website, accessed July 1, 2009 at http://www.ul.com/global/eng/pages/corporate/aboutul/.

For more information on the alleged bribery at the Gemological Institute of America see "Leading diamond appraiser in bribery inquiry," by Patrick McGeehan, New York Times, December 21, 2005. It is available at http://www.nytimes.com/2005/12/21/business/worldbusiness/21iht-nydiamond.html.

Searching the web nine years later, I see that both the Gemological Institute of America and the European Gemological Laboratory are highly regarded.

Thalidomide was a drug that, among other desired effects, relieved the symptoms of morning sickness in pregnant women. Tragically, it also caused terrible birth defects, though that consequence was not understood for many years. Thousands of deformed children were born in Europe as a consequence of wide use of the drug there. In the United States, only seventeen children were born with thalidomide-caused deformities because the FDA refused to allow its use in the U.S. until more testing was done.

For my understanding of the problems with the FDA's authority to ban drugs I am indebted to Professors Dan Klein and Alexander Tabarrok of George Mason University. This discussion draws extensively on their FDAReview.org, a fine source of information on the FDA and alternatives.

Another fine discussion of the FDA is in Milton and Rose Friedman's *Free to Choose*, in a chapter entitled "Who Protects the Consumer?", pp. 203-210. On the related topic of the licensing of physicians, see Milton Friedman's discussion in *Free to Choose*, "Who Protects the Worker?" pp. 230-241, and Shirley Svorny's "Licensing Doctors: Do Economists Agree?" in the online journal, *Econ Journal Watch*, Vol. 1, No. 2 (August 2004) available at http://econjwatch.org/articles/licensing-doctors-do-economists-agree.

The quotation from Henry I. Miller is from his 2000 book, *To America's Health: A Proposal to Reform the Food and Drug Administration* (Stanford, Calif.: Hoover Institution Press, pp. 42-43), as quoted in Klein and Tabarrok's, "Why the FDA Has an Incentive to Delay the Introduction of New Drugs," available at http://www.fdareview.org/incentives.shtml.

The examples in Table 6.1 come from Noel D. Campbell's "Replace FDA Regulation of Medical Devices with Third-Party Certification," *Cato Institute Policy Analysis* No. 288 (November, 1997) available at http://www.cato.org/pubs/pas/pa-288es.html. The sources Campbell cites are, for thrombolytic therapy and Misoprostol, Sam Kazman, "Deadly Overcaution: FDA's Drug Approval Process," *Journal of Regulation and Social Costs*, No. 1 (August, 1990): pp. 43 and 44; for Interleukin-2 and the AmbuCardioPump, Alexander Volokh, "Clinical Trials—Beating the FDA in Court," *Reason*, May, 1995, p. 23; for the home HIV test, Robert Goldberg, "The Kessler Legacy at the FDA," *IPI Insights*, January-February 1997, p. 1.

My source for the statement that estimates of the annual number of preventable deaths attributable to FDA over-caution range in the tens of thousands every year is "Theory, Evidence and Examples of FDA Harm," in Klein and Tabarrok's *FDA Review* at http://www.fdareview.org/harm.shtml. Klein and Tabarrok summarize studies of the U.S. experience over time and also studies that contrast the U.S. experience with that of Europe, where drugs are approved much faster than in the U.S. As to the former, they conclude that "The number of victims of Elixir Sulfanilamide tragedy and of all other drug tragedies prior to 1962 [when the FDA's restrictions were much lighter] is very small compared to the death toll of the post-1962 FDA." As to the latter, they conclude, "There is no evidence that the U.S. drug lag [behind Europe] brings greater safety." Those interested in recommendations of what to do about the problem of FDA overregulation might find interesting Dan Klein's low-tech but persuasive video on The Davos Question, at http://www.youtube.com/watch?v=8N_-IHM00cc.

The quotation from Sam Kazman is from his "Deadly Overcaution: FDA's Drug Approval Process," *Journal of Regulation and Social Costs*, No. 1 (August 1990): p. 43; quoted in Noel D. Campbell, "Replace FDA Regulation of Medical Devices with Third-Party Certification," *Cato Institute Policy Analysis* No. 288, November, 1997.

## Notes to Chapter 7
## "Special Interests versus Democracy"

Information on the Milk Income Loss Contract Program was available as of August, 2012, at http://www.apfo.usda.gov/FSA/webapp?area=home& subject=prsu&topic=mpp-mi, on federal milk marketing orders at http://www.ams.usda.gov/AMSv1.0/FederalMilkMarketingOrders, and on the Dairy Product Price Support Program at http://www.fsa.usda.gov/Internet/ FSA_File/dpd_bulletin_090105.pdf.

Figures on the costs and benefits of the dairy programs come from Joseph V. Balagtas, "Milking Consumers and Taxpayers, the Folly of US Dairy Policy," American Enterprise Institute, 2011, at http://www.aei.org/files/2011/07/15/Final-Balagtas.pdf.

For general information about the dairy industry from the US Department of Agriculture, consult http://www.ers.usda.gov/briefing/dairy/background.htm and "Changes in the Size and Location of U.S. Dairy Farms" at http://www.ers.usda.gov/publications/err47/err47b.pdf.

For commentary on and criticism of the dairy programs, see Chris Edwards, "Milk Madness," *Cato Institute Tax and Budget Bulletin* No. 47 (July, 2007), at http://www.cato.org/pubs/tbb/tbb_0707_47.pdf and Sallie James, "Milking the Customers: The High Cost of U.S. Dairy Policies" at http://www.cato.org/pub_display.php?pub_id=6764.

Twenty cents a gallon is the saving created for consumers by Hein Hettinga, the subject of a truly illuminating look at the disgusting politics behind the dairy programs, and the politicians' total disregard for consumers' welfare, "Dairy Industry Crushed Innovator Who Bested Price-Control System," http://www.washingtonpost.com/wp-dyn/content/article/2006/12/09/AR2006120900925.html, by staff writers Dan Morgan, Sarah Cohen and Gilbert M. Gaul for the *Washington Post,* Dec. 10, 2006.

# Part III: "The Housing Boom and Financial Crisis"

## Notes to Part III
## "Introduction"

The quotation from Peter Wallison is from his "Wall Street's Gullible Occupiers," *Wall Street Journal*, October 12, 2011, p. A21. The quotation from Paul Samuelson is from his "Don't Expect Recovery Before 2012—With 8% Inflation," an interview by Nathan Gardels, *New Perspectives Quarterly*, January 16, 2009. Available online at http://www.digitalnpq.org/articles/economic/331/01-16-2009/paul_samuelson.

## Notes to Chapter 8
### "Mortgage-Making in a Free Market"

For a very interesting discussion of different kinds of mortgages, the difference between mortgages in the U.S. and Canada, and the way government intervention into housing has shaped the U.S. mortgage market, I recommend the *EconTalk* podcast of July 5, 2010, with Arnold Kling, available at http://www.econtalk.org/archives/2010/07/kling_on_the_un.html. For example, 30-year fixed rate mortgages, which Americans consider standard, are rarely used in other countries. They seem to be a problematical consequence of well-intentioned but misguided New Deal policy.

In the section "Not Enough Investable Resources," I say that "Corresponding to the limited supply of investable resources available at any time is a limited supply of loanable funds." Some readers might question this statement. After all, it is possible for monetary authorities to create brand *new* money, of course, just by running the printing press or writing new deposits to bank accounts. Clearly new loanable funds can be created easily, even if new investable resources cannot. Although that is certainly true, it is a very bad idea to create new loanable funds indiscriminately. As we discuss in Chapter 11, when monetary authorities do lend new money into existence *when there are no corresponding new investable resources* nor any increased desire on the part of the public to hold money in their wallets and checking accounts, damaging inflation results. For now it is sufficient to observe that in an economy where the monetary authorities do not indiscriminately produce new money, banks have only limited amounts of money to lend. Those limited loanable funds correspond to—they represent, in effect—the investable resources that are necessarily limited at any point in time.

## Notes to Chapter 9
## "Boom, Bust, and Turmoil"

Data on which the figures in this chapter are based, along with source information, are available at this book's website, www.freeourmarkets.com.

The quotation from Johan Norberg is from *Financial Fiasco*, Cato Institute, 2009, pp. 8-9.

The data on "shaky" mortgages represented in Figure 9.3 come from www.census.gov/compendia/statab/2011/tables/11s1193.xls. The mortgages I call "sound" are those designated in the figures as "prime conventional loans," and those I call "shaky" are those designated in the figures as "subprime conventional loans." It appears that Alt-A loans are split between the "prime" and "subprime" categories. Here is the relevant statement from the data source:

> While the NDS [National Delinquency Survey] does not identify or track Alt-A loans explicitly, conversations with survey participants have established that Alt-A loans are divided between the prime and subprime groups. Thus, Alt-A loan performance is captured in the delinquency and foreclosure rates estimated in the NDS."

The distinction between "prime" and "subprime" also seems to vary by institution:

> The prime and subprime criteria used in the NDS are based on survey participants' reporting of what they consider to be their prime or subprime servicing portfolio. Different servicers may make different determinations regarding the grade of their portfolios. Participants who service both prime and subprime loans report the results of each separately for maximum precision in the classification. (http://www.mbaa.org/files/Research/Flyers/NDSFAQ.pdf)

It is worth noting here that as housing boomed and attracted people trying to make easy money, there seems to have been some carelessness and dishonesty in the categorization of loans, and many loans that were not technically "subprime" were still pretty dodgy.

## Notes to Chapter 10
### "Why Housing Boomed"

For a short (fifteen-page), clear explanation of the government's role in the housing boom and bust and the Great Recession, I recommend "The House That Uncle Sam Built," by Peter Boettke and Steven Horwitz, Foundation for Economic Education, December, 2009. It's available online at http://www.fee.org/files/docLib/HouseUncleSamBuiltBooklet.pdf. A good book-length discussion is Thomas Woods's *Meltdown: A Free-Market Look at Why the Stock Market Collapsed, the Economy Tanked, and Government Bailouts Will Make Things Worse*, Washington, DC: Regnery, 2009.

For an interesting scholarly discussion of the housing boom and bust, asset bubbles in general, and the possible consequences of the Taxpayer Relief Act, see Steven Gjerstad and Vernon L. Smith, "Monetary Policy, Credit Extension, and Housing Bubbles, 2008 and 1929," in *Critical Review* Vol. 21, Nos. 2-3 (2009). They write, "We think that the upward turn in housing prices that began in 1997 was probably sparked by rising household income (beginning in 1992), combined with a very popular bipartisan political decision in 1997 to eliminate taxes on capital gains of up to a half a million dollars for residences."

The data on which Figure 10.1 is based, along with source information, are available at this book's website, www.freeourmarkets.com.

My source for the statement that as of July, 2011, Standard and Poor's estimates "the total taxpayer cost to keep the GSEs [government-sponsored enterprises] solvent at about $280 billion" is "Fannie Mae and Freddie Mac Update: Recent Weak Performance Hasn't Changed Our Taxpayer Cost Estimate," accessed August 6, 2011, at http://www.standardandpoors.com/ratings/articles/en/us/?assetID=1245314207570, available as of June 2013 at http://www.researchandmarkets.com/reports/1929807/fannie_mae_and_freddie_mac_update_recent_weak.

My source for the statement that "in the housing boom Fannie and Freddie typically could sell their bonds paying interest rates a bit less than half a percentage point lower than their private sector counterparts did" is page 11 of Friedman and Kraus's *Engineering the Financial Crisis*. They write that Fannie and Freddie "typically paid a 0.45 percent lower interest rate than did privately-issued mortgage-backed bonds." In private correspondence with Mr. Friedman, I verified that they mean that Fannie and Freddie's interest rate was 0.45 *percentage points* lower.

Quotations from Russell Roberts are from his monograph "Gambling With Other People's Money," Mercatus Center, May, 2010, p. 25. This very useful article, to which I refer extensively in the second part of Chapter 11, is available online at http://mercatus.org/publication/gambling-other-peoples-money.

Apropos of Congressman Barney Frank's statement that "I want to roll the dice a little bit more in this situation towards subsidized housing," the *Wall Street Journal* has a darkly entertaining collection entitled, "What They Said About Fan and Fred" at http://online.wsj.com/article/SB122290574391296381.html. It will make you shake your head unless you have lower expectation of Congress even than I do.

## Notes to Chapter 11
## "Why the Boom Got So Big"

The data on which Figures 11.1 and 11.2 are based, along with source information, are available at this book's website, www.freeourmarkets.com.

The world's money has been completely unredeemable in any underlying commodity since August 15, 1971, when President Richard Nixon severed the last link between the dollar and gold. He took the United States off the last remnants of the gold standard by refusing any longer to pay foreign governments gold for dollars, as the United States had promised to do in the famous Bretton Woods agreement of 1944. The United States had stopped honoring its promises to pay everyday citizens in gold in 1933 under President Franklin Roosevelt. Indeed, in April of that year, with Executive Order 6102, Roosevelt made it illegal for anyone to own more than $100 worth (face value) of monetary gold.

Readers who wish to study monetary equilibrium further should read Steve Horwitz's discussion of it in his 2000 book, *Microfoundations and Macroeconomics* (Routledge, 2009), especially "Monetary Equilibrium as Analytical Framework," pp. 65-75, 81-2, and 96-103. Another very helpful source is George Selgin's book, *The Theory of Free Banking* (Rowman and Littlefield, 1988), available online now at the Liberty Fund's Online Library of Liberty at http://files.libertyfund.org/files/2307/Selgin_1544_Bk.pdf. Note especially chapter 4, "Monetary Equilibrium."

Readers who would like to learn more about free banking should also read Lawrence White's *Free Banking in Britain: Theory, Experience and Debate 1800-1845* (Institute of Economic Affairs, 1995) to get acquainted with the most important historical case of (mostly) free banking. White's *The Theory of Monetary Institutions* (Wiley-Blackwell, 1999) would be a good next choice. There is now also a weblog called "Free Banking," to which White, Selgin, Steven Horwitz, and other outstanding monetary economists such as Kurt Schuler and Kevin Dowd contribute.

Russell Roberts's paper, "Gambling With Other People's Money, How Perverted Incentives Caused the Financial Crisis," was published by the Mercatus Center at George Mason University in 2010. I recommend it highly. It is available online at http://mercatus.org/publication/gambling-other-peoples-money. Passages I have quoted are from pages 6-12 and 37. Roberts's source for the statement that "Between 1979 and 1989, 1,100 commercial banks failed. Out of all of their deposits, 99.7 percent, insured or uninsured, were reimbursed by policy decisions," is Stern and Feldman's *Too Big to Fail*, page 12. Roberts notes that Stern and Feldman "do not provide data on what proportion of these deposits was uninsured."

## Notes to Chapter 12
### "Why the Housing Bust Led to a Financial Crisis"

The data in this chapter are largely from Jeffrey Friedman and Wladimir Kraus's insightful study, *Engineering the Financial Crisis*. Quotations and data are drawn from pages 13, 67, and 79. This book expands on and refines

Jeffrey Friedman's earlier, "A Crisis of Politics, Not Economics," in *Critical Review*, Vol. 21, Nos. 2-3 (2009), another source I relied on.

A persuasive explanation of how the Basel rules helped cause the financial crisis is Arnold Kling's "Not What They Had In Mind: A History of the Policies that Produced the Financial Crisis of 2008," Mercatus Center, September, 2009, available at http://mercatus.org/publication/not-what-they-had-mind-history-policies-produced-financial-crisis-2008. The statement from F.A. Hayek that "the curious task of economics is to demonstrate to men how little they really know about what they imagine they can design," is found in *The Fatal Conceit: The Errors of Socialism* (University of Chicago Press, 1991), p. 76.

Some readers will wonder how a mortgage-backed security (MBS) based on subprime or otherwise shaky mortgages can possibly get a AAA (not at all risky) rating. The key is what is called "tranching," whereby the income from a given pool of mortgages goes to the holders of different MBSs based on that pool in a definite order. The holders of the AAA-rated MBSs get paid first. That is, as the principal and interest payments from all the mortgages in the pool come in each month, the first payments out are made to those investors who have bought AAA-rated tranches (or "slices") of the mortgage pool. Once all the holders of the AAA MBSs (those in the first tranche) have been paid, the holders of the AA-rated MBSs get paid next, and then, in sequence, the holders of the lower and lower-rated tranches are paid, *as long as there are enough principal and interest payments coming in from the mortgages to pay them.*

Typically the AAA-rated tranche of MBSs held rights to about 75 percent of the principal and interest payments due in from the mortgages. That means that if in such a pool at least 75 percent of the homeowners made their mortgage payments, all the AAA MBS holders would get paid. Because the holders of the AAA-rated MBSs get paid first, they bear less risk; accordingly, they are paid a lower interest rate on the money they have invested. The AA-rated tranche of MBSs typically held rights to the next 10 to 15 percent of the principal and interest payments. Because they bear more risk—they don't get paid anything until the holders of all the

AAA-rated MBSs have been paid—they receive a higher interest rate on the money they have invested, and so on.

Even subprime MBSs can deserve AAA ratings (as not very risky) because even in a pool of subprime mortgages, some proportion of the homeowners will make all their mortgage payments. The AAA-rated tranche of a pool of subprime mortgages can therefore deserve its AAA rating *as long as the tranche is narrow enough*. The key is for the rating agency to make a sound judgment about how many mortgages in a given pool are likely to have their payments made on time. For example, if the rating agency judges that in a certain pool of subprime mortgages, at least 70 percent are all but certain to stay current on their payments, the agency might give a AAA rating to 70 percent of the MBSs based on that pool. If it then turns out that no more than 30 percent of the mortgages in that pool fall behind and go into foreclosure, the holders of the AAA MBSs will still get paid everything they expected. If, however, 31 percent or more of those mortgages fall behind on their payments, there will not be enough income to pay all the holders of the AAA tranche, and we could say the rating agency made a mistake.

As things turned out, the rating agencies did make a lot of bad judgments and made the AAA tranches of many mortgage pools too wide.

In discussion of the FDIC, I call payments from banks to the FDIC not "premiums" but "fees," because to call them "premiums" seems to distort the usual meaning of the word. For most banks these payments are not voluntary purchases of insurance, but a tax. According to the *Congressional Quarterly*, "FDIC coverage is mandatory for all federally chartered banks and all state banks that are members of the Federal Reserve System, but voluntary for other state banks." *Congressional Quarterly Weekly Report*: Volume 43 (1985), p. 1715. Accessed June 17, 2012, at http://books.google. com/books?id=pqhEAQAAIAAJ&q=%22fdic+coverage+is+mandatory%2 2&dq=%22fdic+coverage+is+mandatory%22&hl=en&sa=X&ei=XkXeT6 WXIKfH6gGKrfypCw&ved=0CEUQ6AEwAQ.

The explanation of how federal deposit insurance grew out of small banks' desire to avoid competition with large banks on the dimension of riskiness comes from the *EconTalk* podcast of October 26, 2009, with Charles Calomiris on the Financial Crisis (http://www.econtalk.org/archives/2009/10/calomiris_on_th.html). The relevant portion begins at 17:31 into the conversation.

The shortage of money in the bank panics of 1893 and 1907 was alleviated by the ingenuity of bank clearinghouses, individual banks, and even certain large companies that issued money substitutes. Some of these were certainly illegal, but allowed to circulate by the authorities, who saw that they were filling an urgent need. When the banking panics passed, these money substitutes were just taken out of circulation by those who had issued them. For a fascinating account, see Steven Horwitz's chapter, "Regulatory Chaos and Spontaneous Order Under the National Banking System" in his 1992 book *Monetary Evolution, Free Banking, and Economic Order* (Westview Press).

The quotation from George Selgin contrasting the banking experience of the United States and Canada comes from his "Legal Restrictions, Financial Weakening, and The Lender of Last Resort," in *Bank Deregulation and Monetary Order* (Routledge, 1996), p. 209.

Franklin Roosevelt's opposition to government-provided deposit insurance is clear from a 1932 letter he wrote to the New York *Sun*, in which he said that deposit insurance "would lead to laxity in bank management and carelessness on the part of both banker and depositor. I believe that it would be an impossible drain on the Federal Treasury to make good any such guarantee. For a number of reasons of sound government finance, such plan would be quite dangerous." More discussion and a link to the original letter are available at http://cafehayek.com/2008/12/franklin-fannie.html.

The article referred to by Clifford F. Thies and Daniel A. Gerlowski is "Deposit Insurance: A History of Failure," in the *Cato Journal* Vol. 8, No. 3 (Winter, 1989), p. 680. This article tells brief and darkly entertaining stories of the failures of the various funds. It is available at http://www.cato.org/pubs/journal/cj8n3/cj8n3-8.pdf.

The quotation from George Selgin about private, competitive deposit insurance comes from *The Theory of Free Banking*, page 135, available online

at the Liberty Fund's Online Library of Liberty at http://files.libertyfund.
org/files/2307/Selgin_1544_Bk.pdf. FDIC no longer assesses banks on
their total deposits, but on their assets. See below.

Catherine England provides an interesting discussion of the problems
with government-provided deposit insurance and the expected advantages
of privately-provided deposit insurance in "Private Deposit Insurance: Sta-
bilizing the Banking System," *Cato Institute Policy Analysis* No. 54, available
at http://www.cato.org/pubs/pas/pa054.pdf. She also presents an interesting proposal for making the transition from the former to the latter.

For information on the FDIC's assessment base, see the press release
at http://www.fdic.gov/news/news/press/2011/pr11028.html. It states that
a final rule issued Feb. 7, 2011, changes "the assessment base from adjusted
domestic deposits to average consolidated total assets minus average tan-
gible equity."

For an interesting discussion of a specific proposal for a system of
cross-guarantees and predictable resistance to it by special interests, see
John Allison's *The Financial Crisis and the Free Market Cure* (McGraw Hill,
2013), pp. 48-49. The system was designed by Bert Ely; see his "Financial
Innovation and Deposit Insurance: The 100% Cross-Guarantee Concept,"
*Cato Journal* (Winter, 1994), pp. 413-445, available at http://www.cato.
org/sites/cato.org/files/serials/files/cato-journal/1994/1/cj13n3-6.pdf.

George Selgin's observation on the discipline exerted through clearinghouses is from his "Bank-Lending Manias in Theory and History," page
266, in *Bank Deregulation and Monetary Order* (Routledge, 1996).

# Notes to Part III
## "Conclusion"

How might we make the transition from central banking with fiat money
to free banking and free-market money? While there are many proposals,
the reader would do well to begin with George Selgin's "A Practical Proposal
for Reform" on pp. 168-172 of his *The Theory of Free Banking*. Lawrence H.
White discusses "Making the Transition to a New Gold Standard" in the

*Cato Journal*, Vol. 32, No. 2 (Spring/Summer, 2012), available at http://www.cato.org/sites/cato.org/files/serials/files/cato-journal/2012/7/v32n2-14.pdf.

For a useful discussion of "the leading criticisms of the gold standard," see Lawrence H. White's Cato Briefing Paper #100 (February, 2008), "Is the Gold Standard Still the Gold Standard Among Monetary Systems?" at http://www.cato.org/publications/briefing-paper/is-gold-standard-still-gold-standard-among-monetary-systems.

## Notes to Chapter 13
## "Hope for the Future"

For information about Children's Scholarship Fund Baltimore, see http://www.csfbaltimore.org/. For information about Children's Scholarship Fund nationally, visit http://www.scholarshipfund.org.

Those interested in the benefits of ending government intervention in education should read Sheldon Richman's fine book, *Separating School and State*, published by the Future of Freedom Foundation in 1994.

For a short video presentation by Peje Emilsson, the founder of Kunskapsskolan, see http://www.youtube.com/watch?v=X_6MLZonT3U. A promotional video for the Manhattan school is at http://www.youtube.com/watch?v=_weyT_NyV6U. Kunskapsskolan's website is at http://www.kunskapsskolan.com/.

Information about the origins of Khan Academy is taken from the *Wired* magazine article of July, 2011, "How Khan Academy Is Changing the Rules of Education," at http://www.wired.com/magazine/2011/07/ff_khan/all/1. The quotations from Khan Academy are from the academy's website at http://www.khanacademy.org/about.

Per pupil expenditures in public elementary and secondary schools in the U.S. have increased around 24 percent in the last ten years, 41 percent in the last twenty, and nearly doubled in the last thirty. See the National Center for Education Statistics Fast Facts, http://nces.ed.gov/fastfacts/display.asp?id=66.

The article about Kelley Williams-Bolar is "The Latest Crime Wave: Sending Your Child to a Better School," by Micheal Flaherty, on the *Wall Street Journal* opinion page October 1, 2011, available at http://www.cato. org/sites/cato.org/files/serials/files/cato-journal/1994/1/cj13n3-6.pdf. Flaherty writes, "Only in a world where irony is dead could people not marvel at concerned parents being prosecuted for stealing a free public education for their children."

I arrive at the average spending per child in the Baltimore City Public Schools using figures from the system's FY 2013 Adopted Operating Budget (http://www.baltimorecityschools.org/cms/lib/MD01001351/Centricity/domain/1/pdf/2012 13BudgetBookFINAL.pdf). Total expenditure of $1,302,266,468, given on p. 11, divided by total enrollment of 84,212, given on p. 4, yields $15,464 per student.

The Cato Institute study quoted from is Adam Schaeffer's "They Spend WHAT? The Real Cost of Public Schools," *Cato Institute Policy Analysis,* No. 662 (March 10, 2010), available at http://www.cato.org/publications/policy-analysis/they-spend-what-real-cost-public-schools.

Links to academic papers James Tooley and his colleagues have published on private schooling in poor nations, along with photographs and links to news reports and several inspiring videos, including two BBC broadcasts, are available at the website of Tooley's E.G. West Centre at Newcastle University, http://research.ncl.ac.uk/egwest/.

# About the Author

Howard Baetjer Jr. is a Lecturer in the Department of Economics at Towson University in Baltimore, Maryland, where he has taught since 1996. He teaches courses in microeconomics, comparative economic systems, and money and banking. Dr. Baetjer is also a regular faculty member at summer seminars offered by the Institute for Humane Studies.

Dr. Baetjer earned a B.A. in psychology from Princeton in 1974, an M.Litt. in English literature from the University of Edinburgh in 1980, an M.A. in political science from Boston College in 1984, and a Ph.D. in economics from George Mason University in 1993. His dissertation was published as *Software as Capital: an Economic Perspective on Software Engineering* by IEEE Computer Society in 1998.

He is a founding trustee of Children's Scholarship Fund Baltimore, which, since 1999, has provided partial scholarships to more than 6000 low-income Baltimore children, to help them attend private and parochial schools their parents choose.

You can visit Dr. Baetjer's website at http://www.freeourmarkets.com/.